for
Jeffrey Blum
and
Martha McCahill
who made this book possible

GOT ME ON THE RUN
A Study of Runaways

RICHARD BOCK AND ABIGAIL ENGLISH

A Sanctuary Book

BEACON PRESS   **BOSTON**

Copyright © 1973 by The Sanctuary, Cambridge, Massachusetts
Published simultaneously in hardcover and paperback editions
Beacon Press books are published under the auspices of the Unitarian Universalist Association
Published simultaneously in Canada by Saunders of Toronto, Ltd.
All rights reserved
Printed in the United States of America

9 8 7 6 5 4 3 2 1

Library of Congress Cataloging in Publication Data

Bock, Richard D   1950-
  Got me on the run.
  1. Runaway youth—Boston—Case Studies. 2. Social work with youth—Boston. I. English, Abigail, 1949- joint author. II. Title.
HQ799. 73.B7B63   301.43'1   72-6236
ISBN 0-8070-2582-8
ISBN 0-8070-2583-6 (pbk.)

CONTENTS

Acknowledgments ix
Introduction xi

Part I

1 On the Run 3
2 "I Don't Know Why She Runs Away" 15
3 Can't Find My Way Back Home 25
4 Donna 39
5 David 53
6 "She May Just Be Bad Inside" 67
7 On the Way Out 81
8 "Where Are You Tonight, Sweet Marie?" 101

Part II

1 Home Again 143
2 School Days 171
3 Illegal Persons 187
4 Room to Move 213

Notes 235
Bibliography 237

I didn't see how you could know me,
but you said you knew me and I believed you did.
"Sooner or Later One of Us Must Know"
—— Bob Dylan

ACKNOWLEDGMENTS

The process of researching, writing, and editing this book was long and complicated, and we could never have completed the endeavor without the generous help of many people.

We are extremely indebted to all those who aided us in finding runaways to talk with and in contacting adults who had known them. The Sanctuary counseling staff was especially cooperative in this respect, even to the point of calling us at night when a runaway came into the hostel: Guillemette Alperovitz, Jon Brush, Richard Gressle, Barbara Rich, Ray Thomas, Joe Scorscello, and Heather Wimberley were particularly helpful. David Wittlesey and Joanna Skalzi at the Youth Resources Bureau in Cambridge, Sandy and Peter Clark at Project Re-Place in Lexington, and Richard Bavely at the Division of Child Guardianship also helped greatly by introducing us to the runaways they knew. Above all, the counselors at the Project Place Runaway House shared with us their wealth of experience and the opportunity to have direct contact with the many runaways who came to the House during January and February. Those on the staff at the time included Emmet Folgert, Rich Gehrman, Ben Melanson, Rita McNamara, Don Momforte, Sherry Smith, Lilian Strandemo, Amy Weiner, and Phil Woodbury.

We would like to give special thanks to Ray Bentley, Norman Zinberg, and Leonard Friedman, for their support and encouragement throughout. Our friends on the Sanctuary research and education staffs were very indulgent while we were writing and kindly read drafts of the book. We are particularly grateful to Peggy Rizza, Sandra Sucher and David Bynum for their invaluable editorial suggestions and to Mark Rosen for his tireless and good-humored assistance with the interviewing. Pearl Hughes, Joan Griffin, Margie David, and Jeanne Colbeth were especially kind in helping us prepare the final manuscript. We would also like to thank Linda Scovill for designing the book.

Most of all, however, we appreciate the generosity of all the runaways and adults, who shall remain unnamed, but who talked with us so openly and at great length about such personal matters. Without them this book would never have been written.

R.D.B. and A.E.
Cambridge, Massachusetts
July 1972

INTRODUCTION

This book grew out of conversations about runaways which we had with people in the Boston area during the fall and winter of 1971-1972. From the beginning of our study, we were interested in what these young people had to say about themselves as well as what others important in their lives said about them. While much has been written in recent years about the phenomenon of runaways, we felt there was a need for a book which examined the experiences of the people who live and work with runaways as well as the young people themselves.

From the beginning of this project two questions we were asked were whether our research would reach "conclusions" and whether it would be "analytic" or "descriptive." Perhaps the strongest reaction came from a high school principal who complained that studies which "didn't have enough guts" to draw conclusions failed to do people any good. Others said that descriptions of individual lives gave no idea of how "representative" such individuals might be.

All descriptions have an analytic bias. Ours is that the young people in this book have run away from social environments in which they were in difficult positions. We regard running away as a choice many adolescents make for sound personal reasons and believe that at the time they leave, most know why they have to go. By running away, a young person may find a temporary kind of peace, a chance to make new contacts and grow, a new and more "real" world; he will also be confronted with new decisions to make—Should I stay out or return home? Whom should I ask for a place to sleep? Should I seek "help" or try to make it on my own? Do I want to live away from home for good? Once he is a "runaway," the young person will also find that many others—parents, legal officials, social workers, psychiatrists, and school authorities—begin to make decisions about him. We feel that some understanding of how these young people make decisions for themselves and how others make decisions for them is more important than any generalizations about why kids run away. We have tried to show that it is not only the adolescents who are in difficult positions. Parents, teachers, and other adults also have hard choices to make when a kid runs away.

At times we have deliberately left cases open-ended and simply presented our material with little interpretive comment. Whenever possible and appropriate we have offered interpretations; these should be read simply as two people's ideas of what might have been going on in another person's life. Our interpretations are, after all, our own; others might see similar events in a different light. Although we hope these insights will prove helpful to our readers, they are neither judgments nor "conclusions." Usually we have confined our analysis to what was going on in a particular situation, but in several instances we have discussed the broader social implications of people's experiences.

Several times during the course of this work we were asked what our "qualifications" or "credentials" were. We both graduated from college in June 1971—Abigail from Radcliffe, Richard from Harvard—and joined the Sanctuary research staff at that time. We had worked with young people and adults before, yet never so intensively and over such a long period of time. We quickly discovered that the art of interviewing was listening and not necessarily asking questions. Most of the people we talked with told their stories readily, and only when we were confused about some event did we have to interrupt them with questions. Whenever possible we taped the conversations; otherwise we took notes immediately afterwards. Thus, some of the quotations we include were transcribed from the tapes of interviews while others were written down from memory. We have only quoted people, however, when we were sure that we remembered their words verbatim. Our goal was to listen as carefully as we could do what people had to say about themselves.

In general we took people at their word. When we sensed that someone was exaggerating or embellishing a story for dramatic purposes we would ask whether this was happening. After a four-hour conversation with one runaway, whose story appears in this book, his counselor, who had been present throughout, said, "That was the most honest session he's had. Everything he told you was true." We soon came to realize, however, that the "truth" of someone's story was not as important as how well the account expressed that person's feelings about his situation and the people around him. Thus we have often presented several versions of the same incident in order to illustrate the ways different people experience an event and their contrasting perceptions.

Most of the runaways we met ran away during the fall and winter months and spent some time at Sanctuary, which then ran a hostel and drop-in center in Cambridge, or at the Project Place Runaway House in Boston. Despite the weather, many kids run away during these seasons; we can only guess how this compares to the numbers who run away in the summer—such figures are hard to compute and beyond the scope of this study. It may be that kids who leave in wintertime have more to get away from. We simply do not know. We also talked to runaways at other youth counseling centers in Cambridge, Lexington, and Arlington about their experiences. Altogether we had conversations, that lasted at least an hour and often longer, with sixty runaways. We also worked for two months as part-time counselors at the Sanctuary hostel and the Place Runaway House. We have found the public image of runaways as alienated middle-class adolescents to be misleading. In the Boston area at least, many young people of working-class backgrounds also leave home, yet they receive less attention in the media than their middle-class peers.

We contacted adults involved with these young people either through other counselors who knew them or simply by calling them. With one exception all those we contacted—seventy-five in all—agreed to speak with us. Often, we were more hesitant about talking to these people than they were to talk to us. Maybe, we feared, they would not feel like telling us about the runaway they knew. What right had we to expect them to discuss such personal events? We never ceased to be surprised by the remarkable quality they had of speaking honestly and directly with strangers. Perhaps that is something we ourselves have learned in the course of this study.

We have changed the names of all the individuals who appear in the book in order to protect their anonymity. In most cases we have also changed the names of their home towns, while trying to select "disguises" which preserved important characteristics like size and class-composition. When referring to organizations and public institutions we have left names unchanged because we believe that specific information about such places is valuable and should be public.

The book is divided into two parts. The first is a series of narratives that describe the lives of twelve kids from different points of view. The first chapter in Part I concerns two runaways who tell their own stories; in neither case did we go back to the places they had left—mostly because their homes were far away. In the subsequent chapters we have included the accounts of parents, teachers, counselors and legal officials who knew the young people. In some cases, we have had more extensive contact with the adults than with the young person whom they talk about. Throughout Part I, we have also tried to give some account of the experiences young people have away from home—on the street, in runaway houses such as Project Place, and in juvenile "detention centers."

The second section of the book examines the social institutions which have the greatest impact on the lives of runaways—the family, schools, and the law—as well as the alternatives open to kids who leave home. No one of these institutions is more important than another—all play significant roles in the lives of those we have talked with. All too often, we hear people say that the family is the cause of a kid's running away from home; thus, if something is done to change the family, everything will be all right. To assign blame to one institution in such situations, however, makes as little sense as saying that one person in a particular family is "the problem." Youth is a process of growth in which all are involved—parents, teachers, counselors, as well as the legal officials whose duty it is to maintain the social order.

If there is a message to this book, it is that all these people are related to each other in ways which are only beginning to be understood. Young people have a "culture," yet many of the runaways with whom we spoke seemed very much affected by their parents' beliefs and values even as they were trying to develop their own. In a similar way, parents were affected by their children's actions, often to the point of questioning their own lives, even though as adults they were supposed to be mature and sure of themselves. It is not sufficient, however, to say that if everyone learned from each other, all would be happy again; what we see are two (and sometimes more) generations whose differences have a profound impact on each other and whose common humanness makes these matters issues of everyday life.

GOT ME ON THE RUN

Part I

1
ON THE RUN

WE talked to Nancy Schmidt and Michael Mills at Sanctuary; both had run away from home repeatedly and did not plan to return. Nancy, sixteen, came to Sanctuary with another runaway who brought her to us because she was "mixed up"—he did not specify how—and he thought we might be able to help her. We met Michael one night at the hostel and talked to him for most of the next morning. Both kids were only passing through Cambridge and left within days after we spoke with them.

Nancy was blond with blue eyes. At first she was shy and surprised that anyone would be interested in writing about her, but as the conversation proceeded, she talked more easily, sometimes very quickly when describing a series of events almost as if she were reliving them, then she would grow quiet again. When she talked about experiences that made her particularly nervous, such as her encounters with police or failure at school, Nancy would giggle, and start talking about something else. She went into great detail describing incidents that had gotten her into "trouble," but she did not like to describe what was happening to her as "trouble."

When we talked to her, Nancy was away from her home in Burlington, Vermont, for the sixth time in two years. Her reason for running this time was that her mother had found a syringe in her drawer. "I came home and she showed it to me and she said,

'What's this?' and I said, 'Oop,' and . . . I ran." From home she went downtown, stayed at a rooming house, and tried to find a job; she gave her real name and the address where she was staying to prospective employers, one of whom checked with her high school. When Nancy found out that the police had come to her rooming house, she fled to Boston with another girl; both of them were picked up by Boston police and sent to Lyman School (a detention center where girls are sometimes held while awaiting trial), but within an hour Nancy had escaped out a window and found her way back into the city. Her most recent encounter with the law had been in Cambridge. Arrested with several other kids while sleeping in an abandoned house, Nancy had escaped from the police: "I swung at them and ran out of the station and about two or three of them chased me but I got away and I ran. . . . I hid under a porch and . . . well, that's it."

Being apprehended by the police in Massachusetts was particularly frightening to Nancy because she was "not supposed to be seen" in the state. Less than a year before, she had been arrested for driving a stolen car, sent to reform school for six months, and warned by the judge who tried her case not to return to Massachusetts. While the judge had no firm legal grounds on which to "banish" Nancy, that did not matter to her; she felt all the more in danger because of his statement. Her memory of what the judge had said reminded us of a statement made by a lawyer we talked to: much of what went on in the courtroom was like theater, with judges playing roles that they often admitted to be such outside the courtroom. This phenomenon is discussed more fully in Part II, chapter 3. It is possible in Nancy's case that the judge had told her she should not be seen in Massachusetts again simply for effect (since he had no legal authority to say such a thing). For her, however, it had been all too real and seemed to be the principal motive behind her drive to get away from local authorities. At the time she ran away from home Nancy had been out of reform school for two months and on three years' probation. She feared that if apprehended, she could be sent back to reform school until she was twenty-one for violating her probation.

While it is difficult to figure out just what was going on in Nancy's family from what she told us, two things were clear. Her father, she claimed, was seldom at home—he worked long hours at his auto body shop and spent evenings at bars, while she and her mother seemed to be having a pretty difficult time with each other. The two of them argued about Nancy's friends, the clothes she wore, the way her room looked, and whether or not she would stay in school. This final issue was a bitterly contested one. Although once a good student, Nancy was repeating the ninth grade for the third time and failing. "I wanted to quit school. She didn't want me to quit.... One day I got sick of school and I said, 'I'm quitting,' and she said, 'What?' and I said, 'I'm quitting,' and she threw a vase at me.... I told her I'd been in ninth grade for three years, and she said, 'You've got to pass sometime,' and I said, 'What's the use?' and she got fed up and threw it." Nancy said that she "hated" her mother and had been in several accidents while driving her mother's car illegally.

Nancy felt that one reason she performed so poorly in school was her drug use. "I started taking dope in the seventh grade and from there on the grades started getting lower." The first time she failed ninth grade was also the year she began to use heroin, to which she had been introduced after running away from home for the fourth time. Up until this time "running away" had usually meant going to a friend's house; this time, when her mother came to look for her, Nancy ran farther. "She came to the door and I ran out the back door and kept running and running and running till I ended up at this housing project... and then I met some people there and I asked them if I could stay there for a week and they said... all right." It was while staying with these people that Nancy had first tried heroin. She also learned that by stealing cars she could get money to buy her own drugs. For the next six months she stole cars during the day and spent the nights at the houses of friends she met "downtown." While driving in a stolen car with some of her Burlington friends on the way to Boston, she was arrested by the police, taken to court, and sent to reform school. While there she did not use heroin, but when released, she said she began again. In Burlington she had been involved in a drug treatment program that involved groups and had a social worker as well as a psychiatrist. Part of the reason why she had run, she said, was that since her mother knew she was still using heroin, she might "turn her in."

After talking with Nancy, we were uncertain what kind of "help" we could offer her. Nancy said that she wanted a place to sleep and asked about the Sanctuary hostel; because she was under eighteen and would not call home for permission to stay there, we told her that would not be possible but gave her the name and address of the Project Place Runaway House (where kids can stay for up to twenty-four hours without calling home). Before she left us, she called and talked to a Place counselor; Nancy never showed up there.

From what Nancy had told us, her most serious fears concerned the legal consequences of her actions. If arrested again, Nancy thought she would be returned to Burlington and "locked up" until she was twenty-one. At the time, this struck us as exaggerated, so we asked her if she wanted legal advice. She simply said no and laughed a little. In retrospect, after several months of hearing about kids' experiences with the law and finding out just what "rights" juveniles have (see Part II, chapter 3), we realize why our offer of "legal advice" was of no help to Nancy. Her basic fear did not come from any misunderstanding of the law. She understood all too well what would happen to her. Whether it would be for six months or five years, one can be fairly certain that a girl with Nancy's history would be "locked up" for an extended period of time, and while she was confused about many things, Nancy seemed determined to keep that from happening again. The only way for her to act on this intention was to keep running. Faced with that determination and the reality of what she was running from, there was not much we could do to "help."

Two days later, we ran into Nancy on the street. She was smiling, walking around with a new friend, with whom she said she was leaving for California that afternoon. They were going to drive out in his car with some other people. Wasn't that great? She laughed a little and said she wanted to be gone already.

Michael Mills, seventeen, has been living away from home for the last four years. Except for a few weeks one winter that he spent in the custody of his parents, awaiting trial as a "stubborn child," Michael has lived with other young people around the country, sometimes in reform schools. Although his family name is Mills, Michael has taken the last names of rock-and-roll stars as his own: he has been known as Michael Dylan, Michael Stone, and Michael Lennon to friends and counselors as well as to the police.

Michael is tall with curly dark brown hair that goes below his shoulders. He dresses in violet bellbottoms embroidered with flowers, bright shirts, and high leather boots. The morning we spoke to him, Michael made a point of saying that his appearance was no indication of his political views. He claimed that he was "fairly conservative," by which he meant that he did not believe in civil disobedience or abortion, that he had "complete faith in God and Jesus Christ," though he had been neglecting his church for a while, and that he still believed in working for a living. While he did not have a regular job, Michael supported himself by doing occasional work, like moving furniture.

According to Michael, his initial reasons for leaving home had to do with drugs: he had been "dealing" in his hometown in northern Massachusetts and making money until "things got really hot." Rather than stop his dealing, Michael left his town and went to New York. At the time he was not getting along with his parents, because he did not like their rules—"weekly haircuts . . . shine your shoes every morning . . . and don't go out of the house with your pants not creased neatly." While living at home, Michael did not have long hair; his father, who had limited contact with his family because he worked nights as a desk sergeant in the army, gave his sons haircuts every Saturday morning. Once when Michael told his father that he did not want his hair cut he was told,

"When you get old enough to move out of this house, you can decide how you want your hair cut. As long as you live in this house, it's going to be neatly short. I won't have none of this goddamn long-haired hippie shit in my house." Michael claimed these were "pretty close to his [father's] exact words."

In some ways, Michael remained an obedient son. He went to church all day every Sunday with his family and continued to take haircuts, but in other ways he was defiant. He continued to have friends whom his parents forbade him to see ("because my mother and father didn't like the looks of them") and started cutting school. Michael said that although he was not that interested in school, he went "because there wasn't anywhere else to go during the day," but never did assignments and sometimes slept half the day. Up until the time he left home, however, he had maintained a C average despite his lack of effort. When he began to skip school, his parents found out and "took it really seriously." Shortly thereafter, he ran away from home.

The first time Michael left home, he was arrested and returned, but two days later he was gone for good, all the way to New York City. For the next several months he took part in the New York drug scene—using drugs, dealing them, and making money. The morning we spoke to him, Michael's strongest memories of New York were of being arrested "many times." Although he said that he had no animosity toward the police, and "never even called a cop a pig," every policeman he met seemed to hate him, and since leaving home, he had been repeatedly arrested, sometimes on drug charges, other times for vagrancy, loitering, and disorderly conduct. In New York, when he appeared in court at age fifteen, he used an alias and claimed he was nineteen. Because of the crowded court, Michael claims that no one bothered to check out his case, so both times he was released. Often when arrested he would get bailed out, then fail to appear in court, a method that was "safe" unless the policeman who had arrested him saw him again. Once, however, none of these techniques worked and he had been returned home, sentenced as a "stubborn child," and sent to reform school for six months. Eventually, at age sixteen, Michael was released to the care of a foster parent.

Michael talked about his experience with the law as though, in his mind, the things that had been done to him were of more consequence than what he had done on his own. He recounted his run-ins with the law in a casual, matter-of-fact manner, talked without anger, and did not seem to have that fear of police which makes talk of "paranoia" so common among young people. Rather than frightened, he was fascinated by the law; the process of arrest and trial had a real hold on his imagination. One example of this is a story he told about being arrested: picked up for hitchhiking, he had been charged with vagrancy ("That's just what they decided to charge me with. It happens with me a lot—they bust me for something and charge me with something else."). At the police station he was fingerprinted three times, and posed for mug shots. "There's supposed to be three sets of fingerprints and three sets of mug shots that they've taken. One of each goes to the FBI crime information bureau, one goes to the state police, and one stays in the files of the police station . . . so right now the FBI has my fingerprints." When it was impossible to evade legal authorities, Michael submitted compliantly. There seemed to be no middle ground with him—either he got away or gave in.

While living away from home, Michael had supported himself by working ("I drove a moving van . . . worked in stores") and by dealing drugs. He also said that he used to mug people until he "got sick" of violence and "got into helping people out." In New York he had rented a nine-room apartment with his money and lived with eighteen other people. In addition to living in New York, Michael had been to the West Coast and had lived with student friends in colleges, particularly in Massachusetts. He talked at times about how much he "enjoyed" the life he was living and boasted about the girls he could go and stay with when he left Cambridge.

Michael had spent his most recent summer on Cape Cod where, he said, he and a girlfriend had made several thousand dollars selling newspapers and dealing drugs on a regular basis. At one point, with the help of fake identification and his mature looks, he had opened a bank account, deposited two thousand dollars, and bought a car on credit. The problem with this arrangement was that Michael did not drive that well: he had "habits of hitting things like stop signs, ... fire hydrants, and telephone poles." Consequently, the car was in the shop being fixed for much of the summer, and when Michael missed several payments, it was repossessed by the dealer. This story gives one some sense of how Michael saw himself; it does not matter if the story is true—even if it is fantasy, it indicates that for Michael, what he has done has not amounted to much. Unable to find in driving the sense of self-esteem that teenage boys frequently do, he made a point of saying what a bad driver he was. He had some pride about his success in dealing, but all that success amounted to was money with which he had opened up a false bank account and bought a car that wasn't worth much to him. It does not matter whether Michael was as successful a drug dealer as he claims—he has achieved nothing by it. None of his activities—making money, spending it, driving—has led to the development of any sense of competence on his part.

Except for a brief stay with his family several years ago, Michael has not lived at home since he ran away. After serving time in reform school, he stayed in a foster home near his hometown and started school again; that lasted for several months, until spring came and he began taking off regularly. His foster father was a young man to whom Michael sometimes returned to "talk things over," yet one of the things they had not talked about was why Michael kept leaving. Whatever their relationship had actually been, at the time we talked, Michael seemed to regard his foster home as just one more place he had left behind. Michael had considered returning there and starting school again, but did not like the prospect of being in class with kids three or four years younger than himself.

Recently he had given some thought to returning home, but he had not done so, mostly because he was not welcome there. "The main thing is ... my father doesn't want me back. I know that. ... He's afraid of the influence I have on my little brothers. ... My father feels that if I come home, my brothers and sisters will see the way I am and it will corrupt them." It is unclear when Michael's father forbade him to come home, for in the past few years they have not talked with one another. Michael's main link to his family is his mother, whom he meets in local restaurants from time to time, even though, he claims, his father has told her not to talk to him.

After several years of living in the streets, certain aspects of a "home life" are very appealing to Michael. "I think of how nice it would be . . . having a home to go home to every night. And having my mother cook supper for me every night instead of eating that crummy spaghetti at Hazen's [a local Cambridge hangout]. And have someplace to go where I could just watch TV or something instead of spending the night playing pinball for lack of anything better to do." Last Christmas Michael had bought presents for his whole family and taken them to his mother; he was surprised to find his father with her, but did not get a chance to talk to him. "My father gave me a twenty-dollar bill right on the spot . . . and went back to the car and locked himself in. . . . He didn't stay around long enough for me to thank him for it."

Michael claims to have "lost all feeling" about being rejected by his father ("It's something that exists . . . it's a fact . . . you accept it"), said he was not angry with him, and spoke of his parents with a new respect. "Right now I can understand the reason for everything they did. . . . I'm seeing thirteen-year-old kids running away . . . and I feel they're too young to run away from home. Even though I did the same thing." Michael said that he had left home for "crummy" reasons, "but at the time they seemed quite valid."

Michael's criticism of runaways is an indirect comment on his own situation, for when he first left home, he thought he was old enough to do so. It is difficult to say how he came to that decision, but from what he told us, it seemed to have something to do with his father's telling him, "When you get old enough to move out of the house, you can decide how you want your hair cut"; it is possible that because he wanted to have long hair, and be a "freak," Michael felt that he had to move out of the house because he accepted the family "law." After several years away, he had come to question the things for which he had left home and appeared to be reconsidering his idea of what it meant to be "old enough" to leave.

Returning to school, Michael had had to face the fact that in straight social terms he was not "older"; uncomfortable in classes where other students were several years younger than he, Michael had given up on school, yet he had not abandoned the values of education. Although he had completed only seven years of school, he had "definite plans for going to college" and planned to take a high school equivalency test when he turned nineteen. Nevertheless, thoughts of school made Michael question his own experience. While he thought he had done things in the past three or four years "that were more like living ... than most people do in their whole lives," Michael imagined another kind of life for himself. "Right now ... if I had to start out with thirteen-year-old kids and get back into school and get an education ... it's just like I've wasted the last three or four years.... It keeps bothering me.... I'm not completely straight in my head about what I did that was right and wrong.... If I decide I want to be a doctor or lawyer ... I'll have to start all over from the beginning and ... I have nothing to fall back on."

From what he told us, Michael appeared to be in the midst of trying to figure out what he would do in the future. Difficult as this task is for all adolescents, it was particularly confusing for him. By running away for such a long period of time Michael had lost touch with those connections which others could turn to for support and guidance and against which one can measure oneself. He had neither the day-to-day physical support that a family can provide nor had he had the experience of standing up for something he believed in in spite of his parents' objections. Instead he had run away, and now, when he wanted to return, found himself excluded. (Counselors at Project Place who had tried to get Michael and his family back together said that his parents were firm in their resolve that he not come back home.) It was not surprising that Michael still identified strongly with his family's values and called himself "conservative." His own attempts at self-definition had left him confused and adrift, a feeling which led him to suspect that he had been "wrong" and they had been right in the conflict that occurred while he was at home. Consequently, he had taken on their values as his own.

2
"I DON'T KNOW WHY SHE RUNS AWAY"

JOANNE EVANS first ran away at the age of sixteen, returned home, and then left again several times during the next few months. We met her at Project Place when she had just taken off, and talked briefly with her at that time. Later we visited her mother at home one afternoon and spent a morning at her school.

Joanne's mother, Mrs. Evans, seemed quiet and reserved, even shy, on first meeting. Nevertheless, despite her difficulty in speaking English, she talked readily about her anxieties and confusions of the past few months, during which Joanne had left home several times. Mrs. Evans came to the United States from Mexico and lived in Florida until her husband died. Eleven years ago she moved to Boston with Joanne, and lives in South Boston, where she works for a clothing manufacturer as a stitcher. Her apartment, where we talked to her, is stark in its simplicity, extremely neat, clean, and dimly lit—even on sunny days—because the curtains were drawn. Mrs. Evans told us that the first time Joanne ran away she left after a big argument. In response to our question, "Did you look for her or wait for her to come home?" she said, "Where could I look? It doesn't make sense just to walk around in the street. I wouldn't know anywhere to look."

Mrs. Evans wanted Joanne to discuss problems with her and expressed strong disappointment that most communication between them turned into fights. Since Joanne was in the room throughout our discussion with Mrs. Evans, they would occasionally contradict each other and a disagreement would erupt. Mrs. Evans's confusion about Joanne's behavior and her longing to be understood by her daughter were apparent. Many times while we were there Mrs. Evans repeated, "She never tells me anything. I always say to her, 'Tell me, tell me, whatever it is, good or bad; if we talk it over we can work it out together. We'll figure out a way. But if you won't talk to me there's nothing I can do. You must tell me.' I always tell her *my* problems but she never tells me anything." It seemed that many of the arguments between Joanne and her mother occurred because Joanne would not explain where she was going or what she was doing, and Mrs. Evans disapproved of what she suspected or imagined Joanne was doing.

The conflicts between them arose mainly over issues of curfew and drinking. Mrs. Evans expressed sympathy for Joanne's need to have friends and do things away from home: "It must be boring for her here if she stays inside the house all day. She needs friends. She should go outside." The tensions resulted from a strong discrepancy between Mrs. Evans's idea of "fun" and Joanne's notions of how she wanted to spend her time. Mrs. Evans had been quite happy a year or two earlier when Joanne had visited with friends to do things like going bowling. She would go out at a definite time and one of her friends' parents would bring her home after dark so that Mrs. Evans had no reason to worry about her safety. This kind of entertainment seemed far more appropriate to Mrs. Evans than merely "going out" with friends to an undetermined destination for an uncertain length of time.

Joanne's mother felt particularly uneasy about her daughter's walking on the street alone or with just another girl at night. "Maybe I'm old-fashioned," she said, "but I don't think two girls should be out alone late at night. What could they be doing?" Mrs. Evans worried and brooded over fantasies of what they might be doing. "Besides, the streets are dangerous. Waiting for the subway, taking the subway late at night—it's not safe." Mrs. Evans explained her frustration in trying to control Joanne, saying that although she realized Joanne was young and wanted to have her fun, she didn't like her friends because they had "too much influence" on her: "I tell her to stay home sometimes and then a friend comes over and says 'come out' so she goes out.... Her other friends, they were nice girls. I always knew where she was and where to call." Recently she had been bewildered, wondering where Joanne could be and when she would come home. Several times Joanne was out when her mother came home from work in the afternoon, and Mrs. Evans had waited and waited, thinking, "Where is she?" and expecting her to come home, at least by dinner time. Finally Joanne would call at nine-thirty to say, "I'm at a friend's. Can I stay longer?" to which her mother would reply indignantly, "*Where* have you been?"

Mrs. Evans's disapproval registered most strongly against Joanne's suspected drinking. "Drinking I don't like," Mrs. Evans said, "and I know she's been drinking. At home it's one thing. If you want to have a drink here at home and have a good time that's okay. But out in the street—no. I don't like it. Oh, I know boys do it, and boys will be boys, that's okay, but for girls it doesn't look nice." Mrs. Evans's notions of what Joanne should and should not do were clearly governed in part by a rigid sense of propriety—what someone who is a nice girl does or does not do. It seemed to us in one brief contact with her that she applied her ideas of what was appropriate as rigorously to herself as to her daughter. From the way she told us that she had not yet been outside that day, although it was a lovely afternoon, we sensed that she left the house very little except to go to work or on a specific errand. That Joanne might want to "hang out" with friends on a street corner was incomprehensible to her. "What is there to do on the street corner?" It seemed probable to us that because of her difficulty in speaking English and because she has only one child, her contacts with adolescents were rare and therefore her opportunities to become accustomed to their ways limited.

Equally strong was our sense that, lonely already, Mrs. Evans felt increasingly isolated as her daughter spent more and more time away from home and talked to her less. This loneliness, as well as her worries about the appropriateness of Joanne's behavior, was greatly intensified at the times when Joanne actually ran away. Mrs. Evans described in detail one Friday afternoon when Joanne was supposed to meet her at the store after school to do the grocery shopping. She waited for a long time but Joanne did not come. Finally Mrs. Evans went home thinking, "Well, maybe she's mad at me. I yelled at her last night. Maybe she's at home." But at home, no Joanne. "Very late that night when she still wasn't home I found that her jacket, some clothes, and a shopping bag that I'd seen on her bed were gone, so I knew she'd run away.... When she came back I didn't say much, I was afraid to say the wrong thing. She might leave again."

Despite her strong concern, and her disapproval of Joanne, Mrs. Evans assured us that she had never called the police or taken out a runaway warrant against her daughter. Her refusal to call the police seemed to stem from strong pride and a sense of family privacy in addition to a hope that Joanne would eventually come to her senses of her own accord. Mrs. Evans had no wish to involve herself or Joanne in criminal proceedings. "I worried," she said, "but I never called the police. I always think she'll come home. It may be a month, it may be six months, it may be a year, but she'll come." Nevertheless, Joanne was picked up once by the police as a runaway. When asked by the judge whether she would go home with her mother, she refused and was sent to Lyman School for a few days. While there, she broke out with another girl and hitchhiked to Providence. Waiting on a street corner for a ride they were mistaken by police for prostitutes, chased, arrested, called "whores," and taken into the station where they were both badly beaten and then locked up. At her next court appearance, Joanne agreed to go home. She said that she and her friend had been furious at the way the "pigs" treated them, but also frightened. Mrs. Evans told us that at the first court hearing Joanne had seemed "wild," but "the second time she made sense."

One of the things Joanne and her mother had argued about was whether the girl would finish high school. Joanne, as soon as she had turned sixteen, wanted to drop out and get a job, but her mother felt strongly that she should finish school. One of the reasons she had come to Boston was for her daughter to "get a good education." Joanne started skipping classes in the fall, staying away primarily from her business courses, which she found boring. Eventually she stopped going to school altogether.

Mrs. Evans's sorrow and perplexity in the ways she felt deceived by her daughter were strongest when she discovered by surprise that Joanne was staying away from school. "I always asked her why she wasn't doing homework and she said she didn't have homework. I didn't want to call up the teacher. Maybe she didn't have any and then I would make myself or the teacher look bad." Then one day a letter arrived from the school saying that Joanne had not been attending. When Mrs. Evans called up, "the principal said she never had any trouble in school until she started hooking." Seemingly, Mrs. Evans thought that by finishing school Joanne would have an opportunity to fulfill those aspirations she herself had never achieved. Concerned that her daughter finish as soon as possible, Mrs. Evans asked again and again whether we thought Joanne could avoid repeating her junior year if she went to summer school. Joanne herself had other ideas about the way she wanted to spend the summer, but when she mentioned them, an argument ensued which seemed as if it might be typical of the way discussions went between them:

Mrs. E.: What *do* you want to do for the summer?

J.: Maybe get a job. Maybe travel.

Mrs. E.: Travel!

J. (sighing): Well, I only want to go to one place.

Mrs. E.: Where's that?

J.: Ohio.

Mrs. E.: Who do you know there?

J.: I *told* you. Some people from Place. . . .

Mrs. E.: How do I even know who you're going with? Who invited you? Where would you be staying? A hotel, that costs money.

> J.: No, Ma, I told you some people from Antioch who worked at the Place said we could come. We'd stay with them.
>
> Mrs. E.: Is that a rooming house?
>
> J.: No, it's a college.
>
> Mrs. E.: Well, have other people asked their parents?
>
> J.: I don't know. I haven't asked them.
>
> Mrs. E.: There, you see, at Place the kids make plans and when they go home it's all different. You make plans without permission and you don't even know you can go. . . .

Since returning home, Joanne planned to go back to school and possibly attend college, which seemed to please her mother. Nevertheless, Mrs. Evans was wary of pinning too much hope on anything her daughter said for fear of further disappointments. Before we left she told us, "I don't know why she runs away. It seems she purposely won't do things that make me happy—just to hurt me. I don't know why." Her evident feelings of loneliness and increasing isolation gave her an air of confusion and bitter resignation so that when Joanne said, "Come on, Ma. I've been talking to you since I've been home. I told you everything that happened when we were busted," her mother could only answer "yes" in a very uncertain voice.

When we visited South Boston High School to speak with some of Joanne's teachers, numerous students were standing outside the school looking bored and restless. They directed us to the guidance counselors' office, which was up a flight of worn and dirty marble stairs, in a cramped room divided by makeshift partitions. When Mr. Hartley, Joanne's counselor, returned, he had misplaced the keys to his office and had to ask a student to climb over the partition to unlock it for him. Mr. Hartley, an affable, middle-aged man, coaches baseball and football in addition to being a counselor. He did not know Joanne at all. "Joanne

Evans.... I'll have to get her records. We have 2,200 kids here. I only see the bad ones, the ones looking for jobs, and those going to college." When he found her file he told us, "She did as well as anyone in the school. Bs and Cs, mostly Cs ... the kids here aren't smart. Her IQ wasn't terrific but it wasn't *too* low. I guess that doesn't always mean something." Since he knew nothing about Joanne beyond what the records showed, he thought maybe we could "fill him in on a little of the background." He showed surprise that all her absences were not due to the fact that she was "on drugs." "I usually assume that when kids drop out, it's because they're on drugs."

Mr. Hartley attributed dropping out and other school difficulties either to the use of drugs or to the absence of one or both parents: "In 20 percent of the families these kids come from, at least one parent is missing. When a sixteen-year-old student is absent for twenty days a registered letter is sent home to find out whether the kid has dropped out permanently." Mr. Hartley assumed that because, to his knowledge, Mrs. Evans had never responded to the letter she received, she did not care about Joanne's absences. He was amazed to hear of her concern. When he was told of the conflicts between Joanne and her mother he asked, "It's normal for kids to have conflicts with their parents, isn't it?" and seemed unable to understand the kinds of strain such tensions can create in kids' lives. His thinking about adolescents in general was limited almost completely to stereotypes: "bad" kids, "good" kids, "smart" kids, "hippies," "athletic types," and so on.

Unable to answer any of our other questions about Joanne, he went off in search of her English teacher, who joined us in the office. Miss Peabody, a teacher of remedial reading, was the only person we spoke with that day who showed an active interest in Joanne. An elderly, kind woman, Miss Peabody told us with a sympathetic chuckle that she first encountered Joanne last year when she "ejected her from the girls' room a number of times for smoking." Last year, she said, Joanne had been "sullen ... unsmiling ... she resented any kind of authority ... but this year Joanne was quite pleasant." She seemed to have changed over the summer. "You know," Miss Peabody said, "when she smiles she has a beautiful smile."

Miss Peabody felt that many of the students in her class thought themselves stupid because they had been assigned to remedial reading. On the contrary, Miss Peabody explained that she assured her students that she only took people who had "real potential" and who could benefit from some help. Joanne in particular could do well in school if she stayed with it. Miss Peabody felt that one can't always trust IQ tests and that more often a student's ability and performance "is a question of background."

When Joanne began cutting classes, Miss Peabody talked with her mother, who had, in fact, come for a conference in response to the registered letter. Miss Peabody described Mrs. Evans as a "very concerned, very lovely woman," but recalled that when she tried to tell Joanne this, Joanne had merely thrown her head back in a resentful way. "I told her I thought her mother cared a lot and that for her to take the trouble to come in to school during the day when she works and all showed that she was making a real effort and that the least she [Joanne] could do was to make as much effort herself.... I think she was ashamed of her mother for some reason. Maybe because she doesn't speak English very well. But she didn't have any reason to be ashamed." A few days after that conversation, Joanne came up to Miss Peabody and told her things were going better at home. Shortly afterwards, however, she stopped coming to school completely and Miss Peabody had no idea what had happened to her. She seemed anxious to have Joanne return to school.

After talking with Miss Peabody, we went to the office to speak with Dr. Kent, the principal, with whom Mrs. Evans said she had spoken. Waiting in the outer office, we were overwhelmed by a feeling of how impersonal a place the school was, of how anonymous most of the 2,200 students who spent three years there were. We could well understand why Joanne, trapped in business courses which bored her, wanted to leave this school. The discrepancy between her mother's ideal of "a good education" and the reality of her daughter's situation seemed particularly ironic. At one point the assistant principal rushed out of his office saying, "Another one just escaped suspension." He barked into the loudspeaker system: "Alan Jones, come to the office immediately." When the boy arrived the assistant principal laid into him because he was supposed to have been suspended the previous week but "had escaped" because they had suspended the wrong Alan Jones!

Finally Dr. Kent appeared, and talked to us over the counter, neglecting to ask us to sit down. A sixty-year-old man, gray-haired and conservatively dressed, he was gruff and threatening in appearance. After listening to us explain the reason for our visit, he went silently to the files and pulled out Joanne's records, asked us a few questions while glancing through the folder, then said tersely, "Okay. That checks out. What do you want to know?" He explained that he couldn't remember Mrs. Evans at all, though he might have talked with her. "I usually write something down in the file if it's important. I don't have that kind of memory." All Dr. Kent could say about Joanne was that she was "not the most attractive girl . . . rather stolid . . . I doubt she had many, oh, *any* friends." As far as he was concerned she was a junior in good standing, and if she came back to school she could probably get her diploma in a year by taking some summer courses. "But she would have to really *want* to," he added.

The time we spent in South Boston High suggested that neither Joanne nor her mother had made much of an impression on the administration and teachers, with the exception of Miss Peabody. As far as most of the staff was concerned, her running away—and leaving school—meant little to them beyond more paper work; she was merely another statistic for the files. It was difficult to get any sense of how the school personnel viewed runaways, or Joanne as a runaway, since they seemed to give very little thought to the matter. While this could be a positive sign— that kids who run away from there are not penalized or singled out for special treatment—it also seemed to preclude a kind of institutional support or personal attention for a girl like Joanne at a time when she was under strain.

3
CAN'T FIND MY WAY BACK HOME

DAN SCHWARTZ AND HEATHER KELLY were two runaways with whom we talked only once and who asked us not to contact their parents. We were, however, able to talk with counselors who had known them. Dan was sixteen, but his slight build and smooth face made him look younger. One Saturday afternoon Tony, a supervisor at the Division of Child Guardianship, brought Dan to our house, and for nearly four hours we sat around the kitchen table talking with him. We first met Heather, who was fifteen, at the Youth Resources Bureau, a counseling center in Cambridge. She had recently run away from the Children's Unit of the Metropolitan State Hospital. We later talked with her counselor at YRB and with a staff member at the children's unit.

Dan was a quick, appealing boy with a flair for the dramatic, who reproduced verbatim arguments he had had with his family. As he reenacted these scenes, taking first his own part, then that of the other person, he became increasingly angry. It seemed to us that he still felt strongly about events that had taken place before he ran away from home.

A few months before Dan ran away, he had an argument with his girlfriend in which she accidentally kicked him in the stomach.

Unwilling to admit that he had been kicked by a girl, he complained of appendicitis and was hospitalized for tests. Although the tests showed nothing seriously wrong with him, he wanted to stay longer in the hospital, and began playing games with the nurses, complaining of dizziness and strange sensations and purposely making references to drug experiences when the nurses were in earshot. They responded to him suspiciously and even asked questions about his drug use, but he denied their accusations while continuing his suggestive allusions.

On the day Dan was discharged he faked a fainting spell, fell as he was walking downstairs, and was immediately whisked back into the hospital. When the doctors gave him all sorts of further tests and could find nothing physically wrong, the nurses explained their suspicions that he was a drug "addict" (Dan's word) and suggested that he was having "flashbacks." He was released from the hospital, but a few days later, while at home, he feigned another dizzy spell. His mother took him to the South Shore Mental Health Center, where he was again accused of using drugs, but this time he responded with a question instead of an outright denial: "What would happen if I said I did?" When assured that they only wanted to help him, he "confessed" that he had been using speed and acid very heavily for several months.

Dan spoke readily and articulately, offering his own interpretations of his actions. With reference to the elaborate scheme he had engineered he said, "I kind of took advantage of the drug issue to get some attention. I was tired of being ignored." Actually, Dan's confession was as much of a fiction as his flashbacks, but both had the desired effect: people were scared enough to pay some attention to him. For several weeks he went to see a counselor at a drug program in Quincy. In counseling sessions, Dan recounted as his own stories people had told him about their experiences on acid and speed, neither of which he had used more than once or twice.

Ironically, despite the anxiety his mother and stepfather expressed about his drug problem, neither of them noticed anything unusual on the rare occasions when he did use drugs. One evening he had taken several "downs" (Seconal) and practically passed out in front of the television. "Why, I could hardly stand up," he said, "and they didn't even notice!" Dan liked putting things over on people and seemed to enjoy his parents' failure to recognize his drugged state as much as his own success at convincing others that he was a chronic drug user.

Unfortunately, however, while paying attention to his "drug problem," Dan's family did not respond to the very real confusions and fears which had led him to fabricate the story in the first place. Two of the dominant themes in his conversation were an uncertainty about who his real father was and the effect which that uncertainty had on his relationship with his mother. Dan had always been told that his father was David Schwartz, although in answer to Dan's repeated questions —"What was Dad like?" —his mother had continually told him contradictory stories. First she said that Mr. Schwartz was dead, then that he was in the service, and later that he was living in California. Dan suspected that perhaps his father had been in jail but that his mother was ashamed to tell him, so he persisted in questioning relatives and others who might have had any information about the man's whereabouts.

While visiting his grandfather in the South End, Dan overheard a conversation which led him to think that Mr. Schwartz was living nearby. When he confronted his mother with the discovery, she seemed shaken and agreed to tell him the real story. She had first been married to John Murphy, the father of Dan's older brother Jimmy, but after she and Murphy were divorced she married Schwartz. The two of them, however, "had problems," and after they separated she became pregnant by someone else and Dan was born. Dan believed her story up to this point, but when he asked, "Who was my real father, then?" his mother claimed that she did not remember. Furious, he insisted that this could not be true and felt that she had been lying to him all along.

Confusion showed in Dan's face whenever he spoke of his searched-for father. These feelings were aggravated by Murphy, whom he was expected to call "Dad" even though this man was only his brother's father. Dan felt neglected and abused by his "dad." "He would call up on the phone and whenever I answered he'd say, 'Hi, Dan, is Jimmy around?' He never asked how I was or invited me along when he took Jimmy places. The only times he ever came over to see me was when my mother was mad and called him up to come over and beat the shit out of me."

Dan thought Murphy was "two-faced" and resented having to consider the man his father. He complained that Murphy never helped him with his homework or asked him how things were going at school as he did with Jimmy. He only punished Dan if he cut school or got bad grades. Dan pointed out that he *needed* to be "pushed" to do the things that he was supposed to do, but resented the fact that instead of receiving any parental encouragement he was usually just "pushed around." Whenever Dan complained about Murphy, saying, "He's not even my real father so I don't see why he has any right to tell me what to do," his brother beat him up.

Dan claimed that his confused family situation made it difficult for him to make friends at school. He remembers being a loner most of the time: "If you don't know someone they can't hurt you," was his motto. Other kids at school considered him strange because he let it be known that he was Jewish, while the schools he attended were predominantly Catholic. Actually, his supposed father was Jewish, but Dan was baptized Catholic according to his mother's religion. In spite of this he chose to be a Jew and often fought with classmates who taunted him about religion.

The loneliness he felt in school, combined with a lack of interest in the subjects he had to take, led him to stay away more and more frequently. He attempted to switch schools by lying about where he lived, but was unsuccessful, and claims he had missed 104 days in the ninth grade since the only class which interested him was the electricity unit of the shop course. After dropping out he worked part time as a busboy for a few months, then quit and spent a great deal of time at home watching television.

The only person Dan was close to throughout this period was his girlfriend, Susan. The two of them spent as much time together as they could, although her parents were strict about her social life and sometimes forbade her to see Dan. Despite these rules Susan and Dan became more involved and began sleeping together. Their mutual unhappiness at home drew them even closer to each other. Once when Susan's father beat her for coming in too late at night, she fled to Dan's house and stayed there upstairs for a few days. They thought about running away together but never actually did so. Finally Susan went to Project Place to try to work things out with her family through counselors there.

At about this time Dan ran away from home for the third and final time (he had previously run away twice to a friend's house for a day or two). He was bored with doing nothing, but he did not want to go back to school. The recurrent conflicts with his family, coupled with the arrival of his mother's new boyfriend, Joe, finally made living at home unbearable for him. One day Joe accused Dan of being a "lazy bum" and Dan retaliated in kind: "He's had lots of chances to do things but he always blows them. He has no right to tell me that I'm a failure." Dan had been thinking of running for several weeks and had packed his bag, so that when the huge argument erupted between him and Joe, he walked out the door.

As Dan walked down the street, his mother followed, asking him where he was going, but he shouted back at her, "Don't bother me. Leave me alone, I want to be alone, I'm never coming back.... No, I'm not going over to Jimmy's, I don't know where I'm going." He thought for a while about going to his brother's house, but fearing another argument with him, he went instead to Project Place.

While at Project Place Dan met Tony, a supervisor at the Division of Child Guardianship, who offered to help him find a place in the Job Corps. Tony described Dan to us as "a very disturbed kid, maybe you could even call him psychotic." He pointed out several characteristics which Dan shared with his mother and which were, from a traditionally psychological point of view, pathological: he thought both of them were masochistic and had "short fuses" which erupted quickly into violence with minor annoyances. He also saw Dan as lazy and manipulative, and thought that his stay in the hospital was a "psychosomatic-masochistic" episode.

While we had reservations about the psychiatric terms Tony used to describe Dan, we were impressed by his work with this boy. Tony approached Dan honestly and straightforwardly as a friend, offered him a place to stay, and talked openly about his own motivation for helping young people. Most important of all, he recognized Dan's strengths and concentrated his attention on these. He responded to Dan as a likable boy with intelligence and a sense of humor, not as a "kid with problems" or a "psychotic." When he noticed that Dan was lying or evading the truth, he pointed it out in a joking manner, making it clear that honesty was important, but doing so in a spirit of acceptance and understanding. His confrontations were friendly and supportive rather than provocative.

Instead of assuming that Dan needed psychiatric help, Tony offered him companionship and helped him follow up his interest in becoming an electrician by suggesting he join the Job Corps. Tony accepted Dan's need to be away from his family, and helped him find something he would enjoy doing. This kind of affirmative support from an adult was startling in contrast to the punitive and hypocritical attitudes by which Dan had felt overwhelmed at home. He came to feel that there was a possibility of release from the feelings of confusion and boredom which he had experienced at home and as a member of his family.

Heather was small and wiry and her curly blond hair was close-cropped, framing a freckled face. Her young appearance contrasted markedly with her tough manner. Wearing corduroy jeans and a leather jacket, and chewing gum, she spoke quickly and somewhat nervously; to our suggestion that she speak with one of us alone in another room, she responded, "Oh, can't we just all stay here and talk together? You know, kind of an open discussion."

Heather had been running away since she was ten. The first time she took off she stayed out only one day. Heather had planned to stay away longer, but at dusk she was questioned by a policeman about her age and returned home. From then on she left with increasing frequency and for longer periods of time, living at friends' houses or with people whom she had met on the streets. By the time she was thirteen, Heather had found a place in the world of Cambridge street people, and spent most of her time "hanging around" with friends, many of whom were older.

For the most part she enjoyed the free and easy life of the street and the sense that she could follow her impulses with few constraints; once she hitchhiked to Washington, D.C., and back with two friends, a girl and a boy. The life was not altogether an easy one, however. Finding somewhere to stay for the night was often a problem, since Heather was a girl, and although many people offered her places, she was never sure what they wanted from her.

Another difficulty Heather shared with other street people was the continual possibility of being picked up by the police. Due to her age and youthful appearance, she was often questioned, but because of her fast-talking and volatile style, the questioning often turned into arguments which led to her arrest on "idle and disorderly" or "drug" charges. Heather admitted that she had experience with drugs, particularly speed, downs, and "some junk, but not too heavy," but resented her treatment by the police. From what Heather told us, it sounded as though some of the regular cops came to know her and singled her out because they recognized her.

One particular evening Heather was standing around on a corner and a policeman told her to go home. "I said 'no' and he said I had to, and I said I wouldn't, so he took me down to the station and called my mother, and while he was waiting for her to come get me he hit me and locked me up and when my mother came I told her what had happened and all she said was, 'You probably deserved it.' "

Heather described her street friends at length and talked about her feelings toward them. What she liked about the street was that people took care of each other, sharing food, clothes, and places to stay. These friends, she said, were the first who really cared about her: "People really worried about me.... Like, if I wasn't around for a few days they wondered where I was.... They really noticed if I was gone and they worried whether I was all right and what had happened to me."

Heather also worried about her friends. Sometimes she would become depressed when she saw so many people on the street who were "really going nowhere." She was particularly upset to see that some street kids were too old to change and had almost given up the chance of doing something with their lives. She thought that she was young enough and not so firmly entrenched in street life that she could do something else. "I remember thinking to myself, I'm only fourteen—I still have time to change, I can make a new start ... but if they're already eighteen or twenty it's too late for them to start again." At times Heather would cry as she walked around the street; "I don't know why I was crying.... There wasn't really anything wrong, I just felt so awful sometimes I couldn't help it."

Despite Heather's mixed feelings about life on the street she spoke more easily about that experience than about her family. She expressed strong resentment that her stepfather never accepted her as a daughter, even though he was the only "father" she remembered (her mother, divorced when Heather was a baby, had quickly remarried). "I know he's never loved me at all, he's never treated me like a real daughter. I don't understand why ... I guess he'd had so much trouble with my older sisters that by the time I was growing up he was just sick of it." Whatever Heather's stepfather's actual feelings were toward her, she experienced him as uncaring, impatient, and often violent. Heather cited several instances of his terrible temper—one afternoon he flew at her in a rage, threatening to tie her to the bed. Heather said, "I love my mother and I think she's mostly on my side, but she will never stand up for me because she's too scared to go against him." Heather recognized that her mother was upset when she ran away, but felt that her mother had made little effort to control her. We are uncertain about whether she really wanted some kind of parental control, for Heather claimed that there was nothing anyone could do to stop her from leaving home.

Heather talked most about her sister Ann, who was three years her senior. Ann was a junkie who lived away from home, and Heather felt that she was closest to this sister because the two of them had grown up together. Heather also had two older sisters who were married and, according to her, "okay, but kind of boring."

We talked at length with Diane, Heather's counselor at the Youth Resources Bureau in Cambridge, who had known Heather for nearly two years, helped her find places to live, and had gone to court with her on numerous occasions. Diane knew Heather's family well and was the only adult outside of her family to whom Heather felt close. Heather called Diane whenever she was in trouble, and at other times stopped by just to talk and let Diane know what was happening.

Diane confirmed Heather's description of her stepfather, who, she said, had never liked any of his stepdaughters but had a particular animosity toward Heather. Diane had seen his violent temper in action and said that there was continual fighting in the family. During these fights the stepfather was infuriated by the way Heather yelled back and refused to obey him.

Although the stepfather was initially in charge of disciplining the children, Heather's mother often played the role of a manipulative conciliator. When the stepfather stormed out of the house after forbidding Heather to do something, her mother would say, "Oh, Heather, he didn't mean it." In an actual confrontation with the stepfather, however, she never took her daughter's side. Thus Heather's mother acted as a catalyst. By refusing to take a firm stand on either side she perpetuated the sources of conflict, allowing Heather to do as she pleased, but refusing to limit her husband's harrassment of the girl.

Eventually the stepfather became so exasperated with trying to control Heather that he decided to leave the matter up to his wife. Diane felt that Heather's mother was a weak and often manipulative woman who cared about her children but had little notion of how to relate to them. She also seemed unable to show any affection. The counselor claimed that Heather's mother was fearful of her husband and too dependent on him to cross him openly. In desperation over what to do about Heather and at Diane's suggestion, she began going to a psychiatrist at a family counseling center. But despite these visits Heather's mother "made no effort to solve her problems or think through issues. She merely used the psychiatrist as a last resort—someone to call and complain to."

Diane felt that Heather was strongly attached to her mother and wanted her love very much. Running away and her life in the street may have represented attempts to test her mother: Will she still love me if I do this? How many times will she take me back? Diane described in detail the way Heather wavered between her desire to continue living away from home and her wish for some decisive response from her mother.

Heather's life on the street ended when she was picked up on a serious drug charge and committed to Metropolitan State Mental Hospital for observation. She remained there nine months. It was shortly after she had run away from the hospital that we talked with her. One of the first things she told us was that she had come to see Diane because she wanted to stay away from the street, where she "would only get back into drugs again." Heather was staying with a young couple in Cambridge who had offered her temporary shelter until something more permanent could be worked out. She had contacted Diane and asked her to help find a group home situation. In working through the Division of Child Guardianship, Diane was able to arrange for a temporary, two-week, foster placement and set up a meeting between Heather and a DCG worker. The day before the meeting was to take place Heather called her mother and dropped hints about her whereabouts and her plans: "Well, yes, I'm staying in Cambridge ... with a couple ... they have two children ... no, they aren't married ... yes, it's a nice neighborhood ... and I'm going to see Diane and someone from the DCG ... well, soon ... actually tomorrow." It was not surprising that Heather's parents arrived at Diane's office the next day in time for the appointment.

Diane was somewhat apprehensive about the outcome of the confrontation, so she told Heather to wait in the next room, but left the door open. She explained to Heather's parents that if, as they claimed, they were determined to take Heather home, there was nothing to prevent their dragging her out bodily but she, Diane, would certainly not help. She tried to persuade them to agree to a foster home but they refused, insisting that Heather was either going home or back to the hospital. Finally the stepfather walked out in a rage. At this point Heather came into the room to talk with her mother. Throughout the conversation, however, she had one foot out the window ready to jump lest her mother attempt to take her away or back to Met State. Finally the mother agreed to foster placement, but two days later withdrew permission until Diane convinced her Heather would simply stay on the run or might even disappear completely if they tried to keep her at home.

Meanwhile, DCG sent in two applications to group homes "because they really felt she could benefit from such a situation." One of these was Massachusetts Residential Homes, a "halfway house" for adolescents. Admission to this program is contingent upon the young person's "motivation," and before the acceptance becomes final, the staff tries to test the applicant's commitment to change. When Heather talked with the director on the phone, she expressed interest in the program and he was impressed with her. He assigned her the responsibility of calling back at an appointed time, but when she failed to do so the arrangements fell through. Diane felt that at the time Heather's "motivation" (to make a complete break from drugs and street life and return to school) was stronger then it had ever been. She had expected that Heather would call. It is questionable, however, how easily motivation for change can be judged by a person's willingness to make a commitment to an unfamiliar program. Asking Heather to make a conscious and definite break with her family and her only close friends—street people—was no small demand.

Diane was extremely worried about Heather, anxious to find her a more permanent place to live, and afraid that she would again become involved with the "heavy drug scene." She was particularly concerned about Heather's boyfriend, a drug dealer, who "encouraged Heather in her continuing involvement with drugs." One day Heather came to see Diane and was almost incoherent. She seemed ill and underfed, could hardly keep her eyes open, and was unable to speak clearly. Afraid that Heather was using heroin, Diane admitted that she panicked. "I couldn't see any help forthcoming from Heather's parents and Heather seemed unable to follow through on any long-term plans. . . . I was the one who initiated the court action. . . . I hoped maybe that way I could get some real help for her."

At the court hearing, Heather's mother promised the judge that she would separate from her husband if Heather could come home. Convinced that this would be the best solution, the judge released Heather to her mother's custody, but the mother did not leave her husband, and Heather moved out once again, this time to live with Ann, the sister who was a heroin addict.

At this time Heather voluntarily returned to the school at Met State Hospital as a day student. During her previous stay at the hospital she had attended the school and said that she "really liked it there." Classes were small and she was able to do things she wanted. There were courses like astrology in addition to instruction in regular subjects such as arithmetic and reading. She enjoyed art classes above all because she was allowed to experiment, unlike art classes in public school where everyone had to do the same thing. She hated the children's unit itself, however, since she had often been locked up in the "seclusion rooms" for talking back.

When we visited Met State Hospital we walked through the wards of the children's unit on the way to the school. In one room twenty kids were sitting around, playing cards or looking dully out the window. The physical plant of the hospital was depressing—corridors dimly lit, halls painted in drab colors, locks on all the doors. The rooms of the school looked the same, but the atmosphere was far more lively.

We talked with Mrs. Anderson, the director of the school, who had known Heather first as a patient, more recently as a day student, and remembered her well. She explained that the program at the school emphasizes working with kids' strengths and helping them develop confidence as well as skills. The classes are ungraded and students design their own program with the help of the staff. Once a program is agreed on it is viewed as a contract which the student should adhere to until he requests a change or revision. We were impressed by the versatility of the staff and the wide range of activities and classes in which students could participate: painting, sewing, reading, math, as well as such unusual projects as extracting sugar from maple trees to make syrup for a party at the hospital. Apparently some of the staff on the wards are amazed that in school the kids don't seem to manifest the same "behavior problems" which they do in the rest of the hospital. Mrs. Anderson felt that in the school they receive enough individual attention and have opportunities to do interesting things which enable them to focus their energy in constructive ways.

The director's impression of Heather was that "she has a tough, sophisticated exterior, but inside she's just a little girl. . . . She can be just wonderful, but she also can make me madder than almost any other kid here." The records from Heather's previous school which Mrs. Anderson showed us reported that she was "impulsive," "inconsistent," and "defensive." This information appeared on a checklist which ranked her on a scale of 1 to 5 for a number of different personality traits.

At the time we talked with Mrs. Anderson, Heather was attending the school as a day student. Some days she came in, on others she did not. The school did not try to force attendance but expected her to participate in the program when she was there. On the day we visited, Mrs. Anderson took us to look for Heather in one of the classrooms, saying over her shoulder, "You know, sometimes when you come to talk to her, she tells you to fuck off, and sometimes she just goes to sleep." We were unable to see her because she had not come to school that day.

Mrs. Anderson was worried about Heather's living with her sister. She felt that her sister's home was unstable, but recognized that the parents' home was equally difficult, if not more so. While Heather's mother claimed to be concerned, Mrs. Anderson sensed that she had rejected Heather; her evidence for this was that the woman refused to come in to the school for conferences and allowed Heather to live away from home. Her refusal to cooperate with them was frustrating to the school staff, who try to work as closely as they can with the parents.

There is a possibility that at the Met State school Heather will find some of the support she needs to develop her own confidence and skills. Although she is living with her sister, the school is committed to helping her stay off heavy drugs and work through some of her family conflicts. Because her stepfather's presence in the house is a source of such extreme tension, it seems unlikely that she will ever return home for long.

4
DONNA

DR. NATHAN BOWMAN *first came to Sanctuary in the early fall looking for his daughter Donna, who had recently escaped from a mental hospital. His daughter, he explained, had often spent time in Harvard Square; perhaps she would be there now. Disturbed about Donna's disappearance, he wanted to understand what it was that made her and so many other adolescents run away from home. When he heard about the runaway study, he expressed interest in talking with us. What he had to say, he hoped, would benefit other parents in his position. He also thought talking might have some "therapeutic value" for himself. We talked with him three times in his office and visited his wife, Julia, at their home. Not until we had heard both parents' stories did we speak with Donna at the Hare Krishna Temple, where she was staying.*

Nate Bowman was a tall, stoop-shouldered forty-year-old man. A fringe of reddish hair surrounded his bald forehead, and his eyes blinked nervously behind tortoiseshell glasses. When we saw him he wore a tweed sport-jacket with frayed cuffs, a wrinkled dark necktie, and baggy cotton trousers. Nate was a psychologist who taught counseling at a graduate school of education. "Being a psychologist may not always have been the best thing for my relationship with Donna," he said, hesitantly, sitting in his office, a tiny room cluttered with papers. Books were piled to the ceiling.

Julia Bowman, Nate's second wife and Donna's stepmother, could have been anywhere from twenty to forty years old in her steel-rimmed glasses, bluejeans, and cotton jersey. Her hair, though, had hints of gray and her face, slightly lined around the eyes, suggested that she was probably over thirty. She was active in women's liberation and taught a course on women at a local college. We talked to her at the Bowmans' home, a six-room apartment in Cambridge which seemed comfortable if chaotic, with toys strewn about the floor and coffee mugs scattered on the kitchen table. Julia seemed as willing as Nate to talk about her relationship with Donna.

After Donna had run away from Massachusetts Mental Health Center in the fall of 1971 for the second time, Nate and Julia were not sure where she was for nearly three weeks. Neither mentioned, or seemed to know of, any specific incident which might have precipitated her leaving the hospital, but they spoke freely of her past life and of the experiences which contributed to her decision to separate herself from her family. Nate and Julia's stories suggested, from their point of view, how Donna's situation developed into one from which she felt forced to run. They also described the ways in which they as parents tried to cope with a problematic relationship.

Nate had married his first wife, Penny, when she was only nineteen. In retrospect he thought that marrying him might have been *her* way of running away from a strict, repressive home. Although he believed in "multilateral sexual relationships" (i.e., having simultaneous affairs with more than one person), Penny did not, so he had not put his ideas "into practice" at that time. He described Penny as young and somewhat flighty; after they had been married for several years she began flirting with other men, and had an affair with one of them while Nate was away at a conference. At the time, Donna was six and the family lived in a small midwestern town. As Nate and Penny fought frequently, their marriage deteriorated, and they finally decided to get a divorce. Although Nate speculated that perhaps they had not tried hard enough to make things work, he added, with some bitterness, that he thought Penny had been "too young" (especially since she "had no previous sexual relationships") and that possibly they should not have had children so soon.

After the divorce, Donna, who was seven, and her brother David, aged five, continued to live with their mother. When she remarried two years later her husband, Mark Alpert, legally adopted the children. For several years the Alperts lived in a suburb of Chicago, but Donna and her brother occasionally visited their father during vacations. Nate remembered that whenever his children left they would ask, as they were getting on the plane, "Why did you and Mommy get divorced?"

When Donna was ten, Nate married Julia and moved to Boston. Although they had a baby daughter of their own, Julia recalled that they planned some day to invite Nate's children to come to live with them for a while. When she was fourteen, Donna stayed in Boston for a whole summer—her first extended visit since the marriage.

Julia and Nate felt that the girl liked living with them because they allowed her more freedom than she had been given at home. "I would characterize Penny and Mark as authoritarian and Julia and myself as permissive," said Nate with a smile. Apparently the Alperts set strict curfews for Donna, and Mark used physical punishment regularly. Julia believed Donna's claim that her stepfather beat her—"she does exaggerate sometimes, but I feel sure that he did at least slap her around." Nate expected only that Donna be in on week nights at ten-thirty and on weekends at midnight, yet he did not strictly enforce these limits. In talking about the decisions they made about controlling Donna's behavior, Nate and Julia sounded uncertain about the stance they had taken as parents, and wondered about the wisdom of having allowed Donna to determine her own limits.

As the end of the summer approached, Donna wanted to stay with Nate instead of returning to her mother. He agreed and when Penny and Mark came to Boston for a conference in August, he invited them to lunch to discuss the possibility of Donna's remaining with him. The Alperts, however, refused the invitation and flatly denied permission for Donna to stay. Consequently, the girl returned to Chicago.

Two weeks later, however, Penny called Nate and said that Donna "had become impossible." He had spoiled her, and she would not accept any discipline whatsoever. If Nate did not take her, Penny was going to send her to reform school. The next day the Bowmans picked Donna up at the airport.

Julia spoke freely about her ambivalent feelings toward Donna and the tensions her becoming part of the family had created. At that time Julia already had one daughter, Hesther, who was two, and she was pregnant with her second child. Her first pregnancy had been a difficult one and she was worried about having problems with the second birth. They were living in fairly cramped quarters and waiting to move into an eight-room house in Belmont in order to have more room for the new baby. Until they moved, Donna had to sleep on a roll-away bed in the living room. This arrangement meant that the family did not really have a living room and that Donna had no room of her own. This was difficult for all of them. Donna was a light sleeper; she liked to go to bed early and would insist that the lights be off and that people not talk. Nate also went to bed early, so Julia would be left to read sitting on a straight-backed chair in the kitchen. She was torn between wanting to be a mother to Donna and feeling that Donna expected things of her (such as hemming skirts) which she had done for herself at the same age. Julia also felt that Donna considered her "convenient to have around to do housework and other chores."

There were added tensions between Donna and Hesther and between Julia and Donna about Donna's relationship to the younger child. Her stepmother remarked, "I've never seen such strong sibling rivalry between two children so far apart in age. Donna would complain at dinner that Hesther always interrupted her and that she never had a chance to say anything." Donna did not like to babysit and the Bowmans rarely asked her to do so. On one occasion she intimated to her parents that she might not be able to control her temper if Hesther annoyed her when they were alone together. Thereafter they always hired a babysitter, even if Donna was at home. At other times, however, Donna was affectionate toward Hesther, playing with her, teaching her how to dance.

Nate's interpretation of Donna's reactions to her siblings (the Alperts also had two young children) was that "with the birth of each new child, Donna felt further and further displaced, as though she were getting less love." He felt that Julia and his daughter did not get along very well. Things had gone smoothly as long as Donna was only visiting for summer vacation, but "Julia had two other small children to take care of and the problems Donna was having with adolescence were too much of an added burden."

Nate said that when Donna came to live with them it was like having his ex-wife return. He and Penny had fought frequently and while Donna was there Nate often fought with her. Julia objected to this because it deflected too much of his emotional energy away from her. "You fight the most with the people you love the most," she said. Nate suspected that perhaps unconsciously Donna wanted to break up his recent marriage so that he and her mother could get back together.

That year, while Donna was with her father, she went to a public high school but hated it. Julia and Nate were sympathetic to her dislike of the structure and the boring classes. They were uncertain, however, about how to respond to her friends there. Julia worried that Donna was hanging around with a tough, "leather-jacket" crowd of kids. Despite her uneasiness about the effect these kids might have on Donna, Julia was hesitant to impose unfair restrictions on the girl, because she did not really know what the friends were like. "I just wasn't very experienced with teenagers. My own children were still very young.... We wanted to give Donna enough freedom and let her be as adult as she wanted.... I don't know ... maybe we were too permissive." Occasionally, Julia said, when they refused permission for Donna to stay overnight at a friend's house, Donna complained that they were preventing her from getting in with the "right crowd" of people. "Maybe she was right. We just didn't know." Nate expressed a similar ambivalence about the way he and Julia had treated his daughter. "We tried to be sympathetic with Donna, to meet her needs and be understanding, but we were confused about the kinds of limits we should set for her."

The couple had particular difficulty responding to Donna's sexuality, which they considered precocious for a fourteen-year-old. Julia recalled that Donna dyed her hair black and wore lots of makeup, "as though she were trying to look like a whore." Nate recounted two sexual experiences which Donna had confided to him during that year. One weekend he gave permission for her to go away with a friend and her parents ("because it sounded well chaperoned"), but Donna got drunk and slept with her girlfriend's boyfriend. On another occasion, when Donna was coming home, two boys offered her a ride. They took her home and raped her. "When she told me those things," he said to us, "I didn't know what to say or do."

At the end of the year Donna went "home" to Chicago for summer vacation, expecting to return in the fall, but the Alperts refused to allow it, claiming that the Bowmans were too permissive. The next spring Donna called to say that things were impossible and she wanted to leave. Julia and Nate encouraged her not to use them "as an escape valve," to "stick it out" and finish the school year. They promised to consider her return to Boston in June. At that time they called to tell her that they were planning to move into a commune and she was welcome to join them. Donna responded enthusiastically. She wanted to live in a commune and had been planning to run away to one if she could not live with the Bowmans. Penny and Mark finally agreed to let her go. Before driving out to Chicago to meet Donna, Nate had adoption papers prepared, but when he asked Donna if she would sign them, her stepfather interfered, saying, "Oh, she's not ready for that, are you Donna?" She replied, "No."

When the Bowmans returned to Belmont, Donna started spending time in Harvard Square, and her parents thought she was taking drugs. By this time, however, she was nearly sixteen and they did not feel they could restrict her activities.

At the end of the summer, when they were about to move into the commune, Donna seemed upset. She was reluctant to give up her "nuclear family" and said she did not want to be around during the move: it reminded her of the ways in which her life had been turned topsy-turvy—divorce, remarriages, new children, moving around—so her parents arranged for her to stay with an aunt while they were moving. One night shortly before they moved, Donna became hysterical, raving and talking incoherently about her mother. At one point she threatened to kill herself. Hesther, overhearing her, said, "Oh, Donna, don't do that. Then I wouldn't have a sister anymore." Donna calmed down for the rest of the evening, primarily to reassure Hesther.

The situation in the commune was a difficult one for Donna, and for the other people there as well. One of the motivations for starting the new living arrangement had been to share child-care responsibilities, and most of the members were "older" couples with very young children. In this situation Donna's dislike of babysitting created some tension. Julia explained that at first people in the commune assumed that Donna was an adult and treated her as such, so they resented her refusal to babysit. Donna's dislike of the commune extended beyond the house and its members. According to Julia, she was afraid to walk around alone in the neighborhood, and seemed dissatisfied with the free school she now attended. The Bowmans had agreed to send her there, even though the tuition was high, because they were sympathetic to her hatred of public schools.

Nate described circumstances in the commune that resulted in further conflicts over sexuality. He and Julia believed in sexual freedom among married couples and both had other relationships. When Julia had an affair with someone in the commune with whom Donna had been friendly—possibly even attracted to—the girl reacted bitterly. On several occasions she brought boys home to spend the night with her—"not really boyfriends," Nate explained, "just guys she had picked up on the street and brought in for one night." Finally they told her that she should stop doing that. She responded that they "did the same thing so why wasn't she entitled to?" Nate accepted the idea of premarital sexual relations but felt that his daughter was too young to take responsibility for choosing a promiscuous lifestyle. He also sensed that she was asking for someone to "set controls for her."

Nate mentioned that at times Donna behaved in ways that were "clearly self-destructive." She had a habit of biting her fingernails and the flesh surrounding the nails. On one occasion she had chewed on her fingers so much that they became infected. Her parents took her to the hospital, where she was treated by a doctor. Although Donna seemed all right when she came home from the hospital, she began behaving very strangely that evening. At first people thought she was just acting or fooling around. It soon became clear, however, that she was out of control—crying hysterically, talking incoherently, and threatening to throw herself out the window. Nate and Julia stayed up talking to her for a long time and finally persuaded her to lie down, but she remained awake, muttering and moaning throughout the night. The next day they took her to a doctor, who advised that she be taken in to a local hospital for "evaluation." Nate and Julia sat in while Donna was interviewed by a psychiatrist, who they thought lacked understanding of young people. Julia in particular thought that his questions were hostile and provocative. "When Donna picked up something off the desk and threw it against the wall, I didn't blame her." Julia remarked, "I probably would have done the same thing myself." The psychiatrist, however, thought this indicated that Donna was "psychotic" and recommended that she be hospitalized immediately.

After one month at Mass. Mental, Donna ran away. For three days the Bowmans had no idea where she was but finally she called, offering to come home if they promised not to take her back to the hospital. They did so reluctantly, fearing that it was the only way they could get her back. It was a promise extracted under coercion and one which they later regretted. After she came home she began to visit the Krishna Temple, where some friends had taken her. She appeared to have mixed feelings about the Krishna movement, saying once after she had been there, "Don't let me go there anymore. They're trying to take over my mind." After a month or so, however, she told Nate and Julia that she found living with them "intolerable" and was going to stay at the Krishna Temple. They felt powerless to stop her, assuming that if they refused to give permission she would run away.

One night the Temple president called to say that he was worried about Donna: she had not slept or eaten for three days, and was behaving very strangely. Nate picked her up and took her to the doctor, who again recommended hospitalization. Nate was shocked at how quickly doctors brought out the pink "commitment" slips. Donna was furious at them for "going back" on their promise, but the Bowmans were frightened and thought that Donna was so disturbed that their promise had become impossible to keep. This time Donna stayed in the hospital through the summer, although she insisted that she was not getting any "treatment" or being "helped" in any way.

In the fall Donna ran away again, and was missing for three weeks. When her parents heard from her, she had decided to commit her life to Krishna and was living at the Temple. They made no attempt to dissuade her and now visit with her fairly frequently. Both Nate and Julia say that she seems healthy and much happier than a few months ago. Julia thinks that Donna's life at the Temple fulfills certain basic needs which otherwise went unmet; Nate says that Donna seems well, but thinks that the Krishna religion and lifestyle are "crazy." Both hope that Donna's involvement with Krishna is a temporary but perhaps necessary stage which she will grow out of.

Donna now lives according to a strict schedule. Members of the Krishna Temple rise at four in the morning to chant "Hare Krishna" together, spend many hours of the day chanting in the Temple and in the streets; they share the work of the Temple, eat their meals communally, and go to sleep at sundown after an early supper. The Temple is rigidly hierarchical. In order to have visitors, Donna had to request permission from the president. In telling the story of her life during the three years before she joined the Temple, Donna said, "That was all *maya*—illusion—until one finds Krishna, one lives in a world of *maya*. Only Krishna is the truth; Krishna consciousness is the only reality."

Donna's own version of the story gave us some understanding of why she chose to separate herself from her past and become one of the followers of Krishna. During the summer and the first year she lived with Nate and Julia in Belmont she "got into bikes and black leather jackets." As she talked about motorcycles her face looked tougher than usual. She claimed that she enjoyed having her pick of many boys—trying to see how well she could get away with turning them on and off. "I was really into having guys run after me." She also started taking a lot of drugs, mostly acid.

Donna said her father made very little effort to control her, and on the few occasions he did, she could easily manipulate him into changing his mind. She told us that she did not respect her father. When she returned to Chicago that summer, and throughout the following year, the limits set on her behavior were much stricter. Her mother was very concerned that she do well in school so that she could go to college, and her stepfather tried to enforce his rules and regulations very rigidly. If Donna dared to break them, he did not hesitate to use physical punishment. Consequently, she became more and more upset with the restrictions placed on her.

Donna felt Chicago was a place where nothing happened, and sought excitement in ways which were clearly in conflict with her parents' expectations of her. For a while she had sex with many different boys but eventually settled into a more extended relationship. She and her boyfriend often tripped on acid and searched for answers to cosmic questions.

Donna remembered being continually preoccupied with philosophical uncertainties that year. Her endless self-examination took the form of questions like "Who am I? Why am I here? Is there any purpose to what I'm doing? Does God exist?" As she withdrew further into her mind these worries would so overwhelm her that she could not sleep at night. Her mother sometimes realized that she was awake and would come in to ask her what was the matter. While Donna usually responded that she was worrying about her poor grades, she insisted to us that she only gave those answers because she knew that was what her mother was concerned about: "I told her I wanted to do better in school and get good grades but that was all bullshit."

Despite her insistence that she did not really care about school and grades, it seemed to us Donna was in some way still concerned about measuring up to her mother's expectations. She accepted the Alperts' values to the extent that, when her mother wanted to know why she was upset, she replied in their terms. Donna may have felt that she was being hypocritical—that the image her mother had of her was not her *real* self—but she never discussed her "real" anxieties with her mother. Despite attempts to live up to her mother's expectations by *voicing* the appropriate concerns, she chose to act in ways—taking drugs and behaving promiscuously—which could only have confirmed the negative images she feared people had of her.

Throughout the year she lived in Chicago Donna was increasingly bothered by the "authoritarian ways" in which her parents tried to control her. Instead of running away she tried to convince the Alperts to allow her to return to Boston and was so persistent that they finally agreed. Despite her decision to leave the Alperts, Donna seemed preoccupied with the role they had played in her life: she talked about them continually but hardly mentioned her father and stepmother.

At the commune, however, she felt she had little in common with the other people and spent many hours alone in her room. While living there she became desperate to find "the answer," and would explore "very far into" her mind. Her search was an agonizing one. Around the commune she started playing different roles: "I'd be an angel, then a dancer, then a singer, then a witch.... I really got into that witch thing." She played these parts for other people but it got to a point where she "couldn't control which person she was" and "kept changing from one to another." Although it is common for adolescents to experiment this way, in Donna's case her role-playing reached a crisis: she was no longer aware that she was playing roles but actually experienced herself as different people. What began as acting became a terrifying journey, incomprehensible to her, as well as to the people around her. Finally she was committed to a mental hospital.

Donna did not talk about the time she spent in the hospital: all that was important to her was that she had escaped. Shortly after her parents agreed to let her come home she went to a feast at the Krishna Temple and sensed that "something was there," although she did not yet understand Krishna consciousness. She continued to visit the Temple, however, and became increasingly interested in the movement.

At the Temple Donna was afraid of not being good enough for Krishna. She stayed up all night chanting "Hare Krishna, Hare Krishna, Hare Rama, Hare Hare," trying to be a better follower of Krishna and achieve "perfect consciousness." She remembered not eating for days and living on a completely irregular schedule. This was when the members of the Temple were so worried about her that the president called her father, who took her back to the mental hospital. In the hospital Donna felt desperate because she wanted to love Krishna and could not. Even though she knew the psychiatrists did not understand, during interviews all she could do was chant "Hare Krishna." She was unable to say anything else. "That's all I could do. I was in the middle of this vast confusing space and saying Hare Krishna was my only support."

When she ran away from the hospital for the second time, Donna stayed for two weeks with a man she had been seeing earlier. The seediness of his apartment bothered her; fed up with taking so many drugs and doing "too much of nothing," she decided to join the Temple and devote her life to Krishna. At the Temple, she said, she found a "real home."

Certain themes emerged in Donna's account of her experience which help to focus on the particular conflicts which made it impossible for her to continue living with either set of parents. The life of a Krishna follower provided for Donna the kind of emotional and spiritual security which she had been unable to find elsewhere. After her parents' divorce when she was seven she had moved frequently between her two families and thus experienced the insecurity of not having constant or consistent emotional support. During the last three years alone, she had moved eight times. Many adolescents are confused by such frequent displacements, which force them to leave old friends and readjust to new neighborhoods. The style of Donna's friendships also contributed to this sense of discontinuity: among the motorcycle crowd and the drug world, friends may be found and forgotten in a day. Nor could transitory sexual relationships and the fast-paced life of a "bikie" provide the kind of spiritual answers for which Donna was searching.

The most confusing and unsettling aspect of her frequent moves, however, was the continual readjustment to the conflicting values of her two sets of parents. Her stepfather's strictness and her mother's rigid expectations only intensified Donna's anxieties and fears of failure. Superficially, Nate and Julia were more accepting of Donna; they did not force her into a mold and allowed her more freedom to experiment with countercultural lifestyles. Yet in a deeper sense they never really accepted her. To them, and to Julia especially, Donna was an adolescent with problems they could not handle, an extra person who had to be taken into account but who never really became part of the family.

The chaos and confusion in the external circumstances of Donna's life may have served only to intensify the uncertainties which she experienced in a kind of probing, philosophical introspection which is characteristic of adolescents. At the Temple she found not only answers to these questions but also real standards against which she could test and prove herself—standards which made sense in terms of her philosophical questioning: "Who am

I?" "I am not important, only Krishna is important." But even in the new family she had found, the warmth and acceptance with which the other members greeted her was difficult to accept. She continued to worry about not being good enough. Hers was not an easy conversion.

5
DAVID

WE were introduced to David McNeill by a Sanctuary counselor who had known him since he ran away from home. During the course of our research, we talked with him several times—twice in the context of "interviews" and more informally at the Sanctuary hostel, where he often spent the night. We also talked to teachers and administrators at David's old school, all of whom remembered him. We did not try to talk to David's father, for their relationship was a difficult one; both David and his counselor felt that our speaking with the father would only complicate matters.

During the nine months before he left home at the age of sixteen, David ran a household of six—his father, two brothers, two sisters and himself—taking the place of his mother, whose sudden death had thrown the family into a crisis. David's father, who spent most of his time working at his auto body shop, asked his son to take care of the younger children until he found a permanent housekeeper. Although this arrangement was to be temporary, it forced David to sacrifice most of the time that he had previously spent with his friends—hanging out on the street, drinking, and sometimes stealing cars—for the sake of this new responsibility: "I'd have to get up in the morning, cook breakfast for my brothers and sisters, go to school, clean up the house, get them out to school, send them out, cook them supper, iron their clothes...."

Taking care of children was more work than David had anticipated. He found himself spending most of his time inside the house and lost track of his friends: "I just didn't see them. I didn't go up where they usually were and I just wasn't around. They were doing different things. A few of them would be out drinking most of the time, but I just couldn't do it. I didn't have the time or the money to go drinking." As compensation for the time he spent with his family, David received a few dollars a week, most of which went for lunches at school.

Before his mother's death, David had seen little of his father, who was either at work or down at the bar. The months he spent taking care of the house were not much different. When they did talk to each other the conversations were one-sided and hostile: "He didn't like any of my friends and when I did go out at night, he never liked anybody I was with, whether it was because of the hair or something, no matter what it was, he always found something wrong with them, like if they were Italian, he got mad at them because they were Italian; if they had long hair, he got mad at them because they had long hair."

In his new role as housekeeper David began to occupy the place his mother had filled as someone his father could complain to or criticize, a role David found particularly difficult. "He'd yell at me about my mother, and he'd yell about me, and he'd yell about me taking care of the house, how I was doing a lousy job and about how much responsibility he had and I used to tell him that he had none, except to get up in the morning and go to work and that was it...." David's father drank heavily, a habit he had tried to control in order to face the crisis in his family, but in time he resumed his long hours at the bar: "He'd never come home and beat me up or anything like that, but he'd come up, bitch awhile, go to bed, wake up a few hours later, bitch a little more, and go back to sleep.... Then he wouldn't go to work for a few days."

The issue of the promised "permanent" housekeeper further strained David's relationship with his father. What was supposed to be a temporary arrangement for David began to look more and more permanent, and every time he approached his father on the subject there was trouble. "I'd say something like, 'What about the kids, you said you were going to get a housekeeper,' and he'd say, 'Jesus, I go out and work five days a week and what am I supposed to do, come home and wash dishes?' and I'd ask him about a housekeeper—and he'd say, 'Well, I haven't found one but I'm still looking.' " David coped with this situation by taking a lot of drugs, especially depressants: "I used to walk around in a daze all the time, but my father never knew because he was never home and when he did come home, I'd be sleeping or watching television. Sometimes I'd be doing so many downs, I'd pass out."

By Christmas, eight months after beginning to run the McNeill household, David was more upset about what he had been doing, and more aware of what his role had become. "I cooked the whole meal, the turkey, the whole bit, while he was bitching at me and I had to go shopping for the kids. I felt like his wife or something, that's how bad it was."

In the months before he left home, the fall and winter of his first year of high school, the school made an exception for David. He was allowed to come in late for homeroom, due to his increased responsibilities at home. School had never been easy and he often stayed away. One counselor told us he had been "passed along" from elementary to junior high school despite low "verbal aptitude" (reading skills) and low grades. He had repeated seventh grade in spite of a "deal" offered to him by the school authorities that if he passed his subjects during the first term of his second time around, he could receive credit for the whole year. The counselor's stance, however, was a double message: he felt David did not belong in the seventh grade in the first place, yet he resented the student for having refused the "deal" that would have promoted him once again.

One year after he left, David's strongest memory was that he, along with the rest of his class, had been known as a troublemaker. "Our section was 3-9, that's the last section you had. . . . It was strictly for kids who wanted to do something with their hands like sheet metal or woodworking or printing . . . if you didn't want to take a business or college course. We were supposed to be dumb asses. If anything ever went wrong at the school it was always somebody from 3-9 that did it.... If they found cigarette butts in the halls it was always '3-9 did it' or if some kid got beat up at school it was always us that did it.... We were always told to shut up. 'You're a bunch of dummies. You can't learn.' "

David acknowledged that his group got into its share of trouble. "I guess you could say it was the roughest kids in the school, the kids that weren't interested in getting a mark, but we got blamed for a lot of unfair things ... like going down to the gym and ripping the gym apart. We never did that! But if it was done, we did it because a few of us got caught smoking in the hallway some time or a couple of us got in a fight one day. They didn't even wait for somebody to say it was 3-9, you know. They automatically jumped up and said, 'If it's wrong, they did it.' "

David's statements demonstrated a complicated kind of institutional scapegoating which took several forms, the most obvious one being the teachers' continual judgment that "bad" behavior goes along with the industrial track, the "worst" group in the school. Teachers do not invent unruly behavior in these kids— David freely admitted that his group often went against school rules by smoking in the halls or getting into fights—they do, however, according to David, identify a certain group in the school as bad and consistently come to expect the group to behave in "bad" ways.

Yet it is not simply the boys' behavior that leads to their being sectioned off and identified as "bad." The whole issue of who does something wrong seems to be related to the hierarchy of intelligence that exists within the school. The assumption that these kids are bad goes hand in hand with the idea that they are not very bright: "We were supposed to be dumb asses ... we were always told to shut up. 'You're dummies, you can't learn.' " According to David, these attitudes came across in the amount of effort a teacher put into teaching a class. "In the classes I had ... if it wasn't copying something out of a book, it was doing a study that didn't have anything to do with the subject.... We had this teacher who'd always assign us studies. [He'd say] 'I'm busy, you all be quiet and work or I'll have you come after school for detention.' And he'd go on making out his report cards for other classes.... The teachers, they were working for the kids from the college course and the business course rather than all of us in the trade course.... They'd more or less pamper the kids who went for foreign languages and college courses.... They'd teach these kids, they'd go out of their way to explain things.... If I didn't understand English, they'd just say, 'Tough luck, everybody else understands so why can't you?' If I asked him to explain something a little deeper—at the beginning of the year, this was—he'd just say, 'Well, sit down and I'll talk to you later.' And he never did."

David was sensitive to the hierarchy of his school. Because he was in the industrial track, he felt that he was being treated differently, as someone less worthy of being taught. Teachers seemed to be less interested in teaching students in industrial shop, were more concerned with running a well-disciplined class, and in some basic way, communicated to their students that they could not learn much.

Interviews with some of David's teachers indicated that to some degree this attitude does exist among them. It is surprising that while these teachers are often well-intentioned, they still unwittingly make kids like David feel dumb. David's English teacher, for instance, had specific goals in mind for his class. "If a student scores low on reading tests, he's weak in reading skills and I want to teach him how to read better. There's no exciting, innovative way to teach someone how to read. I have one student in my class who'll do anything but improve his reading skills. He's a cooperative boy who's great with his hands, but he doesn't want to learn how to read. To my mind, that boy's better off outside school earning a buck-sixty an hour. You have to see this from the teacher's point of view. I'm here to teach a skill."

The "professional" nature of this statement does not hide the teacher's belief that those students who cannot master basic skills, such as "the cooperative boy who's great with his hands but ... doesn't want to learn how to read," would be better off out of school altogether. Behind this statement lies the assumption that such students cannot be educated. They will never go far, and would be better off in the world earning the meager wage they are fated to. David sensed this feeling. "With a lot of teachers, the sooner you drop out of school the better it is for them because they got more room and they don't have to listen to you talking. They tell you to shut up most of the time."

It is ironic that such attitudes are held toward boys in the industrial arts track of a working-class high school, for David had chosen on his own to be in that track simply because he wanted to learn a trade. "At the end of our seventh year, we elect either a language, a business course, or an industrial course.... I elected the industrial course because I like printing.... I figured I'd be able to learn about printing."

While he was failing his other subjects, David was getting straight As in printing and sheet metal; in addition, he found in his shop teachers men he could talk to for the first time, who were not put off by his argumentative manner. "One of my shop teachers, Mr. Maxwell ... I used to argue with him a lot and he used to really like that; so did my printing teacher.... They used to say that I was thinking. It showed that I didn't want to be told this and accept it. They said it was good, but most of my other teachers didn't like it too much." By the time he had left school, questioning and arguing with teachers had become a struggle of wills which David eventually lost. He was proud of challenging his teachers and felt that that quality distinguished him from the other kids in his class. "If I said that I didn't like the judicial system, they'd say, 'How do you know?' You're not supposed to say that, you're supposed to agree with them, and I used to like to disagree with them, see what they'd do. They used to get really upset because this kid disagreed with them." It was only with teachers who accepted David's questioning as valid that the kind of inquisitive self-assertion that he enjoyed did not turn into a struggle of wills.

Mr. Maxwell, David's sheet metal teacher, remembered what an argumentative boy he had been. He said that David was right—he did appreciate it when boys disagreed with him. Disagreement showed that a kid was paying attention and learning. To Mr. Maxwell, questioning was a sign of attention rather than disobedience, as it had been considered by other teachers. He remembered David as a bright boy who had been neglected somewhere along the way. Uncertain of where that kind of neglect began, he said it was characteristic of many of the boys he had in shop. For many, he felt, the shop rooms were a last chance. Consequently, while teaching he often took time out to talk with his students about the broader issues in their lives. He spoke about the importance of each student's finding a satisfying direction for his life. Mr. Maxwell talked from personal experience rather than abstract principles, for he had changed the direction of his life by becoming a teacher after being a salesman, had gone back to school, taken more courses, and passed exams, all of which "wasn't easy by any means." Talking to his students about the direction of their lives gave them a kind of recognition that no other teacher seemed to offer. The direction of their lives was an important matter, one they were all capable of dealing with.

Simply stated, this man had a basic respect for his students that David, who had grown so used to disrespecting teachers, recognized and responded to. This respect was manifest in subtle ways. For instance, the morning we visited David's school, Mr. Maxwell asked his class how many knew what they were going to be doing when they got older. Later, he explained that he avoided saying "when you grow up," a phrase adults commonly use with adolescents: "Saying 'when you grow up' to these kids isn't right." Implicit in this statement is a recognition that his students were already involved with life. This recognition extended to areas of his students' lives beyond their vocational intentions. "I can tell when something's on a kid's mind just by the way he acts sometimes, and when I see that a kid's got a problem, I kind of let up on him because I know that what I do with him in class isn't really what he's got his mind on."

For instance, he had realized during David's final year of school that something was bothering the boy, but did not try to "discover" what it was. Instead he established a comfortable rapport with David and developed a genuine appreciation of his talents, particularly the "verbal ability" that did not show up on written tests. David remembered that Mr. Maxwell once suggested that he become a lawyer; enjoying argument seemed to be one of his natural qualities.

While this kind of recognition was something that David appreciated, it was more the exception than the rule for him at school. The quality that Mr. Maxwell admired was annoying to other teachers, who usually responded to David by telling him to be quiet. Angered by attempts to silence his questions, he would become more vocal and be sent to the assistant principal's office for being unruly. Mr. Wilson, the man who saw David on such occasions, remembered him well. "You could begin to get through to him, see him open up, but then he'd pull away. I always think that when tears start to come to a student's eyes, you know he's opening up. With David that happened sometimes when he was sent down here. I'd say, 'David, your teacher said you were being disruptive in class,' and he'd say, 'Yes, Mr. Wilson, I was talking some,' and I'd say, 'Well, don't you see that makes the teacher's job harder?' and he'd say, 'Yes, Mr. Wilson,' and I had the feeling that he understood. But later in the term he would come in, and you couldn't say anything to him. He'd start yelling about what right does that teacher have to tell me to shut up and go on and on. He wouldn't listen to a word I'd say."

Aware of the difficulties that David was having at home, Mr. Wilson felt that the student was "acting out" against the school for something that was wrong in his family. Another way of looking at this change of behavior, however, is that David was becoming increasingly frustrated and angry with patterns of authority both at home and at school and tired of being "kept in line."

Mr. Wilson had a particularly vivid memory of an incident that occurred sometime in November, when David was found lying on the floor of the boys' bathroom at ten-thirty in the morning. When the assistant principal arrived on the scene, David was talking to himself. Mr. Wilson had had no previous experience with this kind of incident but felt sure by the way that David was acting that he was on drugs. At the time David told him that he had drunk "some bad orange juice." Uncertain about what to do, the assistant principal called the police "so that David could get some medical attention," but instead the boy was taken down to the station for questioning about drug use. David told police he had been drunk in school, an explanation that Mr. Wilson refused to believe. When he had seen David in the hall at ten o'clock, the student was "all right," but just half an hour later he was in the bathroom, unable to walk. Mr. Wilson did not think anyone could get so drunk that fast; also, because of David's actions, Mr. Wilson "didn't think it was liquor he was on."

David's version of the story was different. In talking about what had happened, he referred to a previous incident. The year before, in the eighth grade, he had bought some dope from a friend and the principal had found out. "He came down with two detectives and grabbed the kid who had sold it to us, then called us out.... He had no proof that we had done this. All he could do was say he had heard this, and all we had to do was deny it, but he let everybody know.... Then when I got drunk in school, they all thought I had hit up two bags of junk or something. They really thought I was going to kick off.... They had three nurses down there ... one from each hospital and the school nurse checking my arm for needle marks." David claimed that he had never used heroin.

Ultimately, David was released to his father and not charged with anything. He returned to school shortly thereafter, and no one mentioned what had happened. According to Mr. Wilson, school officials kept silent in order to "cover things up." To his mind there had been "a drug incident" at the school, something that as few people as possible should know about. Yet that was impossible. Several teachers had been present when David was lying on the floor of the men's room. It is likely that they talked to their colleagues, for over a year later teachers remembered that there had been "some talk" of David's being involved with drugs.

At the time the incident happened, David was already thinking of dropping out of school and working full time. Several of his friends had already done this. Returning to an environment where *nothing was said* about an incident so serious in the eyes of the school authorities that he had been sent to the police could only have made school a more uncomfortable place to be.

Shortly thereafter, David was picked up by the police for trying to buy six quarts of beer. According to his probation officer, who believes that David is one of many kids who "get hauled into court even though they don't belong there," the arrest was a fluke. The police had decided to crack down on the liquor store for selling to minors, and arrested the first kid who came along; David McNeill happened to be that kid. Jailed overnight, he was taken to court the next day and given nine months' probation.

This incident was another in a series of encounters David had with the authorities, all of which occurred after his mother's death. "Everybody says all the trouble I've got in since my mother passed away was because she left, but it wasn't. I was doing the same thing when she was around, but I never got caught at it. . . . After she died I got caught attempting to steal a car, I got caught drinking a few times, I got thrown out of school for being drunk. . . . Last thing I did before I left home was I got busted for trying to buy beer. . . ." All of these encounters made David feel, in part, that there was something wrong with him: at home, at school, and in the eyes of the law, he was continually told that he was bad. While some kids take on that judgment as an identity and become deeply committed to patterns of "delinquent" behavior, David was uncomfortable with all of the trouble he was in. One night in January, after thinking about it for several weeks, he ran away from home.

One year later, when we talked with David, he was still living on his own. Unlike many young people who fall into a pattern of leaving home, returning, then running away again, he left only once. After hanging around Harvard Square and living with street people, he looked back on his life in Somerville with disdain. The things he and his friends had done so often—stealing cars, drinking, fighting among themselves and with strangers—seemed ridiculous in retrospect. Two of these friends had recently been killed when their car ran off the road while they were being chased by police. He was shaken by the incident but amazed as well. What they had been doing made no sense to him now. He thought the lives that most of his friends and the kids at school led were "straight"; either they accepted what they were told to do by their parents or by teachers, or they spent time drinking and getting into trouble.

David felt that he had developed values distinctly different from those of his old peers. Having left home, he stayed with friends in Somerville for a while, then began to hang around Harvard Square, but did not look for work because he feared his father had taken out a runaway warrant against him. Instead he panhandled money and occasionally washed dishes in exchange for food at a local restaurant. After spending nights with anyone who would take him in, he found a regular place to stay in a large, unheated house his friends had rented. Many of the people at the house were runaways like himself, others were older, more experienced street people. David thought the house was a good place to live, principally because the residents shared what little they had equally among themselves. David often went without food, sometimes for two or three days at a time. In part the values of sharing grew out of the fact that all in the house were struggling to survive. They shared common goals—food, shelter, and the desire to stay away from home. Having to survive together made dominant culture values such as that of the sacredness of private property less important, at least for a time.

For several months, David had no contact with his family. He simply lived in the house and spent time with his friends. As it happened, the house was located near a Cambridge drop-in center where David formed relationships with several counselors. His first contact with them concerned drugs, but in time he began to discuss other aspects of his life, particularly his family. When counselors learned that David was on probation, they became concerned about the kind of trouble he could get into if he were picked up, and arranged for him to go to court with a lawyer. In one court appearance, a deal was worked out whereby David could live away from home as long as he stayed with his aunt in Cambridge. This arrangement worked well until his father found out where he was staying and took him to court as a "stubborn child." Even after the court had again decided that David could stay with his aunt, the father kept trying to get his son to return by telephoning or looking for him in his new neighborhood. Several weeks after his appearance in court, tired of his father's harrassment, David left his aunt's and went back to his old house.

For the next several months, David alternated between living at his aunt's and with his street friends. He spent much of his time with Linda, a Cambridge girl involved in radical politics who often brought him food. Eventually he found a part-time job delivering packages. When hundreds of young runaways came to Cambridge during the summer, he criticized their inexperience: these were "plastic hippies," kids who ran away because it was "fashionable"; they would go home when they had to face any test of their ability to survive.

As a veteran of the street, David claimed he had found an identity (his word) away from home, but his old life was never far away. Periodically, his father would find him and take him to court again, but each time the court would let David live with his aunt; as far as the law was concerned, David was actually doing "better" away from home. He had not been arrested since his departure. David considered this to be one of the major achievements of his running away; as a runaway he was in part measuring up to the values of his working-class background. He was obeying the law.

We wondered how the new lifestyle that he felt so much a part of related to his strict working-class background in which obedience to authority was the norm. Although it was not immediately apparent by the way he talked about himself, the pattern of what David had done was typical of working-class adolescents. Having dropped out of school, he moved away from home and found himself a job. What was different, however, was that

David left and became part of "hip" culture, which was hated by so many people he had once been close to, particularly his father, who violently disapproved of his son's new lifestyle. This disapproval was all the more vehement because Mr. McNeill was angry about his son's walking out on him. As long as David did the work, Mr. McNeill was able to handle the loss of his wife without further strain on his finances. Once his oldest son left, however, the burden increased. The first thing he talked about with David after not seeing him for months was his increased financial burden. David said, "He's mad at the fact that I left him with the kids. He has to go out and pay a babysitter now. He has to call up somebody to stay with the kids most of the time and that's the fact he's the most upset about. He still raves about that."

The values which David felt distinguished him from his former peers were "countercultural": he preferred nonviolence to the aggressive encounters of his early youth, talked of how he had come to respect black people on the street, and how important communal sharing had been. In his relationship with Linda, he treated her as an equal and tried not to be a "male chauvinist."

David insisted that the way he got along with Linda was different from the way his friends in Somerville got along with their girlfriends. He spent most of his time with her, something that he said rarely happened between a boy and girl where he came from. Furthermore, the two of them were "a couple," responsible first to each other, rather than part of a crowd. At the last party they had gone to in Somerville, the boys and girls had stayed separate much of the time, talking among themselves. Neither David nor Linda had enjoyed that.

The "new" values that David discovered in Cambridge street culture were in part the consequence of the heterogeneous nature of this environment. In Somerville, David met few blacks; the peace movement was considered communist by most people, including his father; the male-female roles were pretty much set among adolescents. He found in his friends and in his counselors people who shared the values with which he was becoming familiar. Many of these people were engaged in putting new values to work in the hope that if enough people followed, a real alternative to the dominant culture might be created. Although David had not come with this goal in mind he was attracted and excited by the mood of social experimentation.

David's decision to run away had grown out of circumstance: due to his increased responsibilities at home, his adolescence came to an abrupt halt, so he went elsewhere and rediscovered it. Yet this extreme situation may be seen as a paradigm for other runaways. At home, David had grown tired of his responsibilities, but he knew no real way to challenge his father. Nothing he told us indicated that he ever defied his father or shirked his duties while at home. Instead he was steadily worn down and grew more and more confused. The conflict between wanting to be an obedient son and finding the role in which he was placed unbearable made his situation intolerable. When he felt he could no longer measure up to that expectation, he left home rather than face his father's direct disapproval.

Thus David's desire to be an adolescent conflicted with his father's expectations of what he should be: a housekeeper, a role not normally required of male adolescents. That David performed that role for nearly a year indicates how strong a value obedience was for him.

Having left home, he resumed adolescent life in a different environment. In the street culture of Cambridge he found support both from peers and from nonprofessional counselors; yet that culture was a temporary one. A year later, many of David's friends had disappeared from the city, and the drop-in center he had frequented was closed down. After a nine-month relationship, he broke up with his "radical" girlfriend. Then he quit the part-time job. Still living with his aunt, he was confused about what to do next. Maybe, he said, he would go and ask his father to help him find work.

6
"SHE MAY JUST BE BAD INSIDE"

MARY KANDINSKI, *fourteen, ran away to Project Place sometime in the winter of 1972 from Chelsea, a working-class city near Boston. She first attracted our attention by her claim that she had left home sixteen times. Later she admitted that she had made no more than six attempts to run away. We talked informally with Mary several times while she was at the Runaway House and observed several groups in which she took part, one of which is described in the following narrative. Others with whom we spoke included her mother, school officials, and her social worker.*

Three times a week, the kids staying at Project Place Runaway House get together with several counselors for a morning meeting. These meetings are among the few mandatory activities at the House. For the most part, discussions are open-ended. Once everyone is in the room a counselor will ask the kids what they want to talk about. Despite this open orientation, kids usually look to the counselor for the topic or expect that there is something the staff wants discussed. Before one of the groups we observed began, Mary said, "I bet we're going to have to talk about what happened last night." Since we had not been around then, we asked what that was. Several kids answered at once and together told about a father who had come into the House, beaten his daughter when she refused to go home with him, and dragged her out. Mary seemed particularly moved by the event, but insisted that she did not want to talk about it, having discussed it the night before for hours with other counselors. Later on in the group, however, another girl brought up the subject again. It was just that way in her family. When she did not want to do something her parents wanted her to do, or if there was something she wanted to do that they would not allow, her father got angry and sometimes hit her. Mary said that during the beating she had seen herself being hit. As they discussed the previous night's incident a new story materialized. The father had *asked* the girl to come home with him, then he *told* her to, then shouted at her that she was going to come, but she had refused to leave. He had grown quiet and, according to several girls in the group, looked as if he were going to cry. Suddenly he had started to beat her furiously, but after ten seconds he had stopped, amazed at what he was doing, and taken her away. Later he called the House to apologize for his actions. In this account a new theme emerged which we had not expected. The kids seemed to be talking about *their* ability to hurt their parents. In the second telling of the beating, the girl was not simply the victim of a cruel father, but rather the object of an uncontrolled rage that she had, in part, provoked.

Sometime after this group meeting, we learned how familiar Mary was with men losing their tempers. Judging from what she told us, it was not surprising that she had seen herself being beaten the night before. The months before she ran away had been difficult ones. She had started cutting school in the fall and had done so more and more as the year progressed. Her descriptions of experiences away from school were animated; having left the building, Mary and her friends would hitchhike somewhere. Several times she had gone to an amusement park and "done the rides"; often they stayed in the neighborhood. For the most part, the girls got away with "hooking" but whenever they were caught, the principal would inform their parents.

Mary said she did not like school because the teachers and the principal thought she was on drugs all the time and selling them to the other kids. Sure, she said, she had done speed and grass and sometimes taken other kinds of pills, but the school officials were *always* after her. For a while it was so bad that the principal had followed her around the building and even waited outside the girls' room for her to make sure she was not taking drugs in school.

Several times during the fall and winter months she had been suspended for cutting, and in her mind each suspension was more serious than the last. Finally she had been barred from school for a week and could only come back after her parents had a conference with the principal. Each suspension brought punishment from her stepfather, who hit her and sometimes restricted her to the house for several days. During this period Mary began to run away. The first few times she had gone to a friend's house to spend the night, then she started staying away longer. The last departure had been spontaneous. A friend wanted to leave one afternoon and so Mary had joined her. Someone they hitched a ride with told them about Project Place, where they went to spend only the night but remained for two weeks.

As Mary talked about the beatings she had received, her fear was apparent. She spoke faster and faster, as if it were happening again. She also joked about the problem: "Oh, he could hit hard." The way she described the school principal, he sounded like a detective and she the suspect who could not be rid of him. Even before she ran away, there was a "running" quality to Mary's life at school, and the more she ran from there, the more persistent her "tail" became.

Somewhat involved with drugs, she felt herself faced with the general label of drug-user by adults at school. Although she admitted that there were things that she and her friends did that justified some kind of discipline (like being loud in the halls, talking back to teachers, or "hooking" school) Mary was confused about the kind of special treatment she had received. The only way to get away from that environment was cutting school, and this set off a chain reaction of beatings and recriminations in her family. The way Mary told the story, this cycle happened many times before she began to run away from home.

Arriving at Mary's school, we were surprised to find the doors locked. After we knocked and rang a bell several times, someone came, asked what we wanted, and let us inside. Although the building was an old one, it had been recently renovated. The floors, desks, walls, and ceilings all looked new, and were painted in brighter colors than those we were used to seeing in public schools. The attractive appearance of the "plant," however, did not allay our uneasiness about the locked doors. It was the first school we had been to where the kids were literally locked in. Later we were told that this was done in order to keep kids from skipping classes, and particularly to cut down on the kind of coming and going that is so common in big-city public schools. Now, if a kid stepped out of school, he had to ring a bell to get back in (and be "discovered") or stay away for the whole day.

Mr. O'Brian, the principal, and Mr. Donahue, Mary's counselor, were the first people we talked to at the school. Mr. O'Brian started the conversation by asking how much we knew about Mary. After we told him that we had spoken to her as well as her family, he started to talk, but in a slow, reserved manner. Yes, she had a lot of trouble at school along with four or five other girls. One of them was the ringleader, the rest were followers. They all took drugs and sold them to the other kids at school. They would go through the halls shouting while classes were in session or head for the girls' room in a group and make noise there. He suspected that while they were in school they were "on something" which made them act so crazy. "For a while back there, we had a crisis almost every day. One of us would have to go after them and take them back to class, or they'd be down in the girls' room making a lot of noise and we'd have to get a woman teacher to go in and get them out." Now, none of the original "group" was in school any longer and the place was much quieter. Mary was the only one about whom he still knew anything. The others had run away from home or dropped out of school.

The principal asked Mr. Donahue what he remembered about Mary. "She was a good kid," he said, "but she was like two different people. When she was on drugs she was obnoxious and loud, but when she wasn't, she was one of the nicest kids, a perfect lady." The counselor had talked with Mary when she first came to school. At that time, he said, she told him she had been on speed for the summer and part of the previous year, and was unable to remember anything that had happened during that time. Consequently, he believed that she was addicted to drugs, "not physically, but psychologically." As he talked, Mr. Donahue seemed puzzled and troubled about Mary's "problem." She had been taking so much "stuff" he did not know what could be done to help her.

Mr. O'Brian interrupted at that moment. He was not sure it was accurate to say that she was "addicted," but Mr. Donahue was insistent. She was "psychologically addicted," she could not live without some kind of drug. Well, the principal said, maybe he was right. In his eyes, Mary was more of an "emotional problem." He did not know much about her family background, only that her mother had been married several times. He had met her present parents and thought they were both "concerned," good people, so he did not know why Mary had the problems she had. There was no doubt in his mind, however, that she needed "help"—a lot of it. During her last few weeks at school, she had appeared particularly upset. "When a kid has an emotional crisis, school becomes less important in his life." His feeling was that Mary's crisis had been an extended one, and that the kind of help she needed was not something his school could offer. He seemed to be going out of his way to say that the school was not responsible for anything that had happened to Mary.

Mr. Donahue then began to talk about how understaffed the school was, particularly in the area of counseling. There were two part-time people for over four hundred and fifty kids. In the past year, he and the other counselor had not even had time to sit down and talk once with every student in the school. They hardly had the time to give Mary the help she needed. In a meeting with Mary's parents, he had suggested that they send her to a special program for drug addicts at a state hospital which he had recently visited. Mary's parents had not followed his suggestion. On the basis of what Mr. Donahue and the principal said, however, it did not seem to us that the school had neglected Mary because they were understaffed. We were struck by the intensity and concern that went along with the attention they had given her. The problem lay in the nature of that attention, rather than the lack of it.

At one point, while the principal was out of the room, Mr. Donahue enthusiastically described the drug program he had seen at the state hospital, then asked what Sanctuary did for kids who took drugs. How did we get them to stop? We said that that was not necessarily one of our primary goals in working with kids. Whether or not a kid took drugs was often secondary to other issues. He was interested, he said, because he had never known anyone personally who took drugs, while we had gone to college when they were a "big thing." He seemed genuinely puzzled about why kids took drugs, but also open to new ideas. We had the feeling that the only reason he had suggested that Mary be committed to a state hospital was that he knew of no other alternative.

The next person we talked to was Mary's homeroom teacher, a young woman who the principal thought had some rapport with the girl. The teacher said she did not know Mary very well; she had not come to school much. There had been talk among teachers that she had a problem with drugs. Someone had heard from the conference with her parents that Mary had been on speed "for over a year." The teacher qualified these reports, however, as hearsay. She did not know what the truth was. There were times when she thought that Mary might be on drugs because she acted strangely and talked very fast, but could not be sure because she did not really know how drugs affected people. She had also heard that Mary had heavy responsibilities at home, but that was nothing unusual for kids in the area. She had grown up in Chelsea herself and knew many homes where a teenager "held the family together" while one or both parents worked. Perhaps that was why Mary had such trouble.

She particularly remembered Mary's temper. When the girl became angry, she could be really hostile. In class, she had always been well-behaved, but she had once taunted several teachers (herself among them) on a bus after school. What Mary said escaped the teacher now, but the girl had kept at it for several minutes, until she got off the bus.

Mrs. Harlow, Mary's gym teacher, had a vivid memory of that incident. Also a young woman, she said that she liked Mary and had a good relationship with her. As she remembered, the girl had announced to the others on the bus, "I have these two teachers, and they think I'm obnoxious," then spoke directly to the teachers. "I'm here to taunt you. I'm going to be loud and obnoxious so you'll hate me." Mrs. Harlow had been stunned by the incident, but she interpreted it as a consequence of the girl's insecurity. Mary felt that everybody hated her, so she would be vicious and fight back.

Mrs. Harlow was sure that Mary had been on drugs regularly before she left school. In gym class, she was often a "kinetic force" with the other girls and stirred them up. At such times, Mrs. Harlow thought that Mary was on speed. The evidence she had for this was the girl's "strange" behavior, her eyes "popping," and the pitch of her activity. Furthermore, Mary had been involved with a social worker in a group of girls "who discussed drug problems." At her worst Mary was "ungodly ... a terror"; the principal had been required to suspend her so that "the teachers could get some peace." What had become of Mary? She had heard that the girl had gone some place to "dry out" for a while. We said she had been at the Runaway House during that time. We were surprised at what Mrs. Harlow had to say, for while she claimed to be sympathetic toward Mary (she herself had been in her own "share of trouble" as a teenager), she was quick to condemn the girl and accept hearsay as truth. Another surprise was the fact that the group in which Mary participated further incriminated her in the eyes of some school people.

Now that Mary and her friends were no longer in school, both the principal and the counselor felt that there was much less of a "drug problem" there. They did not know what would happen to her now; the principal had heard about Mary's plan to apply for the Boston Trade School, but he seemed skeptical of her ability to succeed in that program. In order for her to be admitted, he had to write her a recommendation. He was not sure she could get the kind of "help" she needed there.

While talking to Mary's social worker, Alice, at the mental health center, we asked whether she thought the girl had been treated differently from other students at the school because people thought she was on drugs. Her response was unequivocal. There was "real paranoia" at the school about drugs. "She could literally be clean from even smoking for like four weeks and they'd look at her if she was tired and say, 'You're on drugs.' . . . And it's so ineffective. I think they should do something. I mean half the kids are on really serious drugs, but they just kind of look at them and say, 'You're on drugs.' "

Alice felt that when Mary cut classes the principal was reluctant to dole out the customary punishment, suspension, because he thought the girl was better off in school than at home. The last time Mary was suspended the principal assigned her special work in the office, allowing her not to tell her parents that she had been suspended.

One of the reasons Alice thought the principal gave Mary preferential treatment was that since she had run away before and might do so again, he was anxious to minimize that possibility. In addition, Alice said, "She's just great. You would hate to say no to her. You don't want her to leave school because she really has a lot of potential. And she has so many strengths I bet they just hated to see her not make it through freshman year." Nevertheless, the counselor pointed out, there was confusion in the relationship between Mary, the school, and Mary's family over the issue of suspension. "The principal was going along with her in saying, 'I'm hiding it from your father that you're suspended. You can stay here.' But then the father found out anyway because he called the school and the principal told him. So the principal was playing both sides—he was playing the father's side, and the father and the principal were both pretending that they didn't know, so Mary thought they didn't know. That was really crazy."

Despite all Mary's trouble in school, Alice thought the girl could be very responsible. During the previous summer she had held a difficult job at a local hospital under the auspices of the Neighborhood Youth Corps. "It was really tough. It's very hot to work there in the summer and it's hard to get there. From here I'm sure it's maybe an hour if you make the right bus connections. And she was never late and really did a good job."

Alice went on to say, however, that Mary's parents were unwilling to give her credit for the kind of responsibility she had demonstrated in doing this job, in babysitting for her younger brothers and sisters, and in helping around the house. Both Mr. and Mrs. Ayer were recently reformed alcoholics who, since making a drastic change in their own lives, had become more insistent that their children "be moral and do things right." "They're very concerned about Mary's companions, where she hangs around and what sorts of activity she gets involved in. They're so structured that they can't be flexible. They're so structured into getting themselves together that they can't open up a bit so that the three of them could really work something out.

"In the months before Mary ran away her parents continually told her, 'You're going to be bad . . . there's no way, if you are good for five years, then I'll know it, you will have proved yourself.' It didn't matter what she did, even the pettiest mistake, it was Mary's fault . . . it was really snowballing, especially in her father's eyes. I think he just didn't know what to expect and was feeling like a bad father."

The counselor felt that Mary had not adjusted to the fact that her mother had stopped drinking. When Mrs. Ayer drank, her daughter was rarely away from her. "Now that there's no drinking her mother and father have a very good relationship. . . . Mary is pushed out. Though they're still close, to Mary it's a gigantic change that her mother can get along well without her and has someone else to look to and pay attention to." At the time Mrs. Ayer stopped drinking, about two years ago, Mary started skipping school. "She wanted to be with her mother," Alice said. "I think she sees that but doesn't know what to do with it."

Since Mary had returned home, Alice thought that everyone in the family was making more of an effort to work things out. She remained skeptical, however. The family still viewed Mary's behavior as either "good" or "bad." "There's a lot of buttering up on each side—Mary saying, 'I want to be a good girl,' and them saying, 'We want you to be a good girl'—and that's about as far as it goes. If she went back to school now and started to get in trouble, I think things would erupt very quickly because I think it's just right below the surface. They're not sure if she's going to be a good girl. She may just be bad inside."

Mrs. Ayer, Mary's mother, an attractive forty-year-old woman, had a pleasant though harried-sounding voice and a good sense of humor. In our initial conversation on the telephone she said she probably could not tell us much, but after we said we were interested in *any* of her reactions to Mary's running away, she laughed, "Well, I was mad!" As we sat talking to her in the kitchen of her large apartment she was surrounded by eight children. Mary was the oldest child at home since her brother Richard had enlisted in the Marines a month earlier. The youngest, Mrs. Ayer's child by her most recent marriage, was still a baby. We visited the Ayers during a week of school vacation, so throughout the morning as we sat in the cheery kitchen, the children ran in and out looking for shoes, jackets, and helping themselves to lunch. From time to time Mrs. Ayer interrupted herself, with an apologetic smile, to tell one child to put away the ironing board, another to warm the baby's bottle. Mary was still asleep when we arrived but joined us later in the conversation.

A feeling of warmth and activity pervaded the room where we sat. Mary's brothers and sisters squabbled and joked and came in to ask their mother for stamps for a letter they were writing to Richard. Throughout it all Mrs. Ayer remained at the table talking with us, seemingly unperturbed by the noise and bustle around her. With so many children in the family, Mary, as the oldest girl, had shared many of her mother's responsibilities around the house such as fixing meals and babysitting for her younger brothers and sisters. Mrs. Ayer said that her daughter had always been dependable. Watching the younger children take care of each other that morning we noticed that they had learned a kind of independence though still quite young. Midway through the morning a letter arrived from Richard, which Mrs. Ayer read aloud while all the children quietly gathered around her. Several of them started crying quietly and even Mrs. Ayer had tears in her eyes.

In beginning to talk about her responses to Mary's running, Mrs. Ayer seemed uncertain about why her daughter had left. "She never told me why she ran away ... she always went to Project Place. She said she needed time to work things out, to find herself ... and I guess she did. We'd been coming down on her pretty hard there for a while—she was always getting into trouble—hooking school, telling lies ... and everything she did, she'd get caught—we'd try to keep her in the house and then she'd be gone." Mrs. Ayer seemed to feel that Mary's pattern of bad behavior was a recent development; Mary had changed in the last year or two. Several of the things Mary had been doing lately bothered her: Mary's girlfriends, her drug use, and her increasingly uncooperative attitude toward school.

Mrs. Ayer said several times that she did not approve of her daughter's friends, among them the one Mary had run away with. She felt torn between her knowledge that Mary was old enough to choose her own friends and her suspicion that Mary was "hanging around with a bad set of kids." Mrs. Ayer was particularly concerned because her daughter had changed so much over the past year: "She was always a very sheltered girl ... she used to stay home, very rarely went out; but now she has friends that I don't like at all. This one girl was going out with a married man—I think she's too young to get involved with that kind of thing. Another girl I don't approve of was the one who introduced her to drugs. What can I do? I can't say I like the girl." Mrs. Ayer seemed to feel that through her new friendships her daughter had become bad. "For a while she couldn't do anything right." Mary began to lie to her family about where she went when she was out of the house, whom she had been spending time with, whether or not she went to school, and her use of drugs. Her mother commented: "I think she was lying so much that she didn't even know herself what was true anymore."

Mrs. Ayer had begun to suspect that Mary was using drugs a year earlier in the summer. While she was in the hospital having a baby her husband told her, "Mary has the house all clean and fixed up nicely for you." This in itself was not unusual, the mother said, "but when I came home and saw her rushing around clearing dishes off the table before we were finished eating, I told Sam I thought something was wrong with her. He said he didn't think so, but I knew this wasn't normal. . . . I thought she must be taking something." We asked whether Mrs. Ayer had questioned Mary directly about using drugs and she explained, "It's hard to know how to ask . . . you don't just want to accuse someone . . . but one day when she came home from school she was acting strange so I asked her what she was doing and she started crying and said she was taking pills, diet pills."

In spite of her serious concern about Mary's use of drugs Mrs. Ayer joked, saying, "And her looking like Olive Oyl—she doesn't need diet pills." The mother thought that Mary's drug use was directly related to problems she was having in school: only in the last year or two had Mary started cutting classes and staying away for the whole day. "Mary was acting like a clown in school and I think that was because of the pills," Mrs. Ayer said. But the main problem was that she sometimes refused to go at all.

Sam Ayer, Mary's stepfather, tried to make sure that she went to school every morning by driving her there and waiting outside until she entered the front door, but she still managed to get away. According to Mrs. Ayer, the family punished Mary's truancy by keeping her in the house; she made no mention of the beatings. The mother felt that Mary resented her stepfather's attempts to control her, but admitted that his standards of behavior were strict. "I guess he's really of the old school," she said.

Mrs. Ayer was concerned about her husband's relationship to her children and anxious that they accept each other. She realized that Mary in particular was disturbed by "this new man coming in and joining the family," and even more upset by the arrival of a new baby. Mrs. Ayer felt that Mary had not liked the new baby right from the start. "I don't know why, but I just knew she didn't like him, so I tried not to make her babysit too much. When I was going out I tried to take the baby with me as often as I could. I didn't always want to be carting the baby around with me when I went to the grocery store and out to dinner.... I did it for Mary ... but she kept on thinking that I loved the baby more than her and that's why I took him with me all the time." Mrs. Ayer was unsure of this interpretation of the girl's feelings since Mary never talked to her anymore. "I don't understand why she doesn't want to talk to me but she doesn't. She never talks to me about anything." After the baby was born, Mrs. Ayer said that she became increasingly worried about Mary and finally contacted Alice, a counselor at a local mental health center. Mrs. Ayer hoped that Mary would benefit from seeing a counselor in ways that would ease the situation at home.

When Mary joined us at the kitchen table, the conversation turned to her own plans. She was out of school and did not plan to return until the fall. When she went back, she wanted to enroll in a work-study program her counselor had recommended. She also talked about her older brother, to whom she felt very close, and whose "trouble" (cutting school, staying out late) was similar to her own. "One week it was my turn, the next week it was his," she said. At this point Mrs. Ayer said that Richard had started cutting school in the second grade, but during the last three years "he would often go out the front door, come in the back door, and then go up to his room in the attic ... and when I'd go up later with the laundry at two in the afternoon I'd find a big lump in his bed and he'd be there sound asleep! Sometimes I'd find Mary and a friend up there, too."

Mrs. Ayer was sympathetic to Richard's reluctance about going to school. Her son, she felt, had had a particularly hard time because of all the confusion and racial conflict at the high school, which she said was "mostly colored ... about sixty percent."

Often he had been assigned to tasks such as guarding the fire box so that other students would not set off false alarms, but as his mother pointed out, "If a big guy comes up to you, you can't stop him, and you can't tell on him either. . . . There were always fights outside the school." Mrs. Ayer thought that Richard also had "bad" friends—guys who were "eighteen years old and still in junior high," and could not understand why he spent time with people like that. To her it seemed that "he was not the kind of boy you would expect to go in for the Marines." Since he enlisted, most of his shoulder-length hair had been cut off.

When we asked Mary and her mother how things had been going since Mary had returned from the Runaway House, they answered simultaneously, "Oh, she's been acting much better since then," and became silent. As we were beginning to leave, Mrs. Ayer, watching one daughter putting on her roller skates and another trying to borrow a dime from Mary, joked, "Maybe after this you'll write another book, one on the population explosion." Then she was serious again: "Before all this started Mary was just a baby and all of a sudden she was grown up—maybe they grow up too fast or maybe they're ready to grow up and I'm just not ready to have them grow up. . . . If the situation were to go back to what it was, we'd probably react the same way; it's hard to know what you should do—if you give out too much punishment you're wrong, if you give out too little you're wrong. Where do you find the happy medium?"

7
ON
THE
WAY
OUT

PAUL SILVER, seventeen, was the oldest runaway with whom we spoke. In the course of his two stays at the Runaway House we talked to him several times and sat in on conversations between him and his counselor, Eric. Because we were particularly interested in his school performance, we visited the school for emotionally disturbed boys Paul had attended during the junior high years as well as the high school in which he was presently enrolled. We also spent most of one afternoon talking to Paul's father.

Paul Silver arrived at Project Place one night in February. Having run away from home a month earlier, Paul had been living on his own, part of the time with a college student in Cambridge. His host had grown tired of him, however, and had recommended the Runaway House as a place to go.

Paul spent several hours that first evening with Susan, one of the nighttime counselors, talking about why he had left home. He told one story after another about problems he had with his parents. Unlike many runaways, his departure had not been provoked by a single incident; he complained of a basic pattern in the family. Everyone treated him "special," as if there were something wrong with him. The rest of his family "bothered" him too much; they were always telling him what to do. They even "bothered" him about how much toothpaste he used. While all the others in his family (which included a younger sister and older brother as well as his mother and father) related to him in this "special" way, he seemed particularly concerned about his father, who was always trying to make decisions for him. Their most recent conflict had to do with school: Paul wanted to transfer out of the college course into a trade program to learn electronics, but his father would not allow that.

Talking with Mr. Silver, counselors found out that this was not the first time Paul had been away from home. He had spent four years (from eight to twelve) in a psychiatric hospital being treated for "hyperactivity," and another three (from fourteen to sixteen) in a boarding school for emotionally disturbed boys. At the psychiatric hospital, Paul had been treated with Dexedrine and diagnosed as "brain damaged." A call to the hospital, however, revealed that the diagnosis was tentative at best. Of the several electroencephalograms administered to Paul, one showed the possibility of a brain lesion. While the parents were quick to inform the counselors of what was "wrong" with Paul, they had apparently never told their son about his "illness."

At seventeen, Paul was a tall, awkward boy who talked loudly. When we first met him, he was growing his hair long and wore an army jacket, bluejeans, and tall leather boots. As far as we could tell, the only thing unusual about his conversation was that he "came on strong," talked loudly, and seemed continually excited. Although the things he talked about were the same things that most kids talk about—school, parents, drugs, cars—he did not become friendly with anyone at the Runaway House. Something about the way he talked seemed to turn other kids off. One day in the office, we saw him try to make friends with two girls who were about to travel to Danvers, a town near his. "Danvers?" he said enthusiastically. "Danvers is near Wakefield, you know any kids from Wakefield? That's where I'm from." The three of them started exchanging names and for a moment it appeared that Paul was getting somewhere, but the girls quickly lost interest. He kept on naming people they might know but they ignored him. After several minutes, they left, but Paul was still talking—to no one in particular—about the kids at the high school.

While at the House, Paul went out several mornings to look for work. The first time, he awoke at five-thirty, went to the Manpower employment agency, and waited all day, but there were no jobs available. His luck was better the next few days so that he soon had earned some money. He asked Eric, his counselor, if he was going to take the money. Eric told him no, the money was his. At home, Paul said, his parents controlled his cash, even the money he earned on his own.

During Paul's first week at the Runaway House, Eric talked often with Mr. Silver. According to the father, Mrs. Silver was "too upset" to talk to anyone from the House. Counseling Paul was difficult because he was asking for several things. While he refused to go home, he wanted his father to agree that he could change from a college to a trade program at the high school. This demand seemed to be one condition for his returning home. Yet when Mr. Silver finally agreed to the switch, Paul became more adamant about not returning home. Eric then came up with another plan: Paul could attend a boarding school and take the courses he wanted. Paul was interested in this proposal and said he would think about it. Mr. Silver agreed to pay for the school. If his son wanted to live away from home, that was all right with him. Eric felt that a boarding school would be the best possible place for the boy; a foster home would not be suitable because he was such a "difficult" kid.

After his two weeks at the Runaway House were up, Paul had to decide what he was going to do. Hanging around in the office that morning, he said that he absolutely would not go home, even though his father had agreed to some changes. For a while we talked to him about electronics; he wanted to be an electrical engineer, not a repair man. For the immediate future, he said that he would stay in a friend's apartment; when we asked how much money he had, he answered that his friend was a girl who would support him. "I'll get a broad to feed me and take care of me. . . .

Can you dig that?" During his meeting with Eric, which we sat in on that afternoon, it turned out that Paul's "friend" was a former runaway, now living away from home, who had stopped in at the House that morning. When Paul said he was leaving that day and had no place to go, she offered to let him stay at her apartment for a few days and promised to return to the House that evening.

During their conversation, Eric tried to convince Paul that the plan to stay with the girl was not a good one. He tried to get Paul to see how "unrealistic" his ideas about living with the girl were; the harder he tried to persuade Paul, however, the more frustrated he became. Part of his insistence came from a feeling he had about Paul's family: his conversations with Mr. Silver led him to believe that the family did not want Paul around anymore. Consequently he felt that the residential school was the best of all the alternatives. Paul said he liked that idea and would try it if the apartment did not work out, but Eric would not accept that, so the two became angry with one another. At one point Paul asked Eric why he was looking at him with such disapproval; the counselor was honest enough to admit that it was because he disapproved of what Paul had chosen to do—he was simply "refusing to deal with his situation," as he had done for the past two weeks. Having expressed his anger, Eric gave up trying to convince Paul, and accepted the boy's decision, even though he did not like it. He asked, however, that Paul call his father and inform him of his plans. "If you don't make the call, I'll have to," he said, "and I'm tired of doing your work for you." He also told Paul that he should accept responsibility for the decision he had made.

Paul did not respond to any of this, since all he wanted to know was what Eric would do if he did not make the call. "Will you tell my father where I've gone?" he asked. Eric said he wasn't sure. "You mean you'd tell him where I went? You'd turn me in? Then he'd come down and try to pick me up." Eric then told Paul that if his father wanted to have him picked up by the police, he would be able to do that easily enough—kids with warrants on them were arrested all the time, often when they were just walking around. Paul became defiant. He would not leave the apartment, then no one would ever find him.

This kind of exchange was unusual in the work we saw done at Project Place and other youth counseling centers, yet it points out a problem that could occur anywhere. Eric grew angry with Paul out of frustration; he had worked out a plan which the boy seemed to like, but would not accept. Furthermore, this was not the first time this had happened between the two of them. For a while at least, it seemed that Eric was very committed to the choice he had made for Paul because he felt that it was in the boy's best interest. Trying to convince an adolescent that a decision is in his own best interest, however, is inevitably a losing proposition. At best, a young person will let someone else make such a decision for him, only later to admit his own feelings and reject the decision. Most of the time Eric seemed aware of the limits on the kind of responsibility a counselor can take for a kid's life; there was only so much one could do, and ultimately the kid was responsible for himself.

Toward the end of their conversation, Paul finally stopped fighting with Eric and said that he did not want to call his father because he would only be told that he had failed again. His father had said not to call unless he was going to come home, and now his father would be disappointed, but Paul did not want to hear that, although Eric pointed out that he was already feeling his father's disapproval. When Paul again refused to make the call, Eric said he could have it his way but would have to leave now. Paul then agreed to talk with his father, but before making the call, he described how he would live away from home—he would get stoned as much as he wanted to and if he had to steal to support himself, he would.

When he spoke with his father (who had a "high executive position" in an insurance company), Paul had little to say. Mr. Silver accepted his son's plan and did not come to pick him up. After the conversation, Paul explained that he did not swear while talking with his father because he still respected him.

The girl Paul expected to stay with never showed up that evening, but he had to leave the Runaway House anyway. For the next several weeks he lived on his own, for the most part in Boston, sleeping in basements when he was unable to find someone who would put him up. Then he returned home, but a week later was gone again. The second time out he spent some time in New Hampshire and visited an aunt and uncle in New York City as well. His parents took out a warrant against him as a runaway, so that when he returned, he had to appear in court as well as undergo a "psychiatric evaluation" (standard procedure for "juvenile offenders" at the Boston Juvenile Court). By this time, however, his parents had decided that they did not want him at home, so Paul stayed at Project Place. The "evaluation" involved interviews with Paul and his parents as well as a battery of psychological tests. On the basis of all this, the clinic assembled a "family history" and recommended treatment for Paul and his parents at a mental health center near their home. Most of the kids evaluated by the clinic end up seeing social workers or psychiatrists there, but Paul was an exception because of his class background. Since the family was well-off enough to afford therapy, they were "referred out." Shortly after the referral was made, Paul left the Runaway House once more; neither he nor anyone in his family followed through on the recommendation for therapy.

When this process was over, we talked to Eric and found him bitter. He felt that the court clinic had put in a lot of work to no end; but the findings of the staff had proved once and for all that the diagnosis of brain damage was a faulty one. They also seemed to have developed an understanding of the Silver family that was similar to his own: since Paul's childhood, the clinic felt, the boy had been repeatedly rejected by his parents—why this was, no one knew. "Paul's problems weren't that complicated after all," Eric said, "just seventeen years of being unwanted." While he respected the evaluative work of the court clinic, Eric was angry about the referral. By involving the family, Paul, and himself in a process, the clinic people seemed to have promised something which they did not deliver. Normally such initial interviews as the Silvers had are the first stages in therapy. Chances are that they would have to do the same thing all over again if they followed through on the referral. Eric wanted the court clinic to take advantage of the commitment all members of the Silver family seemed to have made by showing up to be interviewed, but *that*, the head psychiatrist told him, was impossible. Then why had they gone through the whole process, Eric asked when we spoke to him. When the "evaluation" was completed, Paul was no closer to getting help than he had been before it began.

Our visits to the schools Paul Silver had attended revealed that academically he had consistently done well. This surprised us, perhaps because all the talk of "hyperactivity" and "brain damage" had made more of an impression than we cared to admit. Also, seeing Paul around the Runaway House, often in a very excited state, we wondered how he could sit still in class long enough to learn anything. How could he concentrate? After all, wasn't that what had been "wrong" in the first place? If "hyperactivity" was anything, it was a "learning disorder"; hence we expected to find that Paul had had difficulty in school.

Mr. Hill, the headmaster of the boarding school, remembered Paul as a boy with an intense fear of failure. During the sixth through the eighth grades, Paul's marks had been high, and at the end of that time he tested at a ninth grade level. His fear of failure, however, had made learning traumatic. "He would sit in the classroom and cry if he didn't get a ninety on a test," Mr. Hill recalled. Once Paul had come to see the principal because he did not think he could finish a two-thousand-word history paper on time; the principal had reassured him that if he simply wrote a page a day he could complete his work and have time for other activities. Paul finished the assignment two weeks before the deadline. He also had been apprehensive about taking part in sports. However, although at first he resisted becoming involved in activities other than schoolwork, he eventually played on the soccer and basketball teams.

Mr. Hill felt that Paul had "made progress" while at the school; what he mainly needed was just "a pat on the back." Although he did not know what the reasons for Paul's fear of failure were, Mr. Hill thought that the boy should continue to attend school away from home, possibly in a vocational training program. Paul had already expressed interest in becoming an electrical engineer. Mr. Hill thought that was a fine idea: "Vocational training in schools isn't for the less bright as it used to be; he could be an apprentice and eventually run his own business." Paul's father, however, wanted his son to continue in college courses, and his mother wanted him home after three years away, so the next fall he enrolled in his hometown high school.

On our first visit to the high school, we learned that Paul had returned to the town some time after he had last been to Project Place, but not to his home. Mrs. Williams, his counselor, told us that he was staying with the family of a local minister who was friendly with Paul's parents. Since it did not seem likely that he would go back home, she was hoping that a local "group home" would find room for him; at the moment he was on the waiting list.

Mrs. Williams, a dark-haired, articulate woman in her late thirties, had worked very closely with Paul since December of that school year when he was referred to her by the principal for cutting class. Although she was also trying to help him find a permanent place to live and work out other future plans, much of her work with Paul still involved his class attendance; the day we saw her, she had just talked to him about a class he wanted to cut. After several minutes of talking, Mrs. Williams had simply told Paul he had to go to German. "I get like a sergeant with him," she said humorously, "and he goes." Although Paul came to see her daily, often with outrageous requests, she did not mind. What he needed, she thought, was structure and someone who would be kind but firm. His repeated visits were an indication that she was getting somewhere with him; also, since his return, he had been attending class more regularly.

Paul, Mrs. Williams felt, was a bright, demanding teenager who in many ways was still a child. While others had trouble with his insistent manner and did not know what to do with him, she treated Paul in a straightforward way. "Sometimes he comes in first thing in the morning when I've just gotten out of bed and says, 'Mrs. Williams, I've got this problem,' and I'll say, 'Paul, I don't want to hear about it now, come back third period and we can talk.' I let him know when I don't want to talk to him." She was amused by things he did that others might have disapproved of. Once, while she was talking on the telephone Paul had come into her office without knocking. "Who's that you're talking to?" he demanded. "You talking to my mother? She's going to kill me." Mrs. Williams had simply said no, she was not talking to his mother, and asked him to leave. In telling the story she was both startled and amused by what Paul had said to her; the intrusion was of secondary importance.

Mrs. Williams had talked at length with Paul about his experiences as a runaway. Although she thought running away "solved nothing" and told him so, she respected his ability to survive "when thrown to the wolves." Upon his return, Paul had had some difficulty with his chemistry teacher, a woman "from another era" who, the counselor felt, had given him "more make-up work than a college student could do." Consequently Paul had asked Mrs. Williams if he could drop the course and she had arranged for that. Now that he was carrying a lighter load she hoped he would finish out the year and not run away again. The next time he ran would be more serious than the last time because he was now on probation.

For the past several weeks, Mrs. Williams had been helping Paul apply to the local vocational high school. When we first talked to her he had had his interview and was waiting to hear whether he was accepted. She felt good about the trade program—it was what Paul wanted and she thought that he could do well in it "with some positive encouragement ... and a lot of attention." As part of Paul's application, she had to reassure the school authorities that he would not be a danger in the shop. She also discussed the plan with his father, who had agreed to it but was skeptical that his son would be around. The Admissions Board at the trade school was also worried that Paul might run away again.

The meeting with Paul's father was Mrs. Williams's only contact with the Silver family. Although their conversation had been brief, she was moved by Mr. Silver and wrote in a memo to another school official, "His face is etched finely with lines of care and there is an air of stinging sadness that clings to the man like an aura. . . . The family is generally at wit's end of late . . . Paul's behavior is part of the fabric of the family lifestyle. Years of heavy expense and deep involvement have taken their toll." In the same memo, she set down what she thought "the problem" was with Paul and what she was trying to do for him. Because of a "late development pattern" he did not "recognize ill-considered behavior as such. He has matured to the point where these functions are more natural to him. He knows the rules are also for him and . . . is trying to abide by them. . . . His temper runs mostly to loud verbalizations. . . . He is apt to be trying but I think he is a worthwhile young man who, as he gains control of himself, will do well in the field he has chosen." In talking about her work with Paul, Mrs. Williams mentioned that she had "gone out on a limb" for him. While she did not elaborate, it sounded to us as if there were others in the school who did not think he was worth all the difficulty he had created.

While we were talking to her, Paul came into her office and said that he had left German class. She asked if he was skipping and he said no, the teacher had said if he wanted to go, he could, so he had come to the guidance office. "I want to talk to you about some things," he said. Although she asked what, he would not say. She asked if it could wait and he said, "No, when can I talk to you in private?" She said whenever we were through talking, which would be soon; five minutes later he was back inside the office with a form for her to sign that had something to do with a trade school he wanted a catalogue for, not exactly something that "couldn't wait." This time he was more insistent. How much longer would we be? "Five minutes," Mrs. Williams said. When Paul came back, our interview with the counselor was over.

When we visited the school two months later, Mrs. Williams told us that "things hadn't been going so well with Paul." He had been cutting class a lot and was not getting along with the people he was living with. Furthermore he was getting into more trouble at school; his folder had disappeared from her office after one of his visits and he had recently enraged a teacher by eating her lunch. Placement at the local group home was now out of the question. There was no room. The trade school had put him on a waiting list, but she was no longer so sure he should go there. "I don't think he can function in school anymore," she said. What he needed was a program outside school; with "medication and lots of therapy" he would be "okay."

During this visit, we also talked to two of Paul's teachers, both of whom agreed that he "could no longer function" in school. His English teacher spoke at length about how much attention she had had to give Paul. When she gave an assignment, he would continually ask questions to make sure that he got it right. The German teacher had had a similar problem—sometimes he would ask her to explain sentences word for word, although he usually did well on assignments. If he made a mistake on one, he would ask for an explanation right away and be insistent until he understood the error. While he generally understood things correctly, she felt that he was not learning the language and had tried to work more with him. At one point during the year, when a student teacher took charge of the class, she spent more time with Paul and even wrote him a letter in German. He had borrowed her dictionary, translated the letter, and written back to her on his own. Now that the student teacher was gone, however, she no longer had time to go out of her way with Paul and felt that he was not learning much.

Paul's English teacher talked to us about how well she got on with him. They were friends, she said, and often rode home together on the bus. "You have to deal with him in his own crazy way, you can't take him seriously. What are you going to do if he tells you every day he's running away? How can you take him seriously? I tell him send me a postcard." Whenever Paul started to act up in class, she told him, "If you're going to act crazy, leave and come back when you can act normal." Often, he would try to provoke her in class; once he had taken out a cigarette and asked repeatedly what she would do if he lit it. "Make you put it out," she responded. What he wanted to know, she said, was whether she would send him to the principal, which she would not. "It doesn't do any good to send a kid like Paul to the principal or give him detention. He's too smart." Another time he had turned on his radio during class and increased the volume until she threatened to "smash it."

Although she felt capable of handling Paul and made a kind of play out of his behavior, the English teacher felt such incidents were examples of how he could no longer function in school. "You can't expect all teachers to cope with his antics," she said. Uncertain about what made him behave that way, she thought that it might be because of drugs, about which he was continually writing in his essays. Paul was the only student in her class who was so outspoken about drugs; the others ridiculed him for his enthusiasm and called him "Paul the freak." She did not know how many drugs he had taken, but there were times when she thought he was high in class. Because her course was half poetry, half rock music, she often played records; sometimes when Paul did not listen and instead walked around the room or looked out the window, she thought he might be stoned.

When Paul ran away, his German teacher talked with her class about it. Sometimes, she had told them, we need to go away for a while and think. If he came back she would not treat him differently. Afterwards some students came and talked to her about Paul; some were confused and did not understand why he had left. Since his return, he had talked to both teachers about his experiences; like Mrs. Williams, both were impressed with his "independence" and "resourcefulness."

From all we heard, Paul was a difficult, often confusing person to those who knew him, yet we were surprised that the teachers and counselor with whom we talked were so ready to see him sent away from the school, particularly because all three seemed to have a certain affection and respect for him. The counselor's plan—to find a program that involved medication and "lots of therapy" was a real shock. To what end, we wondered, and what had Paul done in the first place to deserve such special treatment? In retrospect, it seems that the worst one could say about Paul was that he was an inconvenience; although he performed well academically, socially he did not fit into the school environment, so his counselor wanted to send him to a place where he could be "helped."

Another factor in all this is the amount of time and energy Paul had taken from those who tried to work with him. It struck us that like Eric at Place, these "helpers" at school had given up on Paul out of frustration. Each of their attempts to help him had taken a day-to-day kind of effort for which they had received almost no return. It seemed to us that Mrs. Williams had had particularly high expectations for Paul and had gone the farthest out of her way for him. Yet when her expectations were disappointed and her work did not achieve the things she had hoped for, she was the most willing to have him sent away. That was one way, it seemed, of being rid of a responsibility she no longer wanted. In retrospect, it seemed that she had taken on too much—trying to keep him in school and in class. To try to do all these things was only human; she had seen needs which no one else was helping him with. Perhaps a more limited sense of what areas of Paul's life she would try to help might have kept the counselor from being so frustrated, but that was difficult to say. For whatever reason, she and others he knew at school had given up on him, and Paul was on the way out.

When we spoke with him on the telephone, Paul's father said he would be glad to talk to us about his son, provided it did not take too long. We thought it might take about an hour and he said that would be fine. The next afternoon we met him in his downtown office, found an empty room, and talked for two hours. Mr. Silver did most of the talking; we asked no more than a dozen questions the entire time and finally had to end the interview ourselves.

Mr. Silver was a tall, slender man who, except that he was growing bald and had a thick beard, reminded us of his son. His way of speaking was a quieter version of Paul's, and there was even a resemblance between the father's and the son's walk. He began the conversation by asking about our research. Once we had given a brief description of the project, he sat back in his chair and began to talk. The family, Mr. Silver said, had not broken any laws, so they had nothing to hide. He was not sure, however, that we would be interested in Paul, for he was not a "runaway case" but rather an "emotional problem," and had been for quite some time. "You see," he said, "he's got brain damage . . . he's a seventeen-year-old with the mind of a twelve-year-old and the behavior of a four-year-old. . . . He wants to do the things a normal seventeen-year-old can do—have a car, smoke cigarettes, go out with girls—but he can't do these things."

The night Paul ran away, Mr. Silver and his wife had gone out for the evening and left their oldest son (who was twenty-one) in charge. After an argument with his brother and younger sister, Paul had left the house. Mr. Silver thought the argument had little to do with the real reason Paul had run away; his son, he thought, wanted to prove his manhood and this was the only way he could do so. At home he was always doing things wrong and dreaming of "impossible things," the same things, he said, he had mentioned before. Because of these dreams, Mr. Silver thought his son lived in a "fantasy world."

For three days Paul had not told his parents where he was. "At first when he left," his father said, "I was really worried . . . he can't take care of himself . . . I thought he might get into some kind of accident." Once his son let them know his whereabouts, Mr. Silver spoke often with him: he was willing to let Paul stay away as long as he wanted even though his being away made both parents anxious. Mr. Silver did not dwell on the matter, but he mentioned that he and his wife had lost a lot of sleep those first few weeks.

After six weeks away, Paul was arrested and returned home; his father told him, "You're back . . . and nothing's going to be different. . . . We're not going to reward you or punish you, just do your schoolwork and follow the rules." The first week Paul was back "everything went okay. . . . He bragged some and made the whole thing into a big adventure. I told him not to do that but he did so anyway." At the end of the week, Mr. and Mrs. Silver flew down to New York for the day; Paul was supposed to visit his college friend in Boston who had agreed to pick him up and bring him back. When the Silvers returned, however, all the lights in the house were on. Paul was having a "pot party" with friends they did not recognize and the house was "a mess." Paul spent all day Sunday in his room and Monday he ran away again. "I had the feeling he was going to do that," Mr. Silver said.

The "pot party" incident was typical of Paul, according to his father. "Leave him alone for a minute and look what he does . . . freedom kills him." A similar incident had occurred the previous summer, when Mr. Silver and his wife had gone to Cape Cod for the weekend with the understanding that Paul would show up Saturday evening after he finished work. When his son arrived during the day, Mr. Silver knew something had gone wrong, and he soon found out that Paul had been drunk the night before, done his job poorly, and been fired. "I try to give him the benefit of my knowledge as an employer and tell him how to behave on the job but he just won't listen."

The second time his son was gone, it was more difficult for Mr. Silver to keep track of him. One night, however, he received a telephone call at eleven o'clock from the Concord police, who had just picked Paul up sleeping behind a motel. "We've got your son here," the police told him, "and we understand he's a runaway. Will you come and get him?" Mr. Silver told the policeman he would not, a statement that the officer could not believe. "What do you want us to do with him, then?" he had asked. Mr. Silver then became angry. "Is he in any trouble?" "No," the policeman responded. "Then release him." "But how's he going to get home?" "How did he get there?" the father asked. "If he got there on his own, he can get back the same way."

This incident was a critical one in Mr. Silver's mind for it was during this conversation that he had "won" his "freedom from Paul." Since then he had decided that his son would no longer live with the rest of the family. "I don't want him home ... I don't trust him. ... It gives me pleasure to pay money so that he can live with another family away from home." Mr. Silver seemed angry and spiteful as he described what a "bad influence" his son was on the family: he had introduced his younger sister to cigarettes and stolen fifty dollars from his brother one of the times he had run away. "Who knows what he could be setting us up for ... you don't know with the people he's hanging around with downtown ... anyone might get him to help burglarize the place." There were locks on all the doors to the outside now and if Paul moved back in, they would have to have locks inside as well. He also no longer felt safe leaving Paul alone with his younger sister. "I don't know what he might do ... even though she's smart and could probably find help." Paul, he said, knew from books everything there is to know about sex, but he had never had any experience; such extensive knowledge without experience was not "normal" for a seventeen-year-old boy. "Most boys that age know what you can and cannot do."

As he talked, Mr. Silver seemed to be trying to convince us that almost everything about his son was "wrong." His complaint with Paul was general and extended to all aspects of the boy's life. His son was clumsy and always breaking things: "He's the kind of kid who falls up the stairs." He always did things too quickly and had "a poor attention span." While away at boarding school, Paul had wanted to come home, but once there he wanted to go away to school again; "he can't make up his mind." While his son was the kind of kid other kids made fun of because of his clumsiness, he was also "easily influenced" by the others and sometimes got into trouble over things they made him do.

Mr. Silver also felt that his son had a kind of power over

some people. Paul was "cagey." While away from home he had gained "street knowledge": "He's learned how to get people to do things for him ... he's got all kinds of people jumping through hoops to help him." Sooner or later though, they would get tired of him—Paul got on everyone's nerves after a while. Once you gave him something, he always wanted more, he was always after "instant gratification." At one point in our conversation when we mentioned that sometimes kids interpret their parents' going to look for them as a sign of caring he said, "That's it, that's the way Paul's always been: he wants attention, just like a movie star.... He knows if you get good publicity, you do well at the box office." These qualities made Mr. Silver think that his son was "going to come to a bad end ... he never has enough ... [he's] a perfect candidate for drugs ... he'll start taking them and whoosh, [his hand swept across the table] then just like everything else he won't be able to get enough."

Some of Mr. Silver's antagonism toward his son seemed to have grown out of a feeling of betrayal and frustration. The parents had made real sacrifices so that their son could receive the treatment they had been told he needed. While Paul was in the hospital, the Silvers had been "a family of no weekends"; they had visited him once a week for four years. Mr. Silver had given up "possibilities of advancement" in his career in order to remain in the Boston area. More recently, he had been spending a great deal of his time at work doing things about Paul; "I haven't been able to do my work and if I weren't my own boss and had to punch a clock ... I would have been fired by now."

Mr. Silver seemed to have questions about how much good it had done for Paul to be in the hospital. The life there "spoiled kids." He described black children he had seen there at a Christmas party, surrounded by gifts that rich people from the town had sent. "They get steaks and parties there ... the permissiveness is what's therapeutic ... then at age twelve they have to go back to the ghetto ... what's wrong is not in their minds, but what's out there." Though he did not say so, it seemed to us that some of his feelings about Paul were in that statement.

When Paul was released from the hospital (the program he was in only went up to age twelve), a psychologist had told the Silvers that one of the tests given to their son showed the possibility of a brain lesion. It was this, he said, that might be the cause of their child's "hyperactivity" and that something might be wrong with that part of the brain that normally lets a kid calm down. He told them, however, that it was common for "hyperactive" children to develop the functions they had been lacking during their teenage years, anytime between the ages of twelve and seventeen. About drug therapy, he suggested that kind of treatment might help Paul calm down when he got too excited, but that was up to them. During the next few years, the Silvers periodically put Paul back on his "medicine," which "seemed to help"; but since he was fifteen, they had not given him any. Mr. Silver described the psychologist's diagnosis at length. The "lesion" had prevented Paul from learning skills that other kids knew by the age of five or six. When we asked what those things were, he replied, "The ability to do what society expects of you . . . to follow rules . . . it's the whole business of conformity . . . to stop acting like a child and always expecting to be gratified."

Mr. Silver seemed somewhat awed by the professional knowledge of those people he had talked to at the hospital and took pride in telling us what they had told him. "My wife and I, we've been involved with this thing for so long we're almost professionals ourselves," he said. The court clinic, he felt, had done a "bad evaluation." One psychiatrist had not shown up for his interview with Paul. Once the lengthy evaluation was completed, nothing had been done—no one even submitted a report to the court, so that when the family appeared for a hearing several weeks later, there was no record of what they had been through. Mr. Silver was indignant about the way his son had been treated, yet he seemed particularly affected by the clinic's recommendation. Before he told us what the clinic had suggested, however, he asked what our background was. Were we social workers? When he found out that we were not and had had no previous training in psychology, he said in a reserved tone of voice that the clinic had said that the whole family should seek counseling at a mental health center. He seemed amazed and affronted by the suggestion; furthermore he had been to that particular center years ago and did not want to go there again.

Mr. Silver was uncertain about what would happen to Paul now. He was skeptical about whether or not the trade school plan would work out. Paul had only recently returned from his third time on the run; he had stayed with an uncle in New York who had paid for his flight back to Boston. It was through this uncle that something might be worked out, since he knew of some "excellent" special schools in New York state where Paul could go. Mr. Silver had yet to look into this plan, but there was one thing he was very concerned with: the school had to be "custodial"; he did not want Paul to run away again.

8
"WHERE ARE YOU TONIGHT, SWEET MARIE?"

THIS *final narrative is the story of three girls—Charlotte Green, Bonnie Simms, and Jill Ware—all of whom we met one afternoon at the Runaway House. Having spent some time together and sharing common concerns, the three seemed like a natural group. Charlotte, sixteen, was the oldest and the one we know the least about. After staying at the Runaway House, she returned to the vicinity of her hometown in western Massachusetts and we lost track of her. We came to know Bonnie, thirteen, somewhat better. She spent more time at the House and several times during those weeks her mother came to talk with her. After Bonnie's return home, we visited her counselor at a local mental health center, whose account gave us a better understanding of the events preceding her departures.*

We came to know Jill, fourteen, best of all, and talked to her frequently during her two months at the House. As much as any of the kids with whom we spoke, Jill had been involved with juvenile authorities, having spent time in a detention center and in a boarding school for emotionally disturbed girls—all this because she had run away from home several times. In our research we visited the institutions to which she had been sent and talked with some of the people who had helped make decisions about what should be done with Jill—her mother, school officials at her junior high, social workers at the special school and at the Department of Youth Services, and her counselor at Project Place.

We realize that writing about all three of these girls makes a fairly lengthy case. Nevertheless, we have grouped them together because they were friends and because each represents a different kind of situation with which we have become familiar in the course of our research. All were runaways who came to the Runaway House at the same time, yet one ended up in a juvenile detention center, another returned home to counseling, and the third worked out a viable way of living away from home.

One afternoon in January, while sitting in the basement kitchen at Project Place Runaway House, we got involved in a conversation with three girls about why they would not go home. Jill, a dark-haired, engaging girl, set the tone of the conversation by saying that no matter what happened, she was not going home. She and her mother hated each other and fought all the time; her mother would not leave her alone. Jill had a sharp biting voice and spoke with determination, making blunt, direct statements. Charlotte said she had not gotten along with either of her parents and that they did not get along with each other. She had left home after a big fight between her mother and her alcoholic father, after which he had walked out of the house. Charlotte had been gone for over a week and her father had not yet returned; he was living in a hotel and there was talk of divorce. Jill said she knew about that: her parents had been divorced several years ago.

At this point Bonnie, who had sat quietly watching the others, began to talk in a soft voice about her home life. She did not want to go back because her parents were always judging her friends and sometimes did not allow her to see the ones they did not like. Charlotte said her parents had tried to do the same thing only she had argued with them until they left her alone. It had not been easy, the fights had been vicious, but after a while they no longer tried to control her acquaintances. Jill had handled that problem differently. She "corrupted" one of the friends her mother had selected by turning her on to dope and glue; then the friend started to do worse in school. After that Jill's mother had nothing more to say about her friends. Jill told Bonnie she should try to turn some of her "good" friends "bad"; Charlotte said she should fight harder with her parents. Bonnie smiled at their suggestions and said in her sad, quiet voice that she would not go home unless her parents agreed to stop trying to choose her friends.

We spent several hours that afternoon talking to the three girls as other kids wandered in and out to join in the conversation and listen to music on the radio. Bonnie talked about the other things she was dissatisfied with at home—her four o'clock curfew and the way her parents pressured her about school. She also felt that her parents treated her like a child. Away for a week already, she was going to have a family conference in several days. After that she would see whether or not she would go home. Charlotte was apprehensive about a meeting she would have the next week with a probation officer and her parents back in her hometown; she was angry about the meeting and cursed a lot, but curious as well. What could the courts do to her? Would they try to send her to jail or make her go home with her parents? If they did that it would not matter, she would only go on the run again. They could not make her live at home. Jill said that if it was a conference, they would probably just talk about the things that might happen to her. The probation officer could not send her away—she had to appear in court for that. Charlotte said that made her feel better but she still did not know what her parents were going to do.

In addition to discussing "problems," the girls talked about life at the Runaway House. All three belonged to a group of kids there who spent time together walking around the South End, sitting in restaurants, and mixing with the Hornets, a local gang. There were about ten kids in the group and all had new names, which we saw written all over the walls of the Runaway House; Jill was "Sapphire," Bonnie was "Dawn," and Charlotte, "Satin." While we were there, the girls called each other by their new names. Some were involved with boys from their "in" group when we talked to them, others were going out with members of the local gang even though the policy of the Runaway House discouraged that kind of relationship. As long as they were there, kids were expected to be thinking through their "situation," deciding whether to go home, look for alternative living arrangements, or stay out. From what we saw over several months there, most of this kind of thinking took place within the counselor-kid relationship. Among themselves, kids rapidly made friends (and enemies), went out to do things together, kept each other awake into the night—except for the absence of their parents and their familiar environments, they continued to lead "normal" adolescent lives. Listening to Jill, Bonnie, and Charlotte talk that afternoon, we had the sense that this part of their experience away from home was as important as the reasons for their departure and the feelings they had for what they had left behind. All three had had conflicts with their parents over who their friends would be and what they would do with them; away from home, they were able to make friends without being judged by parents.

Our conversation that afternoon ended when Charlotte and Jill left to get ready for Friday night dates. When we returned to the Runaway House a week later Bonnie had gone home. The conference with her family had been an emotional one which ended with the father taking the girl into his arms: there had been some agreement that her curfew be extended but for the most part the family talked about how much they had missed each other. Bonnie's counselor was optimistic—both parents were midwestern and had only recently moved east. They were rigid and particularly restrictive because they were scared of the things their daughter might become involved with (i.e., drugs and sex), yet they seemed warm and loving and that made a difference—particularly to Bonnie. Her father's desire that she come home had affected her strongly and she had cried a lot. The family might seek some kind of counseling. In the meantime, Bonnie would continue to see a psychologist at a local mental health center.

Charlotte was enthusiastic about the conference with her parents and probation officer. Everyone had agreed that some alternative living arrangement should be worked out for her, at least for the time being. Her parents' willingness to cooperate had surprised Charlotte; also she liked her probation officer. As yet, nothing had been worked out but there were several possibilities—a group home near Worcester where her mother might come visit her, one in Cambridge, or perhaps a foster home. She was uncertain about any of these arrangements: group homes had particularly strict rules about when boys and girls could see each other and she did not know whether she wanted another set of parents. Nevertheless, she was hopeful that she would soon have a place to live. Charlotte was glad that her father had returned home and mentioned that he was going into a state program for alcoholics. After "drying out" in a hospital, he would see a counselor once a week. She was skeptical, however, about his ability to stay sober, for he had done the same thing once before, and had been drinking again within a year.

This week, it was Jill who was nervous about a meeting with juvenile authorities. The next day, all those involved in her "case"—which included her mother, a supervisor, and a social worker from the Department of Youth Services (the agency which is responsible for juvenile "offenders"), her probation officer, and Leslie, her Place counselor—were going to meet and decide who would have primary responsibility for her.

Jill had a long history of involvement with the Department of Youth Services, all of which had to do with her running away. Almost a year earlier, her mother had committed her to the state agency as a "stubborn child" in order that she might be "placed" in a Catholic boarding school for children with "emotional" problems, but because the placement took longer than expected, Jill had been held in a detention center for several months. Shortly after she enrolled in the boarding school, she began to run away again. The first few times, she was caught and brought back, but by midsummer, she was determined to leave for good. She hated the school, she said; she had not liked having to be in bed at nine-thirty every night, and objected to being forbidden to talk to her friends in their own rooms (each girl had a private bedroom). Sometimes she had been punished for sitting on a friend's bed and talking to her before the lights went out. One nun told her that these rules existed to prevent lesbianism among the girls.

In August, Jill had run away to Project Place with several other girls. Social workers and teachers from the school had followed them there and told them they were going to come back to the school, but Jill refused to go. When they tried to "reason" with her, saying that they were only trying to help her and it was "for her own good," that she had to come back, she had cursed at them and said simply, "I'm not going back to that prison." The other girls returned to the school but Jill continued to refuse to go until the social workers decided that it would be better to let her stay for a while at least rather than drag her back. After a call to a Department of Youth Services administrator (officially, the state had custody of her), who "approved" their course of action, the social workers had left.

Despite this "clearance," several officers of the Department of Youth Services had showed up at the Runaway House a few days later in order to arrest Jill. Before they could apprehend her, she had run out the back door and disappeared into the South End of Boston. The officers only stopped their search when the administrator who had given permission for Jill to stay was contacted. He had not ordered them to arrest her and was not sure who had, but by talking to him, Leslie got the search called off. To this day she does not know who sent those men for Jill. After several weeks at Place she decided to return home rather than go back to the boarding school.

While living at home, Jill continued to see a parole agent from the Department of Youth Services, Miss Young, but the conflicts with her mother went on and became more intense. Sometime in December, after getting into an accident while driving her mother's car illegally, Jill ran away from home once again, and had been living at the Runaway House up until that January when we first met her.

The second time we talked to her, Jill was uncertain what she would do. She had already stayed at the Runaway House for two weeks (the maximum time allowed by House policy), but by agreement between her mother, Leslie, and herself, she would be staying longer, until she had someplace to go other than home. It was unclear just what this place would be, for Jill did not want to go to a foster home and was unsure about whether or not she would stay in a halfway house. Although there were many such "group homes" in the area, most were full in wintertime and spaces were hard to come by. Jill's doubts about the possibility of getting such a placement had a firm basis in fact; placements in both foster homes and halfway houses are difficult to find.

Charlotte also wanted to stay at Project Place until something definite was worked out, but each day her parents became more insistent that she return to Worcester and wait—either at home or at the regional juvenile detention center. Her probation officer had made the center sound attractive to her: as juvenile "facilities" go, the Worcester center was known as one of the better ones, which simply meant that the food was decent and fewer kids got beaten up there than at other places. Jill told Charlotte she had heard some good things about "Worcester" but warned her against believing what her probation officer said. No matter how good it was inside that place, you had to *stay* inside. "Those places are jails," she said. "Don't let them tell you anything else." Charlotte's counselor had been trying to find a place for her in some halfway house or foster home but so far he had had no luck.

The next day was significant for both girls. Jill sat silent throughout the Runaway House meeting that morning. She left with Leslie shortly after noon and traveled an hour by car to the regional office of the Department of Youth Services, which still had official custody of her. Leslie had worked hard preparing for the conference, spending long hours on the telephone with Jill's mother as well as with Miss Young. While it looked as though all parties were willing to have her take responsibility for Jill's case, nothing was definite yet. She had a particularly good relationship with Jill's mother, who accepted the idea, but it was unclear what the Department of Youth Services would finally decide. It was one of the first times counselors from Project Place had collaborated with this state agency, hence the negotiations were delicate.

The result of the meeting, which lasted for over an hour, was an agreement between all those present that Jill could not live at home right now, that she should go either to a group home or get a foster placement and that Leslie would work most closely with her. This final point had been Jill's decision, which everyone else agreed to respect. In addition, the Department of Youth Services agreed to provide funding for whatever arrangement was worked out. At the meeting, Jill's mother said she hoped all this would only be a temporary arrangement, but Jill herself thought of it as permanent. She was quiet during the meeting and, according to Leslie, scared; yet she remained polite throughout and did not lose her temper. When it was all over, she returned to the Runaway House, and sullenly joined her friends. After a dozen times on the run and half a dozen counselors, she would have a chance to work out where and how she would live.

By the time Jill returned in late afternoon, Charlotte had run away from the Runaway House in flight from her parents, who had told her over the telephone that they were coming to pick her up the next day. Her day had begun like Jill's; she had been at the House meeting and taken an active role in a discussion of whether kids who stole things should be punished. Her feeling at the outset was that people who were "into ripping off" were "people with a problem," consequently they should get help rather than be punished. Other kids felt that anyone caught stealing should be thrown out of the House. When someone said that each case should be handled separately, Charlotte said she was not sure, maybe it would be a good thing if anyone caught stealing were thrown out of the House; she would have to think about it more. Eventually the group decided against setting any rule, and instead would discuss each incident individually.

When the discussion of stealing ended, Charlotte asked one of the counselors what he thought about foster homes; it was now clear that no place could be found in a halfway house; consequently a foster home was her only alternative to going home, going to reform school, or running away again. When the counselor replied to her question by saying he knew of some cases that had worked out well and some that had not ("it depends on the situation and how the placement is made"), Charlotte began to express her doubts. What would her parents think of her living in someone else's house? Why did she have so few choices and all of them bad? That was the problem with her life, always having to choose between bad alternatives. "I guess I just have bad luck or something." As she talked, however, she changed her mind. Maybe a foster home would be a good thing, especially if she could get away from her hometown.

When the meeting ended, Charlotte rushed to the telephone to call her probation officer and tell him of her new plan. He said that a foster home was a possibility—it would take time to work out—and informed Charlotte that her father was going into the hospital that Sunday. Suddenly it was very important for her to get back to western Massachusetts before Sunday; by the end of their conversation, the probation officer had scheduled a Saturday court appearance for Charlotte and her parents. Because of what happened after this phone call, it was unclear who was responsible for the idea of a court appearance on such short notice. It was clear, however, that Charlotte both wanted and feared the meeting.

Charlotte talked briefly with her counselor (who was at home on a day off), then called her parents to tell them that she *could* get into a foster home (even though everyone she had talked to had only said they would *try* to arrange such a placement). Her mother started shouting at her—she would do no such thing, she had been in Boston long enough, it was time she came home—then Charlotte began to cry and called her mother a liar. "You said you would accept what we worked out, now you're going back on your word." For the next several minutes, Charlotte's mother did most of the talking until Charlotte refused to listen anymore. She talked to her father, still crying and saying only that they could not make her go home. Then she said that she could not talk anymore but would have her counselor call them.

After she hung up, Charlotte began to make plans to run away. She simply would not be around when her parents came to get her, that would show them. The probation officer had said she would be in the detention center for at least two weeks. Therefore she decided to run to New York City and went out to the street with other kids from the House to try to "panhandle" the bus fare. For the rest of the afternoon, Charlotte came in and out of the House. She would smoke cigarettes, count her money, talk to the kids in the House or a counselor, then be gone again. By evening she had left "for good," but later that night returned. The next day she was there when her parents came to pick her up.

Both Charlotte and Jill spent most of Friday afraid, trying to work out an alternative to living at home that the juvenile authorities as well as their parents would accept. For Jill, the fear was a familiar one; her many conflicts with authorities and her mother had led her to expect little mercy from either party. She had seen, however, the worst of what either could do to her. Her mother had taken her to court as a "stubborn child" and the state, in turn, had kept her in one of its worst detention centers, Roslindale. By the time she went to the conference, she had been involved with the Department of Youth Services for almost a year, and when she returned from the meeting, she was in a sense free of them for the first time. Yet in order to become so, she had been required to listen to them pass judgment on her. Her past experiences had taught Jill that there was no way that one could trust these authorities. At the same time, there was no way of getting around them. She had taken the only course she knew: to be stubborn in her insistence on her own wishes until those "responsible" for her recognized them as valid. Charlotte, however, was away from home for the first time. Having departed in the middle of a family "crisis," the pain of which she could no longer tolerate, she found herself in a corner, being prosecuted as a juvenile offender. Her actions that Friday were a direct consequence of her position. Up against something she had never known before, her only alternatives were going to jail or running off again into stranger territory with no way to support herself.

Charlotte tried to find a way out through every possible opening. She interpreted the counselor's cautious suggestion of a foster home as an assurance that she could live away from home, agreed to a Saturday hearing in court in order to see her father once more, and tried to get to New York in order to get away from everything. One might imagine her turning from one choice to another, spinning herself around the way children do to get dizzy. Although she tried to run again, Charlotte chose the most familiar course of action and went back home with her parents to be sent to the detention center. Several weeks later, Jill told us of a letter she had received from Charlotte. The food was terrible and the place was crowded, but the worst thing was that she couldn't see any of her friends. Only her parents could visit her.

Two weeks after she had returned home, Bonnie Simms ran away once again and came to Project Place. Already a thin girl, she ate little while she was there and came down with a bad cold shortly after her arrival. Steadfast in her determination not to go home, she seemed equally determined not to be healthy. She visited a free clinic several times, but that did not seem to help. For the most part she sat around the office and in the kitchen, listening to the radio. She complained of a fever and sometimes wrapped herself in a blanket.

Bonnie's return was a surprise to those who had helped her go home after the first time she ran away. Bonnie's counselors thought that in some ways her parents wanted to raise her as they had been raised, but that was not possible. She was of a different generation and had her own ideas about what she wanted to do. Nevertheless, at the family conference, Bonnie and her parents had started to sort through some of the issues. They worked out a contract for her return, an idea of Bonnie's, which stipulated that her parents would let her:

1. choose her own friends
2. stay out until 4:00 p.m. and
3. date

if she would:

1. not lie to them
2. not be pushed around by her friends
3. try to stay away from drugs and
4. try to improve her schoolwork

Bonnie had put in the statement about not lying to her parents. Before she left, she had had to be "sneaky" in order to do those things that were forbidden her (i.e., see "illegal" friends). Lying, she said, had made her feel bad and she did not want to do it anymore. Perhaps the most encouraging thing of all, to Place counselors, was the Simms family's agreement to go into family counseling at a mental health center near their home.

Miss Ray, the psychologist who was already seeing Bonnie, had agreed to work with the family. She had also been pleased with Bonnie's first return and felt that she had had a positive experience at Runaway House. Bonnie, by becoming part of a group of kids, had accomplished something that had been difficult for her to do at home. Now the girl stood up to her parents and told them what she wanted. In the past, when they had forbidden her to see a friend, she had usually gone upstairs to her room and listened to records. In the family counseling sessions following her return, Bonnie began to be more honest about the things that were troubling her. Most of the second meeting concerned drugs. Pressed by her parents, Bonnie had told them the extent of her drug experience (she had tried marijuana several times), and although they had been critical, she had defended herself. Miss Ray felt Bonnie had been particularly "strong" during this session. The next day, however, she ran away from home again.

Miss Ray had begun seeing Bonnie the previous fall. During the summer she had been caught shoplifting several times and had stayed away from home one night (at a friend's house). When she returned home the next day, her father began to reprimand her about "running away"; shortly thereafter, she began to see Miss Ray. In spite of the idea that it had been her father's idea that Bonnie see a psychologist, Miss Ray felt that the girl liked the counseling relationship. In over six months she had not missed an appointment.

Bonnie's family told Miss Ray that their daughter had been "different" for over a year. Miss Ray, however, felt that many of Bonnie's difficulties were a consequence of her experience with the family. For several years, the Simmses had moved frequently because of her father's job as a middle-level executive in a national corporation. As a result of the moves, Bonnie had attended five different schools in as many years before the family came to Boston. For the past year and a half, she had attended the same junior high school, but had experienced difficulty in making friends. This fact surprised us, for she was an attractive girl and despite her reserve had been friendly with other kids at Runaway House. During Bonnie's first year at the junior high, she had been singled out and scapegoated by students in her class (she was a "new kid"), but she had made friends with some older kids who thought of themselves as "freaks." When these friends went on to high school, Bonnie had to start over again. Her next set of friends included some of the "bad" girls at the school. It was with these friends that she had been caught shoplifting the previous summer.

Bonnie's friends became a matter of controversy with her family, for through them she had started to change. She wanted to wear bluejeans to school (which was permitted by the school but not by Mrs. Simms) and began to think of herself as a "freak." She also wanted to go out with some of her male friends and was no longer interested in taking flute lessons. The family was upset about these changes. Mr. and Mrs. Simms had both started dating when they were sixteen and expected Bonnie to wait until that age as well. Mrs. Simms did not like her daughter wearing bluejeans, particularly outside the house, and she insisted that Bonnie continue with her music lessons. According to Miss Ray, Mrs. Simms had once gone to Bonnie's school and counted the number of girls in pants and girls in skirts as well as boys with short hair and boys with long hair. Then she had returned home to tell Bonnie that she did not have to be the way she was; not all the kids were like that.

One week, Bonnie came to Miss Ray and said that she thought she was being followed by a detective while she was at school. At first the psychologist tried to reassure her, and told her that this could not be true. Only later did they both discover that

Bonnie's younger brother had indeed been spying on her and informing her parents about what she had been doing.

It was Miss Ray's opinion that although the parents had agreed on certain changes at the family conference, they had set up new strategies so that change could not occur. For instance, on the issue of friends, they said that Bonnie could choose for herself; however, they would no longer allow her to leave the house on weekends. Her "responsibilities" at home increased and going to church all day Sunday was more important than ever. Miss Ray felt that Bonnie's expectations that her parents would change might have been too high after the first conference. She had run away the second time out of a feeling of hopelessness.

During her second stay at Runaway House, Bonnie did not talk much about concrete issues such as that of choosing her friends. She complained mostly of how she had been treated by her father. She just did not get along with him, she said, but did not elaborate. Since her second departure, Bonnie's father had not talked to her. He felt that she could find her way home on her own. This, Miss Ray said, was typical of the tough and challenging way he treated his daughter. In the fall, when Bonnie had first talked about running away, Mr. Simms had told her that she could not make it on her own "out there." Miss Ray felt that part of what Bonnie did the first time she ran away was to prove to her father that she could survive away from home. Furthermore, she had chosen the city, a completely unfamiliar environment, as the place where she would test herself. Miss Ray described an incident which had occurred shortly before Bonnie left home the second time. It indicated, to her, how strong the tension was between father and daughter. After he found Bonnie smoking a cigarette between church and Sunday school, Mr. Simms had taken her home and punished her by pouring a glass of whiskey, making her drink it, then lighting a cigar and making her smoke it. The girl had been shaken up by the incident and talked at length with the psychologist about it.

Bonnie claimed that she got along well with her mother, which was surprising. Miss Ray felt that Mrs. Simms was particularly worried about Bonnie becoming an adolescent and responded to all kinds of situations with equal anxiety. Once, following her first return, when Bonnie came home an hour late in the afternoon, Mrs. Simms had called Miss Ray and said, "It's happening again, she's letting us down." All drugs were the same in the mother's eyes and all were forbidden. Miss Ray had tried to get Mrs. Simms to begin to "differentiate her reactions," but she felt she had not accomplished much. Miss Ray's description of Mrs. Simms suggested that Bonnie's attempt to be "open" with her parents about her limited experience with drugs might have only made the situation more difficult.

During her second stay at Runaway House, Bonnie talked on the telephone with her mother and saw her several times. The first morning we talked with the girl, however, she did not want to speak with her mother anymore. The night before, Mrs. Simms had called her a "worldly person"; she had denied that she was "worldly" but her mother insisted. Didn't she take drugs and have sex with boys? Bonnie found this insulting and hung up. As she told the story she seemed upset. Her mother's accusation had struck a particularly sensitive side of her.

As she talked, it was hard to believe that Bonnie was considered a "freak" by her parents and classmates in her hometown. She seemed more like a "father's favorite daughter" than a rebel; her bluejeans were new and still stiff, her hair was cut short and she was always soft-spoken. In other situations, however, Bonnie had not been so mild-mannered. According to her psychologist, she had been antagonistic toward her school counselor, an older woman whom she had visited frequently. Bonnie had shouted at the counselor and called her names. She had also, at times, exaggerated her own drug use to her peers as well as parents. One day, she raided her parents' medicine chest and handed out drugs to her friends at school.

One afternoon, while working as counselors at Runaway House, we met Mrs. Simms when she dropped by to visit her daughter. At the time, Bonnie was on the other side of town seeing Miss Ray. Despite her departure from home, she had continued to see her psychologist, traveling across town for over an hour on the subway. Mrs. Simms, a short, light-haired woman, said she brought some schoolbooks for Bonnie and would wait until her daughter returned. The ride in from their home had taken a long time, she said, but it would be worth it if she could see Bonnie. She missed her so much. Everybody in the family did. She just wished Bonnie would get over whatever her "problem" was and come home. She knew her daughter had "problems," but running away was not the right way to handle them. So far, though, nothing else had worked. She had counselors at school as well as Miss Ray, the psychologist. "She's had all kinds of help," her mother said, "but it just hasn't seemed to click."

Mrs. Simms waited in the Runaway House office for over an hour until her daughter returned. The House was crowded that day and some of the kids were shouting at each other. Mrs. Simms tried not to notice what was going on, but the longer she sat there, the less she had to say. When Bonnie finally walked in, her mother started to cry. All the other kids left the office and then the two of them wept together for a few minutes. Finally, Mrs. Simms collected herself and told Bonnie she had brought some schoolbooks. While picking them up at school, she had talked to the principal, who wanted to see that things worked out for Bonnie. Then Mrs. Simms turned on her daughter and said in an anxious voice, "I don't want to see you fail." It was serious that Bonnie had been away from school more than a week; soon, she might be charged with truancy. Bonnie listened to all of this while looking straight at her mother, but had nothing to say. When she started to talk, she spoke of her father. It was because of him that she did not want to come home. At this point, her mother interrupted her and turned to us. There was something Bonnie did not understand about her father. He had been sick several years ago, undergone a serious operation, and had recently discovered that he was sick again. Consequently, he was often disagreeable and had a temper about which Bonnie was not understanding. The girl responded to this angrily: "I've seen him shout at you all the time, the same as he shouts at me." Mrs. Simms ignored this accusation and went on to say that if Bonnie came home, she would have to follow the rules of the house. Bonnie complained about having to be in at five o'clock, to which her mother responded that when Bonnie was doing better in school that would change, but for now she had to be in early to study.

While talking with each other, mother and daughter grew angrier. Mrs. Simms's statement about following rules led to a fight about how responsible Bonnie could be for herself. "You have to realize that you're still a minor," her mother said, "so you have to do as you're told by your father." "So I'm an infant," Bonnie shot back. "You talk to me like I'm ten years old." Whenever her daughter became contentious, Mrs. Simms would turn to one of us and explain something. In this case, she said, "Bonnie has to understand that the family has rules about drugs and sex and that she must follow them. When she's older and responsible for herself, that's another matter, but now she's only thirteen." Bonnie responded to this by asking, "Am I pregnant?" The conversation ended when Bonnie refused to return home with her mother. "Fifty percent of me wants to," she said, but she would not go. When asked to come out to dinner with the rest of the family, Bonnie looked very sad and did not answer for almost a minute. Then she shook her head and her mother left.

Shortly after this meeting, Bonnie had to leave Runaway House because she could no longer work toward returning home. Her counselor said that she had talked of a "group home" but "really didn't know the first thing about what that meant." Consequently, she was on the run again. Periodically, she called the Runaway House to say that she was all right and that she might return home soon, but for over a week she stayed away, sleeping in basements or crashing with people she met. During this time, Mrs. Simms searched the area for her daughter without success. One day, she dropped by Runaway House to see if Bonnie were there. If she found her, she would take her home. This had gone on long enough. She appreciated their help, but it was time her daughter came home. "No one can understand what it feels like when someone does this kind of thing to you." She got too worried, she said, and was having a difficult time sleeping at night. "Why, she's only thirteen years old—you can't be thirteen and running around the streets the way she is." According to Miss Ray, Mrs. Simms had been reluctant to go looking for her daughter. Once Bonnie had left the House, however, Miss Ray had encouraged her to go into the city. After almost a week of searching, Mrs. Simms found Bonnie visiting Project Place and took her home.

Two weeks later, we talked to Bonnie when she called the Runaway House. Upon her return, she said, her father ignored her and told the mother it was too bad the girl had not come back on her own. The main difference about her home now was that she no longer got along with her mother, who, she felt, was always "after" her. In the kitchen one day she had told her sister that she wanted to have a baby, to which her mother had said, "I hope it comes later than nine months." Her mother was particularly worried about what Bonnie might have done while away from home and had taken her to the hospital to be examined and tested for venereal disease. Bonnie thought this was all a waste of money and chuckled, "Maybe it will turn out positive."

Bonnie said she had worked hard at school and made up the work she missed. Her "curfew" had been extended to six o'clock. She was "thinking" of running away again but didn't really know. Maybe she would wait until spring. As we talked with her, she periodically broke off the conversation to shout something at her friends. She managed to stay in touch with both conversations.

Miss Ray felt that the Simmses were afraid of Bonnie since her return. By surviving in the city, she had proved "tougher" than her father expected. Her mother, on the other hand, feared the girl's experience: "She knows that Bonnie has seen more at thirteen than she has seen in her whole life." Miss Ray had given Bonnie the option of their working together with her parents or alone, and the girl had decided to go on seeing Miss Ray on her own. Someone else at the center would see the parents, an arrangement which pleased Miss Ray. Mrs. Simms had called her constantly to talk about Bonnie, but the psychologist felt that she had not accomplished much with her. She was glad that the "contract" was now clarified. There would no longer be any question of whom she was working for.

At the time we spoke with her, Miss Ray's main concern was that Bonnie find some kind of creative program that would help her direct her "freak" interests in a positive way. One of the reasons she felt Bonnie's experience at the Runaway House (the first time around) had been such a good one was that she had "identified" with the other kids there. In her suburb, Bonnie was isolated. Not many of the kids there liked her. By being so consciously a "freak," Bonnie had made it hard for herself at school and closed off the possibility of being friends with "normal" kids.

If the girl could find another group with whom she could identify, Miss Ray felt that Bonnie would become more comfortable about being accepted by others. She treated Bonnie's talk of having "freak" values as something positive. So far, Bonnie had come up with several ideas including a class in pottery, but had been unable to work anything out. The pottery course had almost been arranged, but at the last moment her parents had decided against it and refused to pay. Bonnie's response to this was a kind of depressed resignation. They had done it again, gotten in the way of something she wanted.

All who worked with Bonnie commented on her depression. Even some of the kids who knew her at Runaway House recognized that quality in her. It was particularly apparent, however, when she talked about her family. She was more than angry about the restrictions they had placed on her. What she seemed to be saying was that they had let her down. As we came to know more about her, it struck us that Bonnie had left home in the midst of an early adolescent crisis that involved a conflict within herself between parental and personal values. The strategies that her parents used against her new values were effective only because Bonnie still wanted to measure up to their standards. Even though her parents had not changed—if anything they had become more disrespectful toward Bonnie—by leaving home for a while she had grown in some way that made it possible to live with them and speak up for herself.

On a gray morning in winter we drove out to Beverly to talk with Annette Ware, Jill's mother. She had explained over the telephone that she worked during the day, but would be glad to see us if we came early in the morning. We had been told that Jill's mother lived in a $60,000 house, and along the road to Beverly we passed many lovely old New England homes. In comparison the Ware's house was recently built, white-clapboard, ranch-style, and badly in need of a paint job.

Mrs. Ware came smiling to the door to greet us, one hairclip still holding a curl behind her ear. Otherwise she was meticulously dressed. She led us into the dining room, asked if we would like coffee, and left us to survey our surroundings while she put the kettle on.

Sliding doors opened out onto a swimming pool in the backyard. The dining room, like the other rooms, was as neat as Mrs. Ware herself. Tables, chairs, sideboard, cabinets—all matched perfectly. The arms and legs of the living room furniture were "antiqued" a rather startling shade of chartreuse. So were the picture frames on the walls. The kitchen had been decorated in coordinated shades of blue, including appliances and Kleenex boxes. The house was spotlessly clean, and so neat that we wondered how anyone could feel comfortable in these rooms. We did not.

Mrs. Ware seemed to be trying to put us at ease. She answered our questions readily and told her "story" so fluently that we could not help thinking that she had told it many times before. She hastened to explain that since her daughter refused to come home, she was finished with her. "I'm happy to do anything I can, indirectly, behind the scenes, like talking with you . . . and I hope it helps . . . but as far as Jill goes, I've had it. I've done everything I can," she said, adding, "Jill's a basically good kid but she's also a really screwed-up child. She has a lot of problems. . . . Let's see, all this mess started when she went to live with her father."

Mr. and Mrs. Ware had been divorced about three years earlier. About the divorce, Mrs. Ware said that her daughter "certainly had a large part in it, not that I would ever blame her, of course." Shortly afterwards Mrs. Ware and Jill began to have continual fights. Their conflicts usually resulted from Jill's resistance to the kinds of controls Mrs. Ware set for her. Complaining endlessly that her mother was too strict and gave her too many household duties, Jill aggravated Mrs. Ware's feelings of resentment and bitterness over the divorce. "I was working all day, for a while I even had two jobs, and when I would come home exhausted in the afternoon and ask Jill to do really minor things like empty the dishwasher—just empty it, mind you—and that's not very much to ask—she would say she didn't feel like it and was too tired. Too tired!" They also had frequent battles over dates and curfews.

Eventually Jill badgered her mother into agreeing to let her live with her father for a while. Mr. Ware, according to Jill's mother, was far more permissive. "Jill was only twelve and he was letting her run around late at night . . . and I know that she and her friends had pot parties right in his house . . . and I mean, he must have known about it." Jill lived with her father for seven months, during which Mrs. Ware claimed not to have seen her even though the parents live in the same town. Jill was caught stealing a book out of the school library; she was suspended for a week and her father was to see that she returned to school the following Friday. When she did not appear, the school called her father, who said that they were "having some problems at home" and that Jill would be back on Monday. "The school called me to find out if I knew what was going on and as soon as they told me this I knew she had taken off." Mrs. Ware claimed that this was the first time Jill ran away.

Mrs. Ware was furious with her ex-husband for not having informed her of the girl's departure. She explained his lying to the school by saying that he cared more about his own image in the community than about what was good for his children. "Why, he wouldn't even tell *me,* her own mother," she said bitterly. She also accused her ex-husband of using "mental punishment on his children . . . he never punished them physically . . . but my friends tell me, 'Oh, Annette, you just don't know what he's saying about you.'" Apparently he would malign the mother in front of her own children. Usually the allegations concerned money ("you know your mother owes me x dollars") and Mrs. Ware's social life. "He tries to tell them that I have boyfriends and run around all the time, which they must know is untrue ... because they can see for themselves that I'm always home at night." Her resentment about the divorce seemed to find an outlet in fights with her ex-husband over custody of the children and money for support. Part of Mrs. Ware's anger seemed to stem from her fear of being thought of as a bad mother and Jill's desire to live with her father seemed to confirm this fear. Furthermore, the court had awarded custody of Jill to him.

Mrs. Ware is engaged to be married again, although she says she plans to "wait until some of this mess is straightened out" before she does. Throughout the confusion over Jill's running away she felt that Alan, her fiancé, was her strongest supporter. Eventually Jill returned to live with her mother when her father became so exasperated with her running that he refused to have anything further to do with her. "He had always thought that Jill was perfect and could do no wrong, but when she kept running away he suddenly decided that she was just bad, and that was all, and he washed his hands of her."

Jill usually ran away after a big fight over whether she could or could not do something. Mrs. Ware remembers lying awake at night the first time Jill was gone, worrying and worrying about where she was. "I had visions of gutters and drugs and rape and dark alleys...." Nevertheless, Jill arrived home safely each time. "After the second or third time I finally realized that she could probably take care of herself, although I always did everything I could to get her to come back." Often Mrs. Ware and Alan went into Boston in search of Jill. They became familiar with the hangouts which kids frequented, although she never grew accustomed to what she considered the unbearable grime and filth of the surroundings Jill chose. She and Alan would go to the Sizzleboard in Kenmore Square. "Sometimes we even paid kids to tell us where

Jill might be.... One time we found her in a terrible apartment with all kinds of disreputable characters. I can understand why a kid might be bored around here, out in the sticks ... but why do they want to go into a dirty city like Boston, pardon me if you live there, but to me that's what it is. You can't be in that dirty city for long without trying more than marijuana." Sometimes Jill would give her clothes away to people she met in Boston and Mrs. Ware would buy her new ones, "only the best, of course; she wouldn't wear things from Zayre's, they had to be high-class things from Jordan Marsh ... I'm still paying the bills for the things I bought her."

In their concern over Jill's persistent absences, people at the school finally encouraged Mrs. Ware to "find help for her." They suggested that Jill be sent to Madonna Hall, a boarding school for "emotionally disturbed girls." When Mrs. Ware agreed, they made a referral through "chapter 750" (chapter 750 is special legislation which provides funding for referrals of "emotionally disturbed" children from public and private schools). The school arranged the referral and Mrs. Ware herself "pulled some strings" in the Catholic hierarchy—Madonna Hall is a Catholic school—to insure Jill's placement there. There was one snag, however. It was her impression that the chapter stipulated that in those cases where the family could afford to pay, twenty-five percent of the tuition is paid by the child's family and the rest would come out of chapter 750 funds. The total cost of one year at the school is nearly $8,000.

Mrs. Ware said that she considered selling her house in order to pay for Madonna Hall, but her friends all advised her not to, saying, "Oh, Annette, you have your other children to think of...." Mrs. Ware retained the house. Mr. Ware also refused to provide the necessary funds, saying, "I'm a poor man." That her ex-husband had even dared to suggest that he was poor or couldn't afford something enraged Mrs. Ware. He was a stockbroker, and she assured us several times during the conversation that he earned at least $50,000 a year. Mrs. Ware continually pointed out how hard she was working, doing everything she possibly could, and how unwilling her ex-husband was to help out financially, even for the children. He held firm and refused to pay, thus postponing Jill's placement at Madonna Hall until some other financial arrangement could be worked out.

Mrs. Ware mentioned that the junior high school's suggestion that she find help for Jill had not been the first sign that the girl was a "problem child," nor was it the first time that Mr. Ware had been reluctant to cooperate with school authorities. Jill had always done well in school and received high grades. (Mrs. Ware said, "She has the mind of an Einstein"), but in the sixth grade she began behaving badly in class, talking back to the teacher and generally causing trouble. The teacher called Mrs. Ware, asking her and Jill's father to come in for a conference. At this point in our conversation Mrs. Ware interrupted herself to say that Jill had always been spoiled by her father, in whose eyes "she could do no wrong . . . every man wants a beautiful little daughter," she said, "and he sure got one."

His answer to Jill's sixth grade teacher's request that he discuss Jill's behavior was, "No." Mrs. Ware explained to the teacher that Jill had always been "the apple of her father's eye." "Well," the teacher said, "tell him the apple has fallen off the vine." Mr. Ware's reaction when he heard this comment was explosive and disdainful. "You just tell him I don't have to pay attention to any lowly schoolteacher."

While the placement in Madonna Hall was held up, Jill continued to run with increasing frequency. Her mother was "at her wit's end" and more anxious than ever to get help for her daughter. Finally an arrangement was worked out whereby if she took out a "stubborn child" warrant against Jill, funding for Madonna Hall would be provided by the Massachusetts Department of Youth Services. With great reluctance, and only after long efforts at persuasion by the school, Mrs. Ware took out the warrant. Jill was sent to the juvenile detention center at Roslindale until the papers for Madonna Hall could be processed, which would supposedly take three weeks at the most. For the next six weeks, however, Mrs. Ware drove to Roslindale every other day to visit

Jill. When first taking her there, her mother had asked to speak to the superintendent "so that I could explain that Jill wasn't a criminal, that she had only run away.... When I said this the nice colored girl I was talking to gave a loud exclamation of dismay. 'What's the matter?' I asked, and she said, 'Good God, when are those judges going to learn that when a kid is on the fence and you send her to a place like this she's a criminal by the time she gets out.'" Mrs. Ware was horrified by the conditions at Roslindale and by the difficulties which beset Jill while she was there. Jill was knifed by some other girls, her clothes were stolen, and on one occasion her life was even threatened.

Mrs. Ware seemed to feel guilty for having sent Jill to Roslindale. "There's one thing I know," she said, "and that is I would never send a child to the Youth Service again.... I wake up at night thinking, 'I did that, I committed her to that place.' That was a sin." In contrast, Mrs. Ware considered Madonna Hall, where Jill finally did go, such a beautiful place, with such excellent facilities—a swimming pool, a beauty shop—that it could not fail to be "the answer." Mrs. Ware herself admitted that Jill hated the place, its authority structure, everything about it. She ran away two or three times while she was there and finally went to Project Place.

When Jill came back from Madonna Hall she was greeted like the prodigal daughter. Mrs. Ware said she "felt bad for her ... she had been through so much, and especially after being in the Youth Service I felt she deserved a good time. We redecorated her room and tried to make things nice for her. I told the other children that they should be understanding and be nice to her because she had been through so much." For a while things were going well, but as soon as Mrs. Ware asked Jill to start doing her share around the house the situation deteriorated. Once again there were fights, Jill would stay out later than she was supposed to, and her brother and sister began to resent all the tension Jill's presence caused around the house. The final blow-up occurred one day when Jill took her mother's car and drove it around for a couple of hours. Mrs. Ware explained the incident in exaggerated and dramatic terms: "I had told her whenever she asked if she could drive the car that she was underage and that it was too dangerous.... I told her again and again ... and my fiancé told her, and her brother told her ... if she ever got into an accident it would be a disaster. I tried to explain to her that the insurance company wouldn't cover it and I would be sued and I might lose the house, and she was a ward of the state and the state might be sued, and she would never get a license and she would probably be locked up until she was twenty-one.... One day I came home and the car was in a different place in the driveway and it was parked in reverse.... I was so mad I could have killed her ... so I told her she was grounded for a month and all she could do was go to school and come home and watch TV and do her homework. The next day she ran away to Project Place."

Mrs. Ware supposed that she should be grateful to Project Place for working so hard for Jill and trying to help her, but she also intimated that if places like Project Place and the Sanctuary did not exist kids would not run so often. She thought Project Place was very dirty and unpleasant, "but then maybe kids don't care about things like that anymore."

At the time we talked with Mrs. Ware Jill was staying at the Runaway House. During that time Mrs. Ware had to appear in court for a custody case involving Jill's younger sister, Alice, who had recently been living with her father. Mrs. Ware called Jill and asked her to come to court. "She had once said to Alice, 'You better get your ass home or the same thing will happen to you that happened to me.' So I asked her if she would come to court and she told me she didn't remember having said it so how could she say it in court ... so I wanted to know what she would say if the judge asked her if I had been a good mother, and she said, 'For me or Alice?' 'For you.' 'Well, in that case I'd have to say no.' ... And then she had the nerve to try to borrow seven dollars from me to go to a camp and I told her, 'Jill, if I had the seven dollars, I'd go to the camp myself.' ... So you see, she'd take the shirt off her back for a friend but she wouldn't do even a little thing for her family."

Mrs. Ware recounted another incident where her image as a mother had been challenged. Jill's brother answered the phone one evening while Jill was at the Runaway House. The police had called to say that Jill had been picked up for loitering in Boston. When her brother tried to explain that Jill did not live at home anymore the policeman said, "What do you mean she doesn't live there? She lives in Boston? ... She's at Project Place? ... What's this all about? ... What kind of mother do you have, anyway?"

Mrs. Ware described the atmosphere around the house over the last two years as chaotic: "It's been all calls and courts and schools and jails and police and Madonna and trouble and cells and more phone calls ... my son is the only one who's never given me a minute's worry—but Alice is very emotionally mixed up ... she's very sweet and naïve and I hope she stays that way."

Although Mrs. Ware verbalized a great deal of caring and concern for Jill's welfare, she gave the impression of being a nervous woman, and not very warm. Many of her actions—redecorating Jill's room and buying her new clothes, for example, seemed like attempts to appease her own guilt and to compensate in material ways for her inability to provide real emotional support. Her final comment was, "If only they knew the agony they put us through, they would never run. ... Just wait until Jill has children of her own to worry about, or maybe if she's lucky she won't have any. If she doesn't shape up by the time she's sixteen or seventeen, she'll be dead. ... Now she has everything exactly the way she wants it: she's not living at home, she's not in school, and she's walking the streets."

Throughout our discussion with Mrs. Ware she kept emphasizing the great number of counselors Jill had had and how much help she had been given. How Jill could fail to be "straightened out" when there were so many people doing everything they could was a mystery to her. In talking with Mrs. Ware and many other people who had been involved with Jill's case, we learned that she had expected someone to have "the answer"—the perfect solution to Jill's problems.

Initially the guidance counselor and assistant principal at the junior high school had urged Mrs. Ware to get help for Jill. Both were willing to discuss with us what they had tried to do for her. Miss Adelberg, Jill's guidance counselor for the seventh and eighth grades, was a middle-aged, fifty- or fifty-five-year-old woman with bleached blond hair and an absentminded manner. Despite her position, Miss Adelberg admitted that she had little understanding of either adolescents or counseling. In forming her judgments of the children in school who seemed to have "problems" she relied heavily on the authority of others and seemed to jump to conclusions like "Johnny is on drugs a lot. . . . The mental health center's evaluation showed that he's a very sick boy." Because the guidance department at the junior high was understaffed, Miss Adelberg said that her load of clerical work has increased so much this year that she "hardly had any time to meet with the kids." Most of her time was taken up with checking over the attendance slips to discover who had been truant. When she talked to students it was usually about schedule changes.

Miss Adelberg told us with pride that the teachers and guidance counselors have a meeting every two weeks with a clinical psychologist. Although her own knowledge of psychology seemed limited, she was convinced that Jill needed "therapy." "Well, I don't know too much about psychology," she said, "but I do know about Jung, and I don't think she needs Freudian therapy. . . . What's this about reality therapy I keep hearing about? What kinds of therapy *are* people doing these days?"

Miss Adelberg had several conversations with Jill and with Jill's parents. Apparently Jill had caused some consternation at the school when she stole a leather coat from a nearby shopping center. Mrs. Ware was unwilling to make Jill return the coat, and Mr. Ware refused even to discuss the matter. All he was interested in were Jill's grades which, Miss Adelberg had to admit, were very high. Mrs. Ware came in to talk voluntarily, but Mr. Ware had to be "coaxed." On the basis of what Jill's mother told her, Miss Adelberg thought Jill's father was a very frightening man who had a terrible temper.

Thwarted by both parents in handling the incident of the stolen coat, Miss Adelberg confronted Jill, but the girl was no more willing to talk than her parents had been. All she would say in response to Miss Adelberg's admonishment that "it's never right to steal," was, "It doesn't matter, I wasn't wearing it or anything." Miss Adelberg implied that when Jill came in to talk about changing a math class she really wanted to talk about deeper and more important concerns. One day Jill asked a roundabout question which Miss Adelberg interpreted to be: Can a person, once they have a fixed image in the eyes of others, ever change that image? The counselor responded by telling her the story of St. Paul on the road to Damascus. "I assumed that being a Catholic she knew the story. They train the children very well." Since Jill did not know the story Miss Adelberg told her how "Paul, the worst murderer and thief you could imagine, saw the blinding light of Jesus and was blinded for three days, and when he regained his sight he became the most famous missionary in the world." She chuckled as she remembered Jill's reply: "Wow, he must have been on some trip."

Frustrated by her failure to get Jill "to communicate,' Miss Adelberg decided that the problem was twofold: "Jill had a very bad attitude" (about school) and "her home situation was very unhealthy." The counselor wanted to place the girl in a residential treatment center—residential because "she needed to be out of her home" and treatment because "she needed therapy for her bad attitude." She chose the Protestant Youth Center in Baldwinville, a girls' correctional facility, but two difficulties arose. Placement at the youth center was contingent upon a psychological evaluation of the child and a finding of "stubborn child" by the juvenile court. Miss Adelberg set up the evaluation but Jill refused to talk to the evaluator. Mrs. Ware, equally uncooperative, could not be convinced to take out the stubborn child warrant, "because she was afraid of her husband." In desperation Miss Adelberg took the problem to Mr. Holton, the assistant principal. "Mr. Holton," she explained, "has a lot of pull."

A pleasant man in his forties, who had recently been promoted from math teacher to assistant principal, Mr. Holton was proud of the school and rather bewildered by the increasing numbers of runaways and truants among the junior high students: "I really don't understand why kids run away from here. This school isn't rigid or authoritarian." He felt, however, that the school had nothing to offer Jill, that she was too "sophisticated," "worldly," and "far more advanced" than most of her classmates. "She was really a ringleader for a while."

Mr. Holton's function in the school was primarily disciplinary. The punishments which he could use in cases of truancy, skipping classes, and drug use were detention, suspension, and court action, although recently sensitivity groups had been instituted as an alternative to detention. He recalled having given Jill detention on a number of occasions and even having suspended her once or twice. His view of kids who run away was that they were "serious discipline problems, use drugs, or come from homes with divorced or alcoholic parents." Jill was no exception in his mind. He was careful to point out that she was extremely bright and had excellent grades, but in other respects was far from a model student. His approach in talking with Jill was to try to change her behavior by expressing sympathy with what he thought were her basic concerns, and then pointing out the flaws in her attitude. "One day I asked her if I was missing something by not taking drugs and she assured me that I was. So I told her, 'Jill, I think it's important to respect the authorities—the health authorities—so that when they tell me marijuana is dangerous I believe them.... When I want to escape from reality I go to the package store and buy a bottle and take it home and enjoy it; and I suggest that when you are old enough I would highly recommend your doing the same.'"

Mr. Holton had extensive contact with both of Jill's parents in handling the incident of the stolen coat and in trying to arrange for Jill's placement at Madonna Hall. His feeling was that both Mr. and Mrs. Ware were very selfish and unwilling to face up to their real responsibilities as parents—those beyond merely meeting the children's material needs. "Mrs. Ware seems superficially very concerned," he said, "but underneath the façade she's actually rather cold ... and Mr. Ware ... well, I knew him back in high school, his name was Warzinsky then, they changed it a few years ago . . . he was always a nice, athletic guy, but now he cares only about himself."

Mr. Holton thought that Jill should be referred to Madonna Hall though chapter 750 and convinced Mrs. Ware of the wisdom of doing this. According to Mr. Holton, Mrs. Ware took the initiative in the court action, whereas she maintained that only at the school's insistence had she done so. Mr. Holton was satisfied that in making the referral to Madonna Hall he had done a good thing—"Madonna is one of the finest schools in Massachusetts, in terms of facilities and personnel." He realized that Jill had not wanted to go there, but thought that it was a bad idea to ask kids whether they wanted to go to such places—"far better to send a kid there and then see how he likes it after six months or so."

The setting of Madonna Hall is bucolic and serene. Located in a secluded area of a town west of Boston the school consists of one main building and several smaller cottages, all built in 1963 at the instigation of Cardinal Cushing. The spare lines and pale green clapboard give an air of sterility emphasized by the complete absence of any sign of life or activity. On the day we visited, the silence of hallways and waiting rooms, presided over by portraits of Cardinal Cushing and statues of the Virgin Mary, was broken only by the rustling of nuns' robes on the linoleum floors. Miss Parker, Jill's social worker, met us, and led us into a room marked "Group Therapy." She had requested that we bring written permission from Jill for her to talk with us, but when we presented this, it was insufficient. Miss Parker asked if we had a note from Jill's mother. We did not. She retreated to consult with the Director of Social Work and returned saying, "I'm afraid this won't do. We need *written* permission from Mrs. Ware. . . . You understand, our problem is one of confidentiality, and Jill being a minor, well. . . ." She was very apologetic and offered to tell us a little about the academy and show us around while were were there. She was meticulously dressed; extremely formal in demeanor, despite her youth and her girlishly attractive looks.

A few days later, when we had procured the necessary written permission from Mrs. Ware, we returned to speak with Miss Parker. Sister Celine, the director of Group Living, who had also known Jill, joined the discussion. Miss Parker volunteered little information and sat back with her mouth tightly shut waiting for questions. Her opinion was that Jill had not been "motivated" to come to Madonna Hall, thus she was unready to accept the kind of therapy the school had to offer. Nevertheless neither Sister Celine nor Miss Parker could remember any specific problems which Jill had with schoolwork or group living; furthermore, she had regularly attended her "social services" sessions (therapy with Miss Parker). The social worker thought Jill was "an angry child" who tried to "look hard despite her baby face." She believed this anger was a result of her mother's lack of "warmth" and "nurturance." In therapy she allowed Jill "to vent this anger in acceptable ways, ... though of course I wouldn't let her curse at me in our sessions." Because Jill was at Madonna Hall for such a short time (only six months) Miss Parker felt she had not been able to establish a trusting relationship with her. Sister Celine considered Jill "very restless with a low level of self-esteem. . . . She never really got settled here and therefore we could not even get to first base with her."

Miss Parker added that the Ware family had been another "stumbling block" in the school's attempts to help Jill. She believed the mother and father used the kids in the conflict between them—Mr. Ware "put down the mother by saying she was a lousy mother" and Mrs. Ware continually played a martyr role, telling Jill in great detail about all her difficulties with her ex-husband. In conferences Miss Parker had with the parents, Mr. Ware would insist that Jill "was just *bad*" and that anyone who thought differently was naïve, while Mrs. Ware insisted that if Jill could see the staff psychiatrist every week, everything would be fine. Miss Parker saw Mrs. Ware's desire for a "magical cure" as stemming from her own feelings of guilt. In any case the effect of these attitudes on Jill was negative: "In divorce situations kids learn to manipulate and Jill was a pro."

While Jill was at Madonna Hall she ran three times. Both

Sister Celine and Miss Parker said that some girls who run practically announce it ahead of time and walk down the main road, saying, "Come get me," but Jill was "slick" and "sneaky." Her runs were clearly premeditated attempts since she took clothes with her. The third time Jill ran she went to Place but never returned to Madonna Hall since the Department of Youth Services allowed her to be "paroled home," a solution which Miss Parker thought highly unsatisfactory although she seemed relieved at having lost such a difficult case.

We also talked to Miss Young, Jill's parole agent at the Department of Youth Services, and Mr. Carpenter, Miss Young's supervisor, who were officially responsible for Jill after she was paroled from Madonna Hall. Miss Young had "investigated" the home, when Jill wanted to return there from Project Place, and she had "okayed it." Mrs. Ware, she thought, was a "very clever" woman. Her evidence for this was the decorating of the house and the antiquing Mrs. Ware had done to the furniture. Mr. Ware, on the other hand, was more "confusing." She could not understand his claim that he earned only $10,000 a year, especially since the Ware's house was "on one of the most exclusive streets in Beverly." Her view of the family situation was that the parents were vying for the affection of the children, but otherwise she had few criticisms of them and seemed rather impressed by how well they had provided for the children. Several times she said, looking puzzled, "Well, I wish I could answer the question why Jill ran away" (a question we had not asked).

Mr. Carpenter thought Jill was a "beautiful girl," and Mrs. Ware "a wonderful woman," but pointed out that both of them were spoiled. He thought perhaps Mr. Ware had been unable to say no to his wife, thus creating conflict between them and setting the stage for conflicts between Jill and her mother. In his opinion, "Kids these days get too much," but his tone in saying this was mild and he seemed rather amused. Generally his view of kids broke down along the lines of "good" (Jill was one of these) and "bad" (kids who don't want to help themselves because "sin can be pretty attractive"). His final comment was that Jill would have to learn that "there are other people in the world." It seemed to us that Jill must already have discovered that there were other people, too many of whom were anxious to "reform" her. One night,

One night, while we were visiting with Jill's counselor, Leslie, at her apartment, talking about her experience with runaways, Jill dropped by unexpectedly. After over a month in the Runaway House she was no longer very involved with its social life, partly because many of her first friends had already left and she had lived through a succession of groups of kids.

Jill sat down on the couch and looked around the living room; she seemed more quiet and reserved than when we had seen her at the Runaway House. Leslie asked her what was going on at Place. Not much, she said. Everyone was just sitting around talking. Then they discussed the idea of a foster home for a while. Jill had already visited a group home and decided against it. Consequently she and Leslie had decided that a foster placement would be best for the time being and set to working on that through a local agency that had a possible opening for temporary placement; they would hear for sure in the next few days. Both liked what they knew about this family. The couple was young, lived in a Boston suburb with several children of their own, and had been foster parents before. In order for Jill to move in with them, the girl would have to visit the family and decide whether she liked them, and Leslie would have to get the approval of Jill's parole officer for the move, something she had been trying to do unsuccessfully for the past week. Miss Young was always "busy" or "out" and had yet to return one of her calls.

After they had discussed the placement situation, Jill grew quiet again. Leslie offered her a Coke, but she did not want one. Soon it was time for Leslie to go do her night shift at the Runaway House, so we all got into the car and drove to the South End.

After a warm winter day, the weather had turned cold again. No one was out on the street anywhere in Boston, yet the neighborhood where the Runaway House was located seemed more deserted than the rest of the city. Many of the houses were condemned; there were lights in only a few of the windows. By day, the appearance of the nineteenth-century red-brick townhouses gave the neighborhood a character which one finds less and less in American cities. The city's last remaining delicatessen, The Premier, which people from all over Boston still flock to for lunch—was there, as were ethnic restaurants and grocery stores—Oriental, Greek, Turkish, Spanish, Italian. By day, except for the drunks, it was the children of these immigrant groups who were most visible, playing on sidewalks and in alleys, in empty lots and on the steps of abandoned buildings. At night, however, everything was silent. There was no sign of the activity that made the area so attractive during the day. As we drove through several one-way streets to get to the House, no one in the car had much to say. Jill played with the radio until she found a song she liked. When we arrived at the House she got out quickly, said good-bye, and headed back inside. "It gets to me sometimes," Leslie said. "Jill really doesn't have a home. Most of the time, I forget that. She seems so independent and strong, but whenever I remember that she's been living at the House for two months and doesn't know how much longer she'll have to live there, it amazes me. I'm sure it must get to her too, but she rarely lets on."

Leslie had first met Jill the previous summer when she was on the run from Madonna Hall. At the time, Leslie was struck by the girl's fierce insistence on not going back there and the way she had stood up to the women who had come to retrieve her. The incident that involved Department of Youth Services officers had made her recognize the gravity of the situation. After Jill had run out the back door of the Runaway House, the officers let Leslie know that she herself might be subject to prosecution (for "contributing to the delinquency of a minor"). Somewhat shaken, she accompanied the officers around the South End, looking for Jill, then set to calling up the others in charge in order to straighten things out. Soon, however, Jill went home to live with her mother.

Several months later, she had run away again and come to the Runaway House; this time, she was determined not to go back home. According to Leslie, Jill never said *why* she ran, but the precipitating event was, this time as others, her being grounded by her mother, a punishment she could not tolerate because "her friends were of crucial importance to her and she refused to be kept in the house away from them." Leslie told us much about Jill's family that we had already heard, yet one detail was new. Shortly before the girl's return from her father's house, the mother's fiancé had moved into her home. Jill ran three times the first week she was back.

Leslie interpreted Jill's refusal to return home as a reflection of the position she had played in her family. The counselor's opinion was that Jill had been caught in the conflict between her mother and father while they were married and was still used as the object of their disagreements. Despite the divorce, the two had continued a relationship with each other and were frequently contesting something in court. Jill had been the object of one of their court appearances, and while she was away from home, another suit had developed concerning custody of her young sister. Leslie felt that Mrs. Ware's asking Jill to testify in court was a good example of how the mother "used" her daughter and set herself up for rejection.

While Jill was at the Runaway House, Mrs. Ware called Leslie two or three times a week and the counselor kept her informed about what was happening to the girl. At first Jill had objected to the conversations and even went so far as to tell her mother to "stop wasting Leslie's time; don't you think she has anything better to do?" Leslie had let Jill know she would continue the conversations and called up the mother to reassure her that Jill had spoken only for herself. Leslie considered Mrs. Ware's calling as evidence of "caring." Her request that Jill testify in court, however, led Leslie to criticize Mrs. Ware for the first time about the way she treated her daughter. She told the mother that she felt it had not been a good thing to ask so much of Jill—it was too much to ask a child to take that kind of stand between her parents. The response she got kept Leslie from trying to do anything like this again. Mrs. Ware insisted that the problem was not with her but with Jill: she owed it to the family to testify. After all they had done for her, what had she done for them? Besides, Mrs. Ware said, Jill was not a child, she said she was independent and grown up enough to be on her own, so she should be able to testify in court. Leslie then said to the mother that although Jill talked so much about how she was independent and adult, "you and I know that's not true." Kids still needed and had strong feelings for their parents. Mrs. Ware simply went on talking about how selfish her daughter was and repeated that she was old enough to appear in court. This made Leslie take a tougher approach—she asked Mrs. Ware why she took Jill's talk of independence seriously in one situation, yet continued to treat her like a child and be overly restrictive when her daughter was at home. The mother responded to that by saying her daughter needed the rules that had been set down for her. Leslie found it frustrating to talk to Mrs. Ware about Jill's "independence"; the woman's reasoning was "circular" and she did not seem interested in what Leslie had to say.

Leslie felt that Jill's experience with her family had made her extremely mistrustful of adults and contributed to problems she had at school. (Before being sent to the boarding school, Jill had argued fiercely with her teachers and sometimes been truant.) Consequently, she listened only to those adults with whom she established some kind of trust; the others she fought with or ignored. Leslie supported Jill's desire to live away from home and do things on her own but also talked with Jill about the self-destructive ways in which she felt the girl tried to assert her independence (stealing her mother's car, getting into "trouble"). She was careful to let Jill know what was going on in her conversations with the Department of Youth Services and Mrs. Ware so that the girl would not think that decisions were being made behind her back. She appreciated the difficulty of the situations Jill had been placed in over the past few years and said after the big meeting with Juvenile authorities, "She's on her own for the first time; no one's telling her what to do anymore." Leslie had confidence in Jill. She told other counselors that of all the kids she had worked with, Jill could "handle herself better than most."

Jill took some of the initiative in trying to arrange alternate living arrangements; she made an appointment to visit a group home, went there on her own, and concluded that was not what she wanted. Consequently she decided to try a temporary foster home and went through the same procedure. This plan turned out to be more to her liking, so, when a placement became available, she took it. After a month in a "temporary" placement, she decided to look for a more permanent situation and found another foster home, this time with a family that agreed to take her in on a permanent basis. Several months after running away from home, living in a Boston suburb with a family of several kids, she decided to try school once again but quit after a week, not because she got into "trouble," but because she felt restless there and had difficulties concentrating on schoolwork.

Leslie thought it was best that Jill live away from home. In this case family counseling did not seem to be the answer. Jill's mother seemed too deeply committed to giving her daughter double messages, which made the girl generally antagonistic toward adults. In a foster home, by living in a more normal situation, Jill might learn to trust adults once more.

Once Jill moved out of the Runaway House, she saw less of Leslie; the two agreed that she could visit every other week and call up whenever she felt like it. While Jill was "in transition" from the Runaway House to her new home, Leslie tried to serve as a "consistent figure," but once she was in a permanent home, a social worker from the agency that had placed her started seeing her most regularly. When, late in April, Jill told Leslie that she missed living at home for the first time, Leslie arranged for that worker to begin seeing Jill and her mother together. Although Leslie had always felt that Jill should "keep in contact with her mother" and work out "competitive feelings and mistrust toward her," she had respected the girl's desire not to do either of these things. This attitude contrasted sharply with that of other "helpers" who worked with Jill and may be explained, in part, by the fact that Leslie was working more *on Jill's* behalf than any of the others. Both Miss Parker and Miss Young were involved with Jill in specific institutional contexts; Miss Parker was primarily responsible to the boarding school and Miss Young worked with her as a juvenile offender. While some of Leslie's ideas about what was going on were similar to those of other "helpers", she allowed the girl to take more initiative. She worked with her to achieve a specific goal—to find a legal way of living away from home. Instead of thinking of her as a "headshrinker," "social worker," or "counselor," Jill once told Leslie that she was more a big sister than anything else.

One of the things that struck us about the way Leslie worked with Jill was the restraint she exercised when applying her psychological knowledge to the real person she was helping. Trained as a psychiatric social worker at one of the most traditional hospitals in Boston, she sometimes talked of Jill's running away as a consequence of the return of "strong Oedipal feelings" at the beginning of puberty, when she had left her mother after heated arguments and gone to live with her father. When we first heard her state the problem in these terms, we were curious as to how such an understanding might affect her relationship with Jill. After several months of hearing about the work she had done with Jill and her mother, it seemed to us that the value of having such an insight was that it gave her a point of view independent of both parties.

Perhaps the most striking aspect of Leslie's work with Jill was the role she played in convincing juvenile authorities to let the girl play a more active role in dealing with her situation. This was by far the most time-consuming part of her work, and often involved several phone calls a day. While the laws concerning "juvenile offenders" are strict and those in charge of enforcing them often rigid, both betray occasional signs of flexibility. In this case, Leslie was able to get the cooperation of those officially responsible for Jill by establishing a trusting relationship with her and gaining the mother's support. In doing so, she succeeded where others had failed. By the time Jill ran away to Project Place the second time, she had a reputation as a "difficult" kid to work with, because she would not stop running away. Thus, although the juvenile authorities were strict, they were also confused about what to do and therefore were willing to negotiate. When Leslie and Jill came up with a plan for an alternative living arrangement, it was in their interest to cooperate, for their own approach to Jill had not worked after almost a year. Such negotiations are not a simple matter; the professional pride of those officials one talks to is a potent factor. Sometimes authorities may not be willing to relinquish control and in other cases, when it comes to the test, a kid may choose to remain in the control of legal officials rather than work out her own situation the way Jill did. (Leslie told us of one girl who came back to the House after running away and asked to be sent to reform school; she preferred a structure in which decisions were made for her.)

Ultimately, the system of juvenile justice must be changed, a matter we will deal with later in this book (see Part II, chapter 3). As long as such categories of deviance as "runaway" and "stubborn child" remain, however, the best work a counselor can do is to help extricate an adolescent from the web of "correctional" institutions in which he is involved, support his attempts to make real decisions about his life, and talk through whatever past experiences he chooses to discuss. Leslie's ability to do all these things with Jill seemed to us to be a consequence of the awareness she had of her own role in Jill's life as well as her very specific sense of who Jill was and what needs of hers she was able to help her with. While adolescents talk extensively about being independent and on their own, it is only by doing things in the real world that they gain faith in their ability to be so. By helping Jill do what she wanted, Leslie helped her make a difficult beginning.

Part II

1
HOME AGAIN

We have found a number of family "difficulties" that have gone along with a young person's departure from home: value conflicts between kids and parents, conflicts over social issues such as dating, dress, friends, restrictive discipline of kids by parents (e.g., being kept in the house for a long period of time), kids' reactions to parental discord, pressures to achieve in school, physical sickness in the family, rejection of a kid by his family. Our goal in this chapter will be to examine particular kinds of family crises, most of which have to do with events related to one member's adolescence. Although all the "adolescents" discussed here are teenagers, it is not only with growing young people that families have trouble. When one member of a family goes through basic changes in how he or she sees him or herself, there may be resistance from others in the family who want to keep that person the same. The recent phenomenon of "dropout wives" strikes us as similar (see *Life,* March 15, 1972). At a time when people at all levels of society are questioning their social roles, the sharp increase in the rate of divorce also suggests that growth may create severe difficulties for families. With time other members of the family may adapt to the person's new self-image or even grow with him or her. In many families, however, growth creates strains that can make reconciliation difficult or even impossible. A person may find it so uncomfortable to be in the family that he or she will choose to leave—either temporarily or for good.

Adults who leave their homes, like teenage runaways, may be taking the first step toward a permanent separation. Most, however, can support themselves financially, are recognized as being socially competent, and have probably lived on their own before. Teenagers who leave home have never been away before, and may be "growing" in a self-conscious sense for the first time. While they may have strengths equal to those of adults, they are not "socially competent." If an adolescent wants to make a permanent separation from his family, he will find that jobs are scarce and can only be found by lying about one's age and using an assumed name. Furthermore the "youth culture" to which some kids run is unstable; nowadays, competition for scarce resources is more common than positive peer support.

After some time away from home, many young people return voluntarily. Others, however, come from families which they will stay away from at all costs. Some may deliberately get in trouble with the law to be sent to reform school. A few have the nerve and tenacity to make it on their own in a city and may indeed start new lives. The success of these kids makes us wonder about the legal determination of social competence. Such kids have been the exception in our research, yet that may well be a consequence of the fact that most of the young people we talked to had sought help from social service agencies because they could not "make it" on their own. In addition to the few "successful" runaways we talked to, there were others we knew of by reputation, often the older brothers and sisters of kids who had just left home. The social pathways taken by these adolescents included getting married, joining the army, becoming a prostitute, doing many temporary jobs or holding down a permanent one, and becoming involved in social action programs such as the Job Corps or youth counseling centers.

Most of the kids we talked to, however, were *not* making it on their own away from home. They had sought shelter, companionship, and counseling either for a brief rest before making another attempt to survive in the outside world or to ease themselves back into their families. Most of them were on the run—in flight from homes by which they were troubled. Sometimes they claimed to have long-standing difficulties which they were tired of coping with; in other instances, the "trouble" was recent. All were afraid of being returned home against their will. While working as counselors at the Runaway House we often heard kids talk about what they would do if their parents came to take them back. The plans usually involved more running—out the back door and into the South End. Many were reluctant to call their parents and get their permission to stay at the Runaway House (as required by law) for fear that once they knew where they were, their parents would come and try to take them home. We have heard these fears interpreted as subconscious wishes by the kids to be taken back home; our own feeling, however, is that they are afraid of going back to the confusing situations which they are trying to leave behind.

What was it these kids were afraid of at home? While individual situations varied, we found in many runaways a common fear of the names they had been called by their parents. The conflicts described by these kids almost always went beyond the issues at hand. Attributions of badness, immaturity, incompetence, meanness—something being "wrong" with a kid—were common in the families of the kids we talked to. (We cannot say with whom such name calling began since we have not lived in these families; yet we should point out that the kids are as good at doing this kind of thing as their parents.) The striking thing about these attributions is not simply that they have been made—though some, like the accusation of a child's being responsible for a parent's disease, are startling—but that the kids believe them so completely. The names always made a strong impression. Sometimes the first thing a kid told us was what his parents thought of him at the same time as he insisted that it was not true.

In thinking about the families of the runaways we knew, we were faced with several problems. What made some parents see their children so negatively, and why did their judgments have such a powerful effect on the kids? Another question that came up here was why these kids had run away while others faced with similar problems had not done so. Also, what did running away mean to a kid? At the beginning of our study, we had asked a group of runaways at Project Place what should be included in a book about them and they had unanimously offered advice to other kids *not* to run away. What did that kind of response say about the way runaways saw themselves?

Early in our research, we realized that running away was connected to the first years of adolescence. Most of the kids we talked to were from thirteen to sixteen years old and many of the older ones referred back to their early teenage years as the first time they had run away. In an attempt to understand this phenomenon, we considered the process of adolescence from the points of view of the kids and families involved in it, of our own and our friends' rather recent experience, and of psychologists. Why was it that neither of us nor most of those we knew had ever even considered the possibility of running away from home? Although we were by no means a "control group," we compared our own teenage experience to that of the kids we talked to and found the contrast striking. Some of the conflicts kids described between themselves and their parents sounded very familiar. Fights over what time one would return home at night, what one wore, who one's friends were—all these incidents reminded us of our own teenage years. Yet the conflicts we heard kids describe sounded much more involved than our own. More seemed to be at stake over the issue of whether or not these kids wore bluejeans and had long hair than had been in our own families.

"SHE WAS TRYING TO CHANGE WHAT I UNDERSTOOD"

Ellie, a girl from western Massachusetts, was typical in this respect. Before leaving home, she said, she and her mother, a divorcée, had been fighting regularly; she had not been doing well in school and had had to lie regularly to her mother in order to see the friends she wanted. Most recently the two had fought over Ellie's wearing dungarees to a family dinner, and her mother had said she was a "disgrace to the family." When we talked with Ellie, she did not seem troubled about having left her mother. After she spent the night at the Sanctuary hostel (where the conversation took place), she planned to begin driving west with some other kids she had met in Boston. Now that she had left, she said, her mother could have some peace. Ellie did not express any bitterness; this was simply the way things were: her mother did not want her as she was, so she would leave. Perhaps in six months or so, she might return.

Something of what we mean by so much more being at stake may be apparent from this story. Ellie and her mother were not simply fighting over dungarees. In some families, fights between a teenager and her parents over appearance may be just as heated, yet not involve so many concealed issues. One friend of ours described similar disagreements with her mother, yet felt they had been relatively unimportant, since in areas other than appearance—particularly school performance—she was living up to and accepting parental expectations of who she should be. When Ellie's mother accused her of being a disgrace to the family for wearing bluejeans, she was also saying something about the rest of the girl's life. The issue of appearance was so complicated because much more than Ellie's appearance was, in her mother's eyes, going "wrong" with the girl's life.

Although she did not seem troubled when we spoke with her, it is probable that Ellie had been very much affected by her mother's judgments. Now that she had left home, it seemed to us that it was Ellie rather than her mother who would have some peace for a while. This was the second time she had run away. She had left because her mother caught her lying about the friends she was seeing. Her earlier departure followed a similar discovery of wrongdoing. Having skipped school repeatedly, Ellie was finally picked up by truant officers and returned home. Before this arrest, her mother had not known that she skipped school.

As she told her story, Ellie seemed at ease in her surroundings. Her new friends sat around in a circle and listened while she talked. Something about the way she spoke suggested that the conflicts she and her mother had been through were affecting her more than she admitted. Perhaps kids are as surprised as parents by the intensity of such fights as Ellie described. Now that she had left home, those troubles were still with her. The vividness of some of her stories was proof of that, but the daily demands of living away from home took precedence in her mind. Rather than face the constant censure of her mother (though inside herself, Ellie might still believe that she was "a disgrace"), she was involved in making new friends, finding someplace to stay, selling underground newspapers, and planning what to do next.

Ellie was the exception among the kids we talked to in that she had few criticisms of her mother. In most of their accounts of parent-child conflicts, parents were described as the villains. One runaway responded to our asking him how he would explain to an adult why kids leave home by saying, "I'd tell them that if a kid runs away it's because either the mother or father in his family is crazy." Other adjectives we heard used to describe parents were "hypocritical," "bigoted," "sick." The intensity with which we heard such terms expressed made us think at first that some of the kids had permanently rejected their parents, but the more we heard kids talk, we found that deep attachments can remain beneath the strongest conflicts and resentments.

Julie, a runaway from Georgia, began leaving home when she was thirteen and spending time with friends at a local beach. Several times her mother had found her there and dragged her home "by the hair"; she had also been returned twice by the police. Some kind of argument about the mother's or Julie's values had preceded each departure. "She was really prejudiced . . . she doesn't like colored people and she doesn't like freaks. She doesn't like me in general because I was different from everyone else in the family . . . I wore my hair differently. I wore wire-rim glasses, I wore bluejeans all the time. She expected me to change . . . not to have any colored friends . . . [or know] any people with long hair.

She was trying to change what I understood." According to Julie, her mother expressed her disapproval dramatically. The talks the two of them had often ended with the mother throwing things, calling Julie a freak, and saying that she did not want any hippies in her family. Julie always took refuge with her friends: "They all thought my mother was a bitch, they knew my mother was a bitch . . . it was really nice." Finally she was taken to court by her mother as a stubborn child and sent to a girls' reform school where one could only be released after earning a certain number of points. According to Julie, her mother testified in court that she was "always bringing strange people home and really upsetting the family and the neighbors"—as well as running away. She herself told the judge that she no longer wanted to live with her family. "My mother thought that I was a juvenile delinquent and a child in need of supervision and all this when it was that I wasn't happy at home. I couldn't be with anybody that was prejudiced against the people who were so good to me. She didn't understand this."

While in reform school, Julie thought she was pregnant and ran away once more. This time, however, instead of heading for her friends, she tried to go back to her mother. "I wanted to go home so bad and I told her that . . . and then when I tried to go home I found they had a search warrant on the house and that they could go in the house and search . . . for me if they thought I was there. . . . My mother had told my friends that I better leave the state before I got put away in a mental institution [by the courts for escaping from reform school]." At first we were surprised that Julie had wanted to return home after all the fighting that had gone on, so we asked her again if she had wanted to go home. "I did," she said, "really did . . . I just wanted to go home and I figured . . . maybe my mother would listen to me. I figured I could really talk to her and get it through to her that people with long hair and dark skin weren't bad." After Julie's escape from reform school her mother moved the family back to Italy, the land of her birth. At seventeen, Julie could not rejoin them as she wished, since she was a "fugitive" and could not get a passport.

It seemed to us that Julie's conflicts at home came from her own desire to be accepted by her mother as well as her mother's strong disapproval of her hippie ways. It was because she valued parental judgments that she tried so hard to change her mother's attitudes toward hippies and black people. In a similar way, the mother had strong ideas about who her daughter should be. Both insisted on a kind of personality change that the other was not prepared to make, not because they did not care who the other was, but because they cared so much. The court-enforced separation—mutually desired by mother and daughter at one time—was a consequence of their strong feelings for each other rather than the lack of any.

Both Ellie and Julie had friends in the environments they left behind, yet their acceptance by these friends did not compensate for the disapproval of their parents. For a time, each had run to friends, but eventually both ran farther and left friends as well as family behind. In this respect, we found the following passage by Jerome Kagan in an article called "A Conception of Early Adolescence" very much to the point.

> The early adolescent wants many friends, for he needs peers to help him sculpt his beliefs, verify his new conclusions, test his new attitudes against an alien set in order to evaluate his hardiness and obtain support for his new set of fragile assumptions. However, he still needs his family; the family provides the first set of adults who communicate their estimation of the child's worth ... youth continues to award the family a special wisdom and legitimacy. The family's respect for his beliefs, taste in music, dress or talk is reassuring for it persuades him that he is able to make reasonable decisions.[1]

Although many of the kids we talked to had attained peer approval through sharing beliefs and tastes with friends, they found themselves criticized for the very same things in their families. The criticisms were not always direct; sometimes parents said their child simply "followed the crowd" and "didn't have his own ideas," but either way the message of disapproval got through. If kids attach as much wisdom to parental judgments as Kagan claims they do, it is not hard to see why so many would want to leave negative judgments behind. Having to face such general appraisals of one's character on a daily basis, a young person could easily believe that he was not worth much after all. Being with friends he would only be reminded of his parents' disapproval. Running away is one way an adolescent may try to resolve this conflict; he may seek a new environment in hopes of finding approval elsewhere. Other possibilities include finding new kinds of adult approval in the same environment, trying to change parental judgments of one's self, accepting a negative evaluation, and acting as if one is not worth much (e.g., by failing school) or changing so that one becomes more like what parents expect.

"MAYBE THEY GROW UP TOO FAST"

Most of the parents we spoke with seemed confused by their child's adolescence and found themselves in difficult positions. For instance, Mrs. Ayer (Part I, chapter 6) said of her daughter Mary: "Before all this started she was a baby, and then all of a sudden she was grown up." Startled by new behavior which she did not understand, Mrs. Ayer began seeing her daughter in ways she thought about herself—"good" and "bad." Her husband, who thought in the same terms, reinforced that perception.

As the girl continued to do things—skipping school, lying, taking drugs—which would be hard for any parent to deal with, the family situation became more uncomfortable for everyone. Mrs. Ayer talked about how difficult that time had been for her and her husband, yet also recognized that their actions had something to do with Mary's running away. ("We'd been coming down on her pretty hard there for a while.") That recognition gave a certain legitimacy to the girl's acts in her eyes.

Mrs. Ware (Part I, chapter 8) thought of her daughter Jill, whose behavior was similar to Mary's, as an "emotional problem."

Unlike Mrs. Ayer, she was unwilling to take any of the responsibility for Jill's actions and placed all of the blame on her ex-husband and her daughter. Rather than recognize that the girl might have reason to run away, Mrs. Ware considered the act another indication that something was wrong with Jill, and, convinced that her daughter was severely disturbed, she kept trying to find a "cure."

The issue of a young person's sexuality was a troubling one for the parents of some runaways. Bonnie Simms's mother and Paul Silver's father seemed excessively worried about their children's new powers. But instead of speaking openly with them about sex, both tried to conceal their confusion. Mrs. Simms insisted that her daughter not date boys until she was sixteen, in effect asking her to deny her attraction to members of the opposite sex. Distrustful of her adolescent daughter's behavior, she went so far as to have another member of the family spy on her while she was at school. Mr. Silver, at the same time that he claimed his son was unable to have a girlfriend, feared the boy's sexuality and thought that Paul might even molest his sister. (While there were certainly other issues in Paul's case, his father's fear seemed very important in how he felt about the boy.)

The strategies these parents constructed to cope with their adolescent children's sexuality involved unspoken messages expressed in circuitous ways. Perhaps because of the indirect forms their parents' communication took, Paul and Bonnie seemed more confused about what was going on in their families than those kids whose parents saw them as bad or troubled. Bonnie, however, by running away, brought a concealed issue out into the open. When we last spoke with her she seemed aware of her mother's fears in a way that she had not been several months earlier.

When we began our research on the kinds of conflict that went on between runaways and their families, we hypothesized that many of the kids would perceive their own values as different from those of their parents. We suspected that the fighting that can accompany perceived differences—particularly in families where some beliefs and values are taboo—might have something to do with a kid's leaving home. Furthermore, there seemed to be more of a trend toward young people's developing values which might conflict with their parents' beliefs. While we talked to some young people who perceived themselves and their values as different from those of their parents (see particularly David and Bonnie in Part I), we found many others who saw no such clear distinctions.

Often the perceived difference was greater from the parents' point of view. In two such cases which we shall describe shortly, a dynamic somewhat related to our initial hypothesis seems to be at work. The social image of young people as freaks who use lots of drugs, are sexually promiscuous, and have no respect for their elders or established institutions, has led some parents to expect these kinds of behavior from their adolescent children and to guard against them. Our experience with runaways makes us think that because of such fears, parents may "misread" their child's behavior or treat him in particularly punitive ways in hopes of keeping him from all the horrible things that are associated in their minds with a young person's "expressing himself." Both strategies lead to severe aggravation of the parent-child relationship and may provoke an adolescent to run away from home.

Brian, a gangly fifteen-year-old with red hair, ran away from Lynn, a working-class community north of Boston, the day he was suspended from school for drinking. When we talked with him at Sanctuary several days later, he wanted to return home but was concerned that he get back the right way. Otherwise, he would just have to leave again and go even farther the next time. In talking some about the suspension, Brian claimed that he had been putting cold paper towels on a friend, trying to sober him up for the next class. The friend had been drinking and he had not, but a teacher saw them together and told the principal. When called down to the office and charged with drinking, Brian "took the rap" so that other friends would not get caught.

In Brian's mind, the suspension merely added to problems

that already existed at home. His parents thought he was bad, "some kind of criminal," and seemed to suspect him—of what he was not sure. He made a point of saying to us that he "kept his nose clean" and stayed out of trouble, but they still bothered him. One example of their suspicion had to do with his main hobby—collecting tapes for his stereo tape deck. Brian and a friend down the block traded tapes back and forth. One day, after he had given the friend another tape, his parents asked Brian what was in the box. Nothing he said could make them believe that it was only a tape. Another time, the same friend called him at eleven o'clock one night to tell Brian he had forgotten one of his tapes. After Brian had thanked the friend and hung up, his parents asked him what the call was about. They would not believe that the friend had called to tell Brian about one of his tapes. Although he did not say so, it sounded to us as though the parents suspected their son of using or selling drugs.

The irony of this was not only that Brian did not take drugs, but that, for the most part, except for his long hair, his values were similar to those of his parents. Like his father, a machinist, he possessed a "natural mechanical ability." "I was born with this skill, I guess. I can take things apart and put them back together just like that. I've done a few motors and an adding machine. I'd never seen an adding machine before but I took it apart and put it back together and fixed it." In school, he was enrolled in the trade course and hoped to turn his manual ability into a marketable skill. One of the reasons he wanted to return home was to get back to the shop. Brian also held down a job as a dishwasher, which he was afraid of losing if he stayed away too long. It was with money earned while working that he had bought his stereo tape deck.

When Brian told his parents of his suspension, they yelled at him, so he left the house and went to a friend's apartment. He wanted to stay away from home for the night and think things through. "Sometimes you just can't think about something at home, you have to go somewhere else," he told us, but when he called his parents and tried to get their permission for him to stay away for the night, they refused. His father said if he had problems to think about, he could do that at home. After two hours of trying unsuccessfully to change their minds, Brian took off.

It seemed to Brian that the suspension was a confirmation of his parents' fears; as much as he objected to their judgments and tried to do the right things, there was still something "wrong" with him. For a long time, he had been able to live with his parents' suspicion, but now that events in the outside world were confirming it, the prospects were too frightening. The possibility that he might be "some kind of a criminal" was enough to make him run away and leave behind an active life that for the most part he enjoyed. In doing so, however, he only further lived up to their negative expectations. If his parents took out a warrant on him, Brian would indeed become "some kind of a criminal."

When Diane first came to Project Place, she said she was on her way to Vermont, where someone had offered her a cabin for the winter. She had left Malden, a working-class community near Boston, the week before; running away had been on her mind for the past six weeks, ever since her parents had become very restrictive with her. Some of the restrictions she talked about were typical: her parents would not allow her to wear bluejeans to school, nor would they allow her to smoke in the house; others, however, seemed particularly harsh. They insisted that she cut her long brown hair, which struck us as attractive, and kept her inside the house after school for days at a time. Just what the reasons for these rules were, Diane would not say. It seemed to us that she simply did not know, but the restrictions had reached the point where she could no longer tolerate them. After being grounded for weeks, she took off, dressed in bluejeans, a coat, and a sweater, and now all she wanted to do was "put as much distance" between herself and her parents as possible; what she wanted was to regain the sense of freedom she had had before her parents had become so restrictive. Freedom, Diane said, was the most important thing in life for her.

Up until the past few weeks, Diane said, she and her parents got along pretty well. Now, however, they fought constantly, and the few times she had talked with them on the telephone, they had hung up on her. Unlike many of the runaways we talked to, Diane was doing well in school. Since the first grade, she claimed, she had only received three Cs—all her other marks were higher. Her school achievement, however, had not kept her parents from seeing her as a "hippie," which was what all the fighting over bluejeans and hair length had been about. Diane said that her parents had particularly nasty words for Project Place, which they had seen advertised on television. Her father, who owned several local garages and a service station as well, was particularly scornful of "hippies."

Her first day at Project Place, Diane refused all offers of help, would not call home to get permission to stay longer, and insisted that she was going to spend the rest of the winter in Vermont. By her second day, however, she had called home and talked her parents into letting her stay there for a while. Diane, her counselor, and her parents spent the next few days talking about the possibility of family counseling. Although the parents were hesitant, they seemed willing to accept counseling if their daughter would return home. Then, unexpectedly, Diane's father showed up at Place one night and insisted that she come home with him. When she refused, he lost his temper, beat her, then took her home (see Part I, chapter 6). Diane's counselor talked to her parents the next day and found they had changed their minds. There would be no family counseling. It was their feeling that the problem lay with Diane, not the rest of the family. During the next week, they took her to a family doctor, who prescribed tranquilizers for her and withdrew her from school. The last thing the counselor heard about Diane (from her parents) was that she was being kept inside the house most of the time.

The reaction of Diane's parents was an extreme one, but it is similar in intent to the strategies of other parents we have heard about who want to keep their adolescent children under control. Our first reaction when we heard stories of kids being kept in the house for months at a time was disbelief. No one we had known as teenagers was treated that way. With time, however, we were no longer surprised by kids' running away from such situations. We also came to recognize that by running away, kids felt they were taking great risks in their relations with their parents, about which they could be both fearful and guilty. Diane stated such fears by talking about a cousin who, after living in Diane's house, married a man whom the family disapproved of. After two years of marriage, the cousin divorced her husband and called her aunt, asking if she could return to Malden. Diane's mother had refused to take the girl back into the family; now the girl feared that her parents might disown her as well. Diane's fears had some basis in fact—she had overheard her father tell her mother on the telephone, "If she wants to run away, let her go for good."

"SHE'S OUR DAUGHTER AND SHE'S BEAUTIFUL"

Some parents of runaways have difficulty in accepting their children's growing away from them. A study done at the National Insitute of Mental Health, entitled "Parental Perceptions of Separating Children," described a group of parents who dealt with their child's adolescence in ways which made it more difficult for him to grow: "The parents in disparaging their adolescent offspring typically tended to focus not so much on a specific lack of skills or experiences which could be corrected through effort or training. Instead they aimed at seemingly deep-rooted and incorrigible character defects which they deemed beyond repair."[2]

Although only some of the adolescents in the families studied by the NIMH group actually ran away, we found their conclusions helpful. We understood how conflicts over specific issues could lead to a young person's departure. Yet some parents seemed to relate to their children simply through chastisement. We do not know why this is, but the NIMH study suggests that parents may recruit children to fill their own needs. For instance, a mother may label her child a "born loser" and "externalize" her negative feelings about herself, rather than cope with those feelings on her own. This idea might explain the persistent quality of the negative attitudes that some parents of runaways take toward their children.

The study points out that in the process of adolescent separation, parents must restructure their lives at a time when it may be difficult for them to do so—middle age. Optimally, they will help the child gain confidence in his ability to grow and become independent of the family, while they deal with feelings of loss on their own. Some parents, however, respond to the event by accusing the child of abandoning and hurting them or by paying more attention to him than usual.

The study also suggests why some of the harsh judgments parents make about kids may be so effective. Although an adolescent is not so dependent on his parents as a child and is moving away from them "toward new relationships outside the family orbit ... he remains vulnerable to parental expectations to the degree that he still lacks a core of autonomy."[3] Adolescents will be particularly vulnerable to those parental expectations which have to do with their becoming independent, their ability to make close friends outside the family, and whether they will be bad or destructive once they leave the family. With the development of autonomy, however, an adolescent "can selectively respond to and refute his parents' perceptions of himself."[4]

Many of the kids with whom we spoke seemed to lack such a "core of autonomy," sometimes to the point that the idea of running away turned out to be more their parents' than their own. One girl left shortly after an argument with her father in which he had told her, "Shape up or pack your bags and leave." More common, however, were cases in which kids responded to more general negative parental perceptions. The complaint about parents' judging friends "bad" is one example of this. With some "core of autonomy," an adolescent would not be threatened by such a judgment; with confidence in his own selection of friends, he could dismiss his parents' ideas rather than insist that they stop expressing such opinions.

Claire, a slight, attractive, fourteen-year-old from Worcester, had problems with her family but they were not very clear in her mind. Upon her arrival at Project Place, it was hard to figure out why she had run away. She talked some about her parents' not letting her play the stereo as loud as she wanted, but that hardly seemed reason enough to travel the thirty miles from Worcester to Boston. Claire's parents were quite restrictive and she was having problems in school, but neither home nor school sounded particularly upsetting; she did say, however, that she wanted to get along better with her parents and that she was afraid of becoming "a failure" like her older brothers and sisters, all of whom had graduated from high school and were now having trouble supporting themselves. Through the work of the Place counselor, Claire's parents agreed to go into family counseling in their home community. They themselves were confused about what to do with their daughter.

When we saw Claire and her parents together, she had decided to return home. The day before, her mother had called and asked her to come back. Now her parents had come down to have a family conference with Claire and her counselor in which we took part. Claire's counselor began the conference by saying that most of the difficulties in the family seemed to have begun when Claire became a teenager. Claire then told her mother that things might be difficult between them "because you grew up differently from the way I'm growing up" (Claire's mother had married while still a teenager). The mother listened, beaming at her daughter, then replied that she might be overprotective sometimes, but she was just concerned. She went on to say that she trusted Claire, she was a wonderful girl. Until recently, the two of them were "like this," she said, crossing her fingers, but now the daughter seemed more withheld. She continued to smile and look right at her daughter while she talked. "She's such a good girl; yes, she is my baby and I love her, but can't a mother love a daughter? She's our Claire and we think she's beautiful." The mother leaned over to hug her daughter, who allowed the gesture but did not smile.

As Claire's mother continued to talk, she described a different daughter. There were problems: she did not like Claire's friends, who seemed to make Claire mean. The mother began to tell a story about how her daughter and her friends had stolen a kitten from another child, then turned the animal over to the local Animal Rescue League, where, if unclaimed in a day, it would be killed. At this point, Claire interrupted her and said that she and her friends had not known that the animal would be killed, but her mother insisted that they had; "that kind of thing" was typical of those friends. Claire's mother had found out about all this through her neighbors. She let her daughter know that she kept track of her.

The girl's mother was also concerned about the boys her daughter was friendly with, one of whom was black. The family had discussed race often, she told us, and while they didn't think that one race was superior to another, she thought it best that people stay with their own kind. But Claire continued seeing the black boy. Someone had even seen her "necking" with him on a street corner. Claire insisted that this was not true, but the mother ignored her. She should be more careful about who her friends were. Several years from now she might be in love with a "nice" boy and what if someone whispered to him, "Claire made out with a black boy?" That could ruin everything. She would have to be more careful about what the neighbors said. "The neighbors can make you or break you."

Claire did not fight with her mother very hard. It was difficult to talk back to her because she had so much to say and spoke with such assurance. She would also not admit her negative feelings about her daughter without repeating how much she trusted her and how "wonderful" she was. Yet to us at least, the message seemed clear. As long as Claire stayed within the family, close to her mother, she would be good. Once outside, she made poor choices of friends, could become mean, and might make mistakes which could do her irreparable harm. Although Claire's father did not encourage her mother or add his own negative expectations to hers, he did not refute her perceptions. Throughout the conference he was quiet. Watching the family together, it was our feeling that part of what Claire had tried to escape from was the double role in which she had been cast by her mother as a "good" girl but a "bad" adolescent.

"FINDING OUT WHAT THE WORLD WAS LIKE"

The act of running away may serve as the impetus for a young person to develop strengths that help him grow in a confusing environment. Even if he returns home after several days, the experience of being away may lead to some change in self-image. In an unpublished study of runaways who had returned home over a year ago, one boy described what he had learned while away: "When my family used to laugh at me, I felt like a chicken and cowered in a corner. I learned how to stand up for my rights and depend on myself. I learned that I was better than some people and worse than others and that everyone's like that." Others spoke of "feeling more independent," "finding themselves," and "finding out what the world was like." In this final respect, disillusioning experiences as well as positive ones helped kids get a sense of who they are. One girl said, "I ran because I wanted to be happy and I wasn't happy and I'm not happy now. The run made me more cold and calculating, more critical, less trusting of people. When I ran I thought the world was sunshine and love. It wasn't like that at all."[5]

The data from this study is all that we know about how runaways look at their experience after it is completed. (Most of the kids we had known were still running away and there was no way to tell how any of them would feel a year later.) All the kids interviewed were from "intact" families, and when contacted by telephone were asked to respond to a five-part questionnaire. Despite (and perhaps because of) the limited nature of this contact, kids gave very precise statements concerning their feelings about the runaway experience.

In addition to talking about how running away had helped them grow, some kids looked back on their experience with disdain. "I think it was stupid now," one boy said. "When you leave home it doesn't help anything out. It's a waste of time. You end up going back anyway." Some still seemed guilty over the effect they had had on their parents. One said running away was a "poor thing to do . . . your parents worry. They don't know where you are. They took care of you all your life." Another thought that the experience was not "really worth it. . . . It cost my parents a lot of money . . . a lot of hassles and made them get gray hair."

Another group of kids felt that running away had helped them improve their relationships with parents. One boy claimed that before he left, he and his parents were in "absolutist places," each insisting that his own ideas were right. "We found a gray area after my run." Another boy simply said, "It brought my parents and me together so we could talk with each other." A third said running away made him "grow up and realize what life was all about. I laugh looking back. . . . It was stupid in a way. It's not hard to listen to your parents. You can compromise instead of walking out." It interested us that what appeared to change as a consequence of his running away was a kid's perception of his family. Having proved themselves independent, some kids were more ready to accept parental guidance. It was significant in this respect that while well over half of the kids said one or the other parent was the "main problem" before they had run (twelve out of nineteen girls and nineteen out of twenty boys), very few felt their parents were still the "main problem" (five of the girls and none of the boys).

Only five out of forty runaways in the study would advise others to do as they had done. Some even felt they would tell others not to leave home, while thirteen "felt both ways." According to interviewers, most kids felt that their reasons for running away had been specific and individual, thus it was hard for them to advise others what to do. We cannot help but think, however, that the large number of kids who advise others not to run may be an indication that despite their positive feelings about the experience (twenty-eight out of thirty-nine "enjoyed" it at the time while twenty-six out of thirty-nine still took a "positive position" toward it in retrospect), kids are not really comfortable with the option of running away. The kids' advice serves as a reminder of the kind of choice running away is—one that a person makes only if he feels he has to.

There is no way of knowing if the kids in this study come from families similar to those in our own. It may well be, however, that these kids come from happier families than those we saw; the kids' talk of better communication with their parents, gaining the ability to compromise, and coming to respect parental points of view makes us suspect this. Most of the kids we talked to did not express such sentiments—they simply wanted out. Some young people who run away may simply be seeking relief from the ambiguities of growing up. The early teenage years are particularly confusing ones, for there is a double standard at work. On the one hand, a young person is experiencing for the first time that he can be an independent human being. With puberty, kids not only become mature sexually but they begin rethinking parental and social values. These processes are the beginning of what may later become a more complete and better established independence, yet in their inception, they are dramatically different from anything the person has known before. Despite this new experience of selfhood, young people are still dependent on their parents and must deal with their authority. The double standard is one of independence vs. dependence, freedom vs. control; it is a difficult situation to be in, particularly when kids are insecure about their new selves. Thus, early in adolescence, after some conflict with his parents, a kid may run away to reaffirm his faith in his own independence. These first years of adolescence were particularly long ones, as we remember them. It seems as if it took forever to get from junior to senior high school or from the time we wanted to drive a car until we were legally of age to do so. Some of the kids who ran away may be trying to prove to themselves as well as to others that they are growing up; for these, running away may be a kind of play at independence which allows them to return and follow the regular social pathways to that goal.

"THEY JUST KEPT DOING IT"

Sometimes when a kid runs away from home, parents take extreme measures in response. Anger is perhaps the most common reaction to a kid's departure; one family counselor told us that before she was able to get anywhere in such situations, she first had to deal with parental anger. For instance, Michael and Paul (see Part I) have both been permanently rejected by their families for running away a number of times. Parents may also have a son or daughter declared a "stubborn child" or "runaway" by the court and sent to a correctional institution (see chapters 3 and 4). While we did not find them used often by the families of runaways with whom we spoke, incarceration in a mental hospital and beatings were two particularly extreme parental reactions to a kid's running away.

We heard of kids who had been put in mental hospitals just for running away several times, but we do not know enough about any one case to discuss it in detail. Nevertheless, according to one article we read, the idea that running away is a sickness is gaining a certain professional legitimacy. The "runaway reaction" has now been included in *The Diagnostic and Statistical Manual of Mental Disorders* of the American Psychiatric Association as one of the "behavior disorders of adolescence." While some psychiatrists disagree, others may have accepted this definition of running away as a sickness.[6]

Joe and Phillip, two runaways with whom we talked, were beaten by their parents for leaving home. Both had run away after particular family crises. Joe was the son of eastern European parents who had recently immigrated to America. Despite his outgoing nature and good looks, he had made no friends in the Boston suburb where he lived. Everyone made fun of him because he was foreign. For his first two years in America, he had worked hard at home as well as at school, spending long hours helping out in his parents' store and getting good grades, mainly to please his parents. One of the reasons for their immigration, they told Joe, was for him to get a good education. Until his third year, he had been able to take purpose from their expectations, but after a long summer of helping out at the store, he told us, he grew tired of playing "their game." Weary of being labeled "teacher's pet," he stopped working in school and stayed away for several days. When the school reported the absence to his parents, they beat him furiously; although physical punishment was common in families of his ethnic background, Joe had never been beaten like that before. His father, he said, cornered him in his room, while his mother blocked the door, then both began to hit him "uncontrollably." While doing this they seemed to Joe to be smiling. When it had ended after what seemed like a very long time, Joe said his nose was bleeding and his face was cut. Then his parents called a policeman and talked to him about what could be "done" with their son. The policeman came to the house and described to the parents the procedure for filing a "stubborn child" complaint. Joe told us that when he tried to tell the policeman what had been done to him, the officer simply said, "If my son stayed away from school, I'd probably give him a good slap across the face too."

The next day, Joe had run away from home and come to Sanctuary. Somehow, his parents found out he was there; when he refused to go home with them, they began to beat him once more—the father with his fists and the mother with her purse. Only the fast work of some counselors got them to stop, and after a long family conference, Joe returned home.

Phillip, fifteen, was beaten by his parents the day he returned from running away. Earlier in the day, he had had a family conference with his parents at Sanctuary. The beating occurred in the evening. Several weeks later he still had a vivid memory of the incident: "My parents beat me ... you see my tooth is chipped. They did that. He socked me, my father, right in the mouth. Everybody in the whole family got on top of me, and they just kept ... I, I don't want to go through that again. They just, just kept hitting me, you know, they just wouldn't stop. My father would hold me and my mother would hit me. And my brothers and sisters were on me and I fell and my father was on me and I was on the floor. He was squeezing me, suffocating me, bending my back. Telling me, 'You went out to tell somebody else our problems. You shamed our family. And what are the neighbors going to think?' Like I was really something criminal. And they just kept doing it. I had a bloody nose and I was coughing up blood ... that was the worst day. And then, I don't know, the police came down. I don't know how they got there. Anyway they took me upstairs. They talked to me. I remember my father saying, 'Oh, I didn't mean to do that. Can't you just scare him or something, he's so defiant.' At that point I really felt like killing my father. So they took me upstairs. I cried for an hour. After everything that had been going on, you know, it built up inside me. And all my emotions just came out at once. Even when the cops were there ... I didn't care who was there ... I just kept crying and I didn't stop. Finally I gave them my promise that I'd come down to the station next day to talk to the juvenile officer. But I didn't want to talk to them, anyway. I just got all my clothes on and left again."

NOTES ON FAMILY COUNSELING

Many people point to the runaway phenomenon as evidence that the family as an institution is breaking down. Our talks with young people have left us with the opposite impression. Those who try physically to leave their families often take along the expectations and judgments of their parents. While they may not want to live with their families, these kids remain involved with them in basic emotional ways: some call home often to find out what's going on and most are particularly curious about what their parents think of their departures. Running away provides opportunities for growth. As kids make new friends, experience their "independence," and talk through things about which they are uncertain or confused, they may come to be less affected by family patterns. Many kids, however, simply stay away for a while, then return to the same situations that they tried to leave behind.

In recognition of factors such as these, family counseling has become a popular way of working with runaways and their families. Unfortunately, it has too often been regarded as a universal solution rather than one of several options open to those who work with runaways. "The Runaway Youth Act" now being considered by Congress, for instance, proposes a two-step procedure for runaways—after a short stay at some "temporary shelter," a kid would be returned to his family. "Once returned home, family counseling would be provided." The problem with this approach is that it is not open-ended enough; some kids need to run for a long period of time, others can make good returns home without therapeutic intervention, or might be better helped by individual counseling. Some kids *ought* to be away from home; thus some alternative living arrangement may be more suitable to their needs than family counseling.

Nevertheless, in a number of situations, some kind of family counseling may be a necessity to help a young person return home. Generally, however, "family counseling" involves a longer relationship in which a therapist and family members work together for change. Often a young person runs away, not to leave his parents, but to set the basis of a new kind of relationship with them, so that this form of counseling may, in effect, be what he is asking for.

One important element of this kind of counseling is that simply by the fact of the whole family's being involved, a young person may no longer be considered "the problem." Although his parents may continue to see him that way, their participation in family counseling is an admission that this is no longer true. Nathan Ackerman, one of the founders of family therapy, described the counseling situation as one that provides an "opportunity ... to unburden a scapegoated family member" so that "the disturbance becomes recognized as a contagion of emotional pain within the whole family rather than the exclusive affliction of one member."[7] In such cases, Ackerman notes, "one member is exploited to preserve a pathogenic family equilibrium," in which "there is no true safety for any family member ... when the therapist counteracts the scapegoating he paves the way for a new and healthier alignment of family relationships."[8]

While this process may not lead to a new intimacy, it can lead to clarity. Since the kinds of "parental perceptions and expectations" we have discussed in this chapter may be particularly confusing to a young person, an important goal of family therapy is to clarify the hidden perceptions and expectations parents have of an adolescent.

Another goal, as stated in the previously cited study, "Parental Perceptions of Separating Children," is liberation: "By liberation, we mean the adolescent's freeing himself of the thwarting impact of his parents' perceptions."[9] As long as a young person accepts his parents' idea of who he is, his own growth may be impaired. The authors point out that with the realization of the situation in which he has been placed, an adolescent may try to get back at his parents by living up to their expectations. This idea partly explained why some of the kids we had known seemed so locked into thinking of themselves as "sick" or "bad." "The implication for therapy here is that the family therapy must analyze the exploited victim's masochism—and enjoyment of power over his parents—which are inherent in his living up to his parents' negative ... perceptions and expectations of him."[10]

The "liberation" that these therapists propose is for parents as well as adolescents. "To the extent that the parents become able to correct their expectations of and expectations for their adolescents in the light of the latters' true needs and capacities, they will promote their own growth, and instead of miring themselves and their children in a vicious circle of exploitation and counter-exploitation, will work toward true separation and liberation."[11]

Among those who have tried to work with the families of runaways, we have found that the issue of whom the counselor is working for comes up often. Because of confusion over this issue, some have chosen to work only with the runaway in order that their allegiance not be vied for. Those who choose to work with the entire family should expect that "taking sides" will be part of the process.

The factors at issue in the families of runaways are not always as profound as those described above; only some of the parents we observed seemed to be actively undermining their children. The counseling process may be valuable simply as a means of keeping communication open at a time of family crisis—for any "kind" of family. One of the kids we talked to explained his need for this sort of communication in the following way. "I sit here and talk about how much I hate my father, but deep inside I need him to tell me what it's like on the other side." In their own efforts at growth, young people may be supported and encouraged by real accounts of what the process has been like by those who are farther along.

2
SCHOOL DAYS

Shortly after we began our research in the fall, we answered a call on the Sanctuary hotline from the sister of a fourteen-year-old boy who had just run away from home. He had left, she said, because of bad marks; report cards had been distributed the day before and he had not returned from school. If her brother contacted us, she wanted him to call her. Their parents were worried. It did not matter what marks he had—they just wanted him home.

Several months later at the Place Runaway House, there was an influx of kids which no one could explain. It was the middle of winter and not close to any particular holiday, yet one of the counselors remembered a similar increase in the number of runaways the same time last year. It turned out to be another report card week. All over Massachusetts kids had received their mid-term grades, and some of them, disappointed, confused, and ashamed of their records, took off.

When we began our research, we suspected that kids who ran away were socially alienated in every way and consequently had rejected the entire educational system. However, the young people who took off, the ones who did not want to bring bad report cards home, were in fact involved in school and fearful of its evaluation process. Specific events, at home and at school, relating directly to education, were often responsible for an adolescent's departure. Most of the students we talked with spoke at length about how they had been treated by teachers, school authorities, and parents but seldom expressed the general disaffection with school we had expected. We came to see that alienation began in the everyday details of these kids' lives. Three kinds of events were of particular interest to us: the ways in which family problems might affect school performance, the ways school personnel responded to these problems, and the more general issue of the roles adults play which contribute to a young person's running away.

In talking with school officials we grew accustomed to hearing that the family and not the school was responsible for a kid's problems. In the same spirit, the parent of one runaway boy responded to a counselor's suggestion that his son was having difficulty in school by saying, "That's it! The school's to blame for what's happening to him." Both attitudes, it seems to us, are inadequate responses to a complicated situation. Most often, we found that school and home problems went hand in hand, so that for one party to blame the other for a student's difficulties did no one any good. "Let's face it," one administrator said, "a kid's got two places, here and at home, and if they both let him down, he's in trouble."

THE FAMILY AND SCHOOL

One study ("Suburban Runaways of the 1960s," done by Robert Shellow and others) indicated that runaways have a difficult time doing well in school, despite the fact that, as a group, their tested intelligence was equal to that of their peers.[1] In our conversations, we came to recognize some of the different ways in which family troubles made school harder for a student. During an emotional crisis at home, school sometimes became less important; worried by what was happening in their families, some kids lost interest in schoolwork. In other cases, the crisis between a kid and his parents concerned specific differences about the value of education. Although these kids, too, seemed involved in family troubles, the issue for them was rooted in the educational process.

Two kids we talked with related poor school performances to events in their families. Linda, a high school junior from an affluent Boston suburb, whom we talked to at a drop-in center in her hometown, had run away a year earlier after trying to erase the bad grades from her report card. She stayed away for a week, traveling from one section of New England to another; part of that time she spent skiing with some kids who picked her up hitchhiking. Upon her return, she fought with her parents about her bad grades; then, for a while, she felt things at home improved.

Her mother, Linda explained, would not allow her to date or even to drive in cars with boys. Although she did not like these rules, she seemed to respect them and felt guilty about breaking them; she blamed herself for the fights she had at home. When we talked to her, she said she was "fucking up again" at home as well as at school: her grades were going down once more and her mother had recently found drugs in her room. Things got bad "in cycles," she told us, and it seemed as if another one was on the way. Although she was a pretty girl who got on well with the kids at the drop-in center, Linda had no friends at school and was sometimes scapegoated by the other kids there. This scapegoating also came and went "in cycles." Most recently she had been beaten up by several girls at a local hangout.

It seemed to us that Linda had grown to accept the idea that since she was bad, bad things would happen to her. She had left home at a time when there was some objective proof of her fears—a bad report card—and continued to find daily reminders of their validity. Her idea of "cycles" struck us as a kind of passive fatalism. There was nothing she could do about her "badness," particularly because she deserved everything that happened to her. Her self-image seemed to derive mainly from what she thought her mother thought of her. Consequently, poor performance in school was just another part of the way she conceived of her life.

John had left home for several days because he was confused about homesexual desires which his mother sensed and ridiculed by calling him a "queer." At the time, he was fifteen and doing poorly in school; his teachers and parents told him he was an "underachiever." After several months of talking to a Sanctuary counselor about his "problem," John started doing better than he had ever done in school. His explanation of the improvement was that before he had run away and discussed his confusion with someone, the "problem" was the only thing he could think about. It "built up inside" him so long that he never wanted to reveal it. "I couldn't concentrate on anything else," he told us. "But when I talked to the counselor about it my real inner self came out.... All through school the teachers would tell my parents, 'John has the brains but he doesn't use them.' Well, I'm using them and I'm getting really great grades." By going away from home and school for help, the boy began to understand a conflict that had kept him from achieving in school.

School performance is also an area in which an adolescent's wishes may conflict with his parents'. Some of the kids we talked to had run away after their parents became more restrictive following a decline in school performance. In such cases, the parental expectation seemed to be that if denied privileges, a kid would improve his schoolwork. It is possible that parents learned these forms of discipline from their own parents. Whether or not such discipline "worked" when these adults were younger we do not know, but the kids we met seemed to obey their parents by staying home and continuing to do poorly in school until they could no longer tolerate the restrictions. In two family conferences, we observed kids who had run away from such situations, and their parents who spoke of "coming down too hard" on them over this issue. It seemed to us that poor school performance could set off strong parental reactions, which were valid expressions of concern but only put a young person in a more difficult position. By running away, some kids made their parents understand that they did not want to be treated this way. The two runaways whom we saw talk this issue over with their parents both agreed to return home after their parents promised not to punish them for poor marks.

In Joanne's family (see Part I, chapter 2), the girl's school education was of far more importance to the mother than it was to the girl herself. From our conversations with Joanne we felt that she was sincere in wanting to work and earn money rather than spend the next two years in a big city high school where she was bored. Her mother's desire that the girl complete high school—that was, after all, one of the reasons she had moved to America—made the girl's wish a source of tension in the family. It was after a fight over whether she could leave school that Joanne ran away. A similar dynamic seemed to be at work in the Silver family (Part I, chapter 7). Ever since he was young, Paul had expressed interest in electronics, yet his father had insisted that the boy direct himself toward a college education. When Paul finally ran away, he got his father to approve the change from a "college" to a "vocational" course, but by running, he jeopardized his chances of being admitted to that program.

In families where doing well in school is valued by parents, a young person's academic achievement may be part of the strategy he takes toward his family. For instance, Joe, in the previous chapter, chose to start doing poorly in school after a summer of working in his parents' store. Before the summer he had understood that the vacation would be his own time. When his parents told him he would have to help out in the store he accepted their authority, but returning to school the next fall, disappointed and resentful about his summer, he did poorly, knowing that they would be affected.

For Bonnie Simms (Part I, chapter 8), doing poorly in school was an upsetting event which she could not understand. After months of trouble with her family, her grades declined, she received several "pink slips" (notices that she might fail a course), and began "acting up." Twice she walked into the school guidance counselor's office and started to shout at the woman. Bonnie had the feeling, she told us at the Runaway House, that all of her teachers hated her. While we never visited her school and do not know if the girl's allegations were accurate, it seemed to us more likely that the way she had been treated by her family—particularly the fact that she had been spied upon—might have made her generally suspicious of adults. Such feelings could make learning more difficult.

Not all kids who ran away were upset by poor school performance. Some actually seemed to make success out of failure, finding in friendships the excitement and activity that were missing in school. These kids described enthusiastically the things they did while cutting school; usually they "skipped" in groups and went somewhere away from their neighborhood. What they did however, was not as important as their enjoyment of doing things together. These kids did not talk much about school performance, but some of their comments made us realize that insofar as school functioned as a source of social evaluation, they respected it, however grudgingly. Although Michael Mills (Part I, chapter 1) had rejected school and become involved in the street life of his friends, when we talked to him he wanted very much to pass a high school equivalency exam. David McNeill (chapter 5) also looked for some kind of social recognition—a year after dropping out of school, he was on his way to the State Employment Office to take aptitude tests. He told us that he wanted to know what his skills were. The first thing Jill Ware (chapter 8) did when she finally settled down to a permanent living arrangement was try to go back to school. She lasted less than two weeks, however, and dropped out once more because it was late in the year. Nevertheless, she told her counselor, she would try again in the fall when she could begin with everyone else.

Not all kids who run away from home have problems at school. Those who were doing well stand out in our minds, for they made a point of saying that they were good students and impressing on us that school was *not* why they ran away. For all the social questioning of the function and value of education, it still means a lot to a kid to say that he has done well. At the same time, judging from the kids we met, it does not seem to be any easier to admit failure these days. Although they may criticize the school and their teachers, many kids seem to place primary blame for poor performance on themselves.

WHAT SCHOOLS CAN DO

Because kids spend so much time at school, the response of teachers and administrators to family troubles can have a significant impact on their school experience. Thus it is important that school personnel understand the pressures which problems at home can place on kids and act, whenever possible, to alleviate rather than intensify those strains. David McNeill (Part I, chapter 5) and Meg Allen, a fourteen-year-old runaway from a wealthy Boston suburb, were particularly affected by the ways in which adults at school responded to their difficulties at home.

David, responsible for taking care of his younger brothers and sisters and household chores, was often distracted and argumentative in class, signs which most of his teachers took as further indication that, like other students in the industrial track, he was not very intelligent and did not care about learning. They noticed specific instances of "bad" behavior—suspected drug use, aggressive questioning in class, smoking in the halls—identified him as a troublemaker, and associated him in their minds with other troublemakers in the school. David's assistant principal told us that he was aware of the boy's problems at home and pressed him to "open up," but without success.

His shop teacher also noticed that David was under pressure at home but explained that when he thought that a kid was upset he tried "to let up on him." Instead of forcing David's confidence, Mr. Maxwell attempted to reduce classroom pressure for the boy so that he would have an opportunity to work through his difficulties without added complications from school. He simply tried to establish a comfortable rapport with David so that, if he wanted, he would have someone to talk to. Most important, however, the teacher's knowledge of family difficulties did not alter his perception of David as a bright, active student. A year after dropping out of school David remembered the concern and recognition this man had shown him.

Meg Allen came from a family in which both parents were alcoholics. Because her mother was often drunk, Meg had to clean and cook for her younger brothers and sisters. She also had to contend with her father's argumentativeness: when drunk he would berate her for doing badly in school and try to provoke fights. After several years of increasing tension at home, Meg began cutting classes, skipping school, and running away to a friend's house for a few days at a time. Meg often felt severely depressed after repeated fights with her parents and would avoid school for a day or two, walking around on the street and sitting in friends' cars in the school parking lot.

When we talked with Meg about school she spoke contemptuously of the teachers there, criticized the irrelevance of many classes, and seemed to resent the pressure her parents exerted on her to get good grades. She mentioned one adult—Mr. Babcock—who stood out in her mind as someone who understood the difficulties she had at home. As her unit chairman, the person responsible for administrative and disciplinary matters, he called her into his office whenever she cut classes or skipped school. One day Meg explained her family situation to him and remembered that he expressed concern; later on he even offered to try to arrange a foster home with the help of a social worker. Meg realized that she could have taken advantage of his sympathy by explaining away absences or late assignments with the excuse that she was upset, but she chose not to. She felt lucky, she told us, to have someone at school who was understanding of her problems and did not rigidly enforce the rules every time she broke them.

When we spoke to Mr. Babcock he seemed genuinely concerned about Meg's problems and tried to make them part of a total picture when deciding whether or not to take disciplinary action at any given moment. Once when he told her to stop fooling around in study hall, she had walked out the door. Instead of running after her, he let her go. The next morning when she came into his office and asked if she was suspended, he said jokingly, "I bet that's just what you want—but I'm enough of a sadist not to give it to you." The matter was settled: Meg stayed in school for the rest of the day and caused no further problems in study hall. It is possible that Meg had been testing Mr. Babcock's limits, trying to see how much she could get away with, but his easygoing response gave her some leeway and avoided making a big incident out of an essentially minor matter.

Both Mr. Maxwell and Mr. Babcock understood that they could respond to troubled students in ways that made school a more comfortable place for them; each acted to keep school pressures from exacerbating other tensions in kids' lives. While responding to David and Meg as kids with family conflicts, neither teacher tried to intervene and solve the problems for the students; instead both gave them recognition of their situations and leeway in which to work things through on their own.

THE ROLE OF THE SCHOOL

The most common school-related cause of a kid's running away was his being thought of as a problem by teachers and other school personnel. Kids often complained that the adults at school thought they were "bad." One boy claimed that all the teachers were particularly hard on him because his older brother had been a problem at the school; they judged him "bad" even when he had not done anything wrong. While we were not able to travel out to this boy's school—located in the western part of the state—to confirm his story, something about it rings true. Teachers can and do make such total judgments about their students, thus almost always affecting how young people come to see themselves, since, except for parents, they are the only adults with whom a young person has daily contact.

In his study *Pygmalion in the Classroom,* Robert Rosenthal demonstrated that a teacher's opinion of a student's ability can be more important than the pupil's tested "intelligence." In the study, teachers were given randomly determined (but false) evaluations of their students' abilities. By the end of the year most students were doing as well or as poorly as the teachers had been told they would. Some of our research (see particularly David McNeill, Part I) has made us recognize that similar dynamics may be at work in the school experience of kids who run away. David's teachers, for instance, by assuming that there was something bad about the boys in the industrial track, linked a general perception of intelligence with a similar perception of behavior.

Some kids who run away seem to have chosen what Erik Erikson calls "negative identities." According to Erikson, adolescents in search of themselves may accept the negative names others give them rather than have no names at all. In our research we recognized some of the ways in which the behavior of teachers and administrators may encourage the development of such negative identities in students.

In thinking about the ways teachers and school administrators relate to these young people we found it helpful to keep in mind the basic fact that these were adults dealing with adolescents. When, for the first time after being that age ourselves, we talked extensively with teenagers we were surprised by the excitement and insistence, as well as the lack of respect and the impatience, these kids displayed. At first these qualities were hard to take, but with time we came to enjoy them. For a teacher who is trying to keep a class in order so that he can fulfill his professional role, such qualities may often be aggravating. We heard several kids (see Mary Kandinsky) describe encounters that did not seem particularly serious to us as a consequence of which teachers came to call them "bad" or even "disturbed."

In a report ("The Way We Go to School") on children who had been "excluded" from the Boston public schools for a variety of reasons, researchers found a similar phenomenon. Although some kids were labeled "problems" for behavior that was "aggressive and often dangerous," others were singled out for behavior such as "using certain language, speaking back to a teacher, clowning around, failure to show 'proper respect,' breaking some rule, and the like."[2] The report went on to say that "normal" children may develop hostile and aggressive behavior patterns if school authorities respond to them too severely or inadequately. In fact such responses may cause the "normal" child over a period of time to become "emotionally disturbed." The report then goes on to quote from a recent Presidential Commission which concluded that in most schools the administrators act as though misbehavior results entirely from the characters of the students, and that since they sought changes in the young person and overlooked the faults of the school, their efforts to cope with misbehavior were ineffective.

The reactions of school officials to Jill Ware's stealing a coat from a local store were typical of another way in which the school may foster the development of a negative identity. Administrators and counselors reinforced the idea that Jill was a thief. Because school officials perceive themselves as responsible for their students' moral as well as academic development, they often judge *all* aspects of a young person's activities. In this spirit the assistant principal at David McNeill's school told us that the boys he hung around with in the town were a "bad group"; Mary Kandinsky's principal thought that the way the girl acted in school was evidence that she would need "a lot of help."

The act of running away may be a cause for school personnel to regard a young person as a "problem." Although some kids are simply absent for a few days, and return to school without anyone's knowing that they "ran away," others leave repeatedly and are noticed. Sometimes school officials will intervene and try to arrange "help" for a runaway. The goal of such "help"—as in Jill Ware's case—is often simply to stop the kid from running away. What happened to Jill is one extreme of what can happen to runaways in school—because officials decided there was something "wrong" with her behavior, she was benevolently pushed out of the school. In contrast, some administrators will go out of their way to ease a kid back into the school environment. For instance, during one runaway episode, Bonnie's principal contacted her mother and said that all the girl would have to do when she returned was catch up on the work she had missed. Within several weeks after she came home, Bonnie had accomplished that task and was involved in school once more.

Running away is often perceived by adults in a "negative light," but to a young person it may be an attempt to get away from a negative identity to which he has acquiesced and finally adopted. It is our feeling that while kids who are put in such positions often live up to the negative expectations of others, they are nevertheless uncomfortable about it and may subsequently choose to leave school altogether. Neither Jill Ware, David McNeill, nor Mary Kandinsky returned to the schools they left when they ran away. Others, however, after staying away for a while, went back to their old environments despite negative associations. These others may, like Bonnie Simms, try to change their negative identities, or like Paul Silver, again act according to the expectations of adults around them.

DRUGS AND SCHOOL

Drug use or suspected drug use by a student often leads adults at the school to relate differently to him. Because many adults still see even the mildest drugs as universally bad, they may treat healthy kids as "problems." One administrator, talking about the way kids refused help, showed us a marijuana cigarette he had found. When the boy to whom it belonged was in his office, he said, he had asked him what he thought about the drug, but the boy had nothing to say. The administrator then "tried to impress" upon the student that the school was willing to help him with his "problem." The boy still had nothing to say.

In situations where drugs represent only a part of a general crisis in a kid's life, the "help" offered so insistently by the school may only intensify the kid's distress. Mary Kandinsky, for instance, seemed to be confused about her own drug use, but by admitting it to her counselor she only made school life more difficult. Word got around that she used drugs and that fact influenced the way adults at school responded to her.

Helen, a fourteen-year-old from a wealthy Boston suburb, talked for several months with a school counselor before she ran away. She had first gone to him to ask for information about "downs" (mostly barbiturates). After she had made several visits, the counselor asked her whether she used these drugs and she said yes. When he asked how often, she replied with a low figure, which he challenged by saying she should be "straight" with him. Helen then admitted she used the drugs more frequently.

What we know of Helen we learned from her counselor, who thought that the girl had a "drug problem" for which she needed help. He recognized that there were other things going wrong in her life: she fought often with her parents and had thoughts of suicide. But in the counselor's mind, it was "drugs" that was the basic problem. Several times she had come to him in school "downed out." On the first such occasion, he encouraged her to seek help from a local drug rehabilitation program, but the second time he told her that the school would have to contact her parents. This prospect terrified her and shortly thereafter she ran away.

In a letter to the counselor Helen wrote, "I'm just afraid to face my parents. I really don't think I could do it." To her parents she wrote, "The only reason I'm taking off is because I know you won't understand. I've got a problem which the school must have informed you of by now. I'm not taking off because of you and Dad... I thought we were getting along pretty well this past week, but it just had to happen. I'm sorry it did... I have no choice."

Helen herself felt that she had a "drug problem" and had sought help from the appropriate person at school. She did not, however, seem to realize the possible consequences of confiding in the counselor. In many schools (Helen's among them), it is a rule that student drug use must be reported to the parents. Thus the counselor was in a difficult position—he was a school authority as well as a "helper." Helen seemed to appreciate him in the second role, but the things he did as an authority influenced her departure. "Please don't be mad," she wrote to him in her farewell letter. "Right now or even later I'm really afraid that if I'm offered anything to take I'll take enough to send me down and never be able to come back. I'll just be dead and maybe that's what I really want. I'm just too screwed up to know what I want."

Helen stayed away for several months and traveled as far as Florida. When she returned, she was beaten so violently by her parents that the counselor arranged for her to go live with a relative several towns away. Although the counselor had talked with the parents and tried to get them to recognize that their daughter shared similar problems with other adolescents, they did not, as she feared, "understand." The last the counselor had heard of her Helen was still taking a lot of drugs.

This incident points out some of the problems involved in school drug counseling. In the first place, the counselor insisted to the girl that using drugs was a problem that she had to do something about immediately. Yet he seemed to recognize that certain drugs served distinct functions in school: he joked that some kids he knew got better grades when they used drugs than when they did not. The kind of drugs Helen was using tend to "block out" unpleasant things and, given the difficulties of the relationship between the girl and her parents, it is understandable that she might want to close herself off from her environment. By insisting that she simply stop taking drugs, the counselor only reinforced the girl's guilt about using them.

In *Coming of Age in America,* Edgar Friedenberg found that what many people expected of counselors or psychologists in schools was that they work on a young person in trouble, "tinker with him and straighten him out." Friedenberg draws a distinction between working "on" rather than working "with" the young person; few people expected those who tried to help kids to do the latter. The same kind of attitude seems to be at work in the area of drug problems: counselors are expected to work on kids so that they stop taking drugs. In Helen's case, despite the strong concern that motivated the counselor's attitude, his primary goal remained that she stop using drugs. She should, he thought, get help from a drug program, a recommendation that confirms one of

Friedenberg's findings that people tend to view a young person's troublesome behavior "as a technical problem, to be referred to the right expert for solution."[3]

Another issue raised here is confidentiality. The counselor's position was complicated by the fact that he had to inform the parents of their daughter's drug use in school. Thus he had not one but three clients. Perhaps such rules exist in order to protect school personnel should anything happen to a kid. Nevertheless, these rules can complicate and even undermine a counseling relationship.

Walking through the halls of a big city school we saw several kids shoving each other on the way to a class. Suddenly a teacher emerged from a doorway, pushed through the crowd of students, and grabbed one of the boys. "Why did you do that?" he demanded, and when the boy did not answer, he took him down to the principal's office. In another school, while waiting to see a teacher, we observed a big open study hall, most unlike the silent, closely martialed "study hours" of our own junior high school days. Several hundred kids were sitting on tables and on the floor, talking, sometimes shouting across the room at one another, some of them playing roughly like the boys in the other school had been doing. All this, while the several teachers assigned to the study hall walked from one group of kids to another, socializing. These scenes were not what we had come to find out about, yet they seemed related to the things we were studying. As we observed kids in school, we came to think that rather than some kids having "problems" and others being "normal," there might be a certain randomness to who got called what. Perhaps some of the adults responsible for educating adolescents needed to think in these terms, while others did not, and thus certain kids were selected. That school life is made arbitrarily difficult for certain kids seems tragic, for the school is the institution through which, problems and all, a young person moves away from his family out toward the larger society.

3
ILLEGAL PERSONS

When a runaway is arrested and taken into court he becomes tangled in a web of legal and quasi-legal processes, institutions, and relationships. We can describe this network with fair accuracy; exactly what effect it has on the young people caught in it we can only begin to suggest. In analyzing the particular legal situation of runaways we shall consider the origins of the juvenile justice system, as well as the specific laws which apply to adolescents who leave home. Comments on juvenile court procedures and observations about the correctional institutions to which kids are sent will reflect the treatment which most juvenile "offenders"—and not just runaways—receive at the hands of the law. The families of runaways, and the multitude of officials, professional and non-professional, who are responsible for the workings of the juvenile justice system hold positions which entail many confusions and difficulties in their own right. An appreciation of these confusions and some exploration of the ways in which these adults and runaways perceive each other as persons can lead to an understanding of what kids' experiences are in the courtroom and in the institutions and agencies they are sent to.

JUVENILE JUSTICE

The present system of juvenile justice seems to have strayed from the "humanitarian" intent upon which it was founded during the late nineteenth century. Until that time, children who broke the law were treated like adult offenders. Tried in adult courts, they were punished as adults and sent to regular jails. In an article on the history of "adolescence" in America, David Bakan suggests that there was a "humane motivation" behind the development of the notion of a *juvenile* delinquent: "a desire to remove young people from the rigidities and inexorabilities associated with criminal justice and to allow wider discretionary powers to authorities in dealing with juveniles."[1]

The first Juvenile Court Act which changed the procedures for handling young offenders was passed in Illinois in 1899. "Hearings under the act were to be informal, the records were to be confidential, the young people were to be detained separately from adults. The aims were to be investigation and prescription rather than determination of guilt or innocence. Lawyers were to be unnecessary."[2] Although there was nothing in these stipulations which would interfere with the intent of the new system to provide *corrective* rather than *punitive* treatment, there was also little to safeguard the *rights* of young people in court. In fact, the practices prescribed for juvenile court proceedings, as Bakan pointed out, "had the effect of suspending the fundamental principles of legality."[3] Depriving children of the right to a lawyer meant that they had to appear in court with no advocate of their own. By permitting the judge to consider offenses for which there was no prohibitive law in effect at the time, and by not requiring that guilt be established beyond a reasonable doubt, the law allowed the court a potentially dangerous latitude. In 1910 Judge Harvey Baker of the Boston Juvenile Court admitted that "the court does not confine its attention to just the particular offense which brought the child to its notice. For example, a boy who comes to court for such a trifle as failing to wear his badge when selling papers may be held on probation for months because of difficulties at school."[4]

Thus the heritage of the present juvenile justice system has been a history of extensive judicial power over the lives of children who are considered delinquent. Although it is certainly possible that this power may be used wisely or kindly, children in court are always at the mercy of the officials; and if those officials choose to wield their authority inflexibly or without understanding, there are no legal safeguards to prevent it. Whether or not the judge acts benevolently in a particular case may well depend on the attitude of the child. Juvenile judges tend to be more kindly disposed toward kids who seem repentant.

According to Bakan the system depended upon and tried to foster a middle-class child-rearing orientation. As a juvenile judge in Colorado said, children must learn to feel "the desire to do right because it is right,"[5] must lose their fear of going to jail and develop a fear of doing wrong. In other words, the system was to focus on the child's motivation, and attempted to instill conscientious values by reform and correction, instead of punishment. The persistence of this attitude to the present day has been responsible for the *rights* of young offenders being left unprotected. Although, as we shall discuss later, there have been some changes in attitude and a few proposed modifications in legislation regarding juveniles, they have for the most part remained extremely vulnerable under the law.

The legacy left by the early juvenile justice system can be seen clearly in the particular legal situation of runaways today. The actual laws governing adolescents who leave home are rather vague and therefore allow maximum leeway to judges and officials involved in such cases. Although the runaway laws vary slightly from state to state, we will consider primarily the Massachusetts laws because most of the kids we have talked with were from that state and those laws provide a fairly typical example of similar legislation in other states. Although the term "runaway" has never been defined by law, there are references to runaways in the General Laws of Massachusetts, one of which reads: "Runaways, common night walkers, common railers and brawlers [and] . . . persons guilty of indecent exposure may be punished by imprisonment in a jail or house of correction for not more than six months, or by a fine of not more than two hundred dollars, or by both such fine and imprisonment" (Chapter 272, section 53).

In order for a runaway to be taken into court, a parent must swear out a warrant for his arrest. A Runaway Warrant is different from a Missing Person's Bulletin, although parents, anxious to locate their children, are often ill-informed and uncertain enough to confuse the two. When a Missing Person's Bulletin is issued, the police have no obligation to search for the child, but many police departments will cooperate by doing so. If the child is found, he is simply returned home and no court proceedings ensue. If parents swear out a Runaway Warrant, however, the child, if found, is arrested and a court hearing must take place. Sometimes the runaway is sent home until the hearing, but this happens only at the judge's discretion, and the kid may be placed in a detention center. The warrant may be withdrawn if the child returns home or is found without the aid of the police, but may not be withdrawn once a kid has been arrested. Thus many parents are unaware of the implications of what they are doing when they sign a Runaway Warrant and become unwittingly involved in court proceedings when their intention in notifying the police was simply to find their child.

We observed one such incident in the Boston Juvenile Court, which involved a fourteen-year-old girl charged with being a runaway. Her father testified that his daughter had always been a "good girl," and "helpful around the house," but that he had contacted the police because he was worried when she disappeared for two days. The girl herself explained that she had gone to her older married sister's house and asked if she could stay for a week. Her sister had agreed and promised to call the father for permission. Before the sister called, however, she heard that a warrant was out for the girl's arrest. Frightened, the sister called the police, who came and arrested the girl. The judge put her on probation for one year.

Another law which is frequently applied to runaways is the "Stubborn Child" law. In the case of Brasher v. the Commonwealth in the spring of 1971, a Massachusetts court defined a "Stubborn Child" as one who "persistently refuses to obey the lawful and reasonable commands of his parent or guardian." In an earlier decision—Joyner v. the Commonwealth, July 1970—the court had ruled that the term "Stubborn Child" could only apply to someone under seventeen years of age. Even as defined by the court, the term leaves the interpretation of "persistent refusal to obey" and "just and lawful commands" up to the judge in any given case. The Massachusetts Defender's Committee has made efforts to have the law thrown out for vagueness, but without success. Although many legal officials, including lawyers and probation officers, feel that the law is anachronistic, it is still frequently applied to kids who have left home several times but have never been arrested while on the run. Occasionally a kid who is picked up by the police on a Missing Person's Bulletin and is sent home will later be taken into court by his parents on a "Stubborn Child" charge.

Major John Bechtel, head of the Investigation and Services division of the Montgomery County Police Department, made the following statement to the Senate Subcommittee on Juvenile Delinquency in response to a question from Senator Birch Bayh concerning the laws on runaways: "Well, the law basically is, unless you have been emancipated by the court, you must be under somebody's care and supervision until you are eighteen years of age. So if you are out on the street and you are not under the control of a parent or guardian or you are not placed, say, in a shelter home or something by the court ... then you are in so-called violation of the law." Senator Bayh then asked, "Let us get as close to specifics as we can so we will know what we are talking about. Let us take a boy twelve, like Richard, who described how his father backed him against the wall and pulled his hair and twisted his arms, or let's take the little girl that the girl from El Paso was referring to who was sexually assaulted by her stepfather. Let us take the law as it applies to them. Are they violating the law when they run away from home?" Major Bechtel replied, "Yes, they are violating the law."[6]

The irony of Major Bechtel's response is scarcely compensated for by the wide latitude given to judges in the dispositions they can make in runaway cases. A judge might decide, in cases such as the ones Senator Bayh mentioned, to assign a runaway to a foster home or other alternative living arrangements, but there is no guarantee that he will do so. The Juvenile Judge in Cambridge, Massachusetts, outlined for us the range of options which he has in deciding the case of a runaway. First of all, he can dismiss the case. In situations where he feels the evidence warrants a finding (i.e, that he decide whether or not the kid is "delinquent") he can "continue" the case (i.e., make no finding at the time), putting the kid on probation, and later either dismiss the case or make a finding. Even if the judge makes a finding immediately, he could still put the kid on probation, and after a few months have elapsed, if he feels that the kid is "doing well" (the judge's words) he might reverse the finding and "file the case," leaving the kid with only an unofficial record. Last of all, at the time he makes a finding he can also sentence the kid to a correctional institution. If this is done, the sentence can either be put into effect immediately, or "suspended" and later revoked or put into effect, depending on the kid's attitude and behavior. What the judge failed to mention in describing the intricacies of his legal options is that a court record is rarely, if ever, erased. Even if the case of a runaway is dismissed, the police retain a record of the arrest and the charge. Thus runaways who are taken into court cannot escape the stigma of having a "record." Many, therefore, emerge from their court experience—whether or not they are actually judged delinquent—as illegal persons, in their own minds and the minds of others.

The complexity of the legal proceedings in the courtroom and the plethora of ways a case may be decided by a judge are particularly significant because of the power a judge has. How a judge acts in the courtroom, and the decisions he makes, can have a profound effect on the lives of those who appear before him. Most of the runaways who are taken into court, especially for the first time, have little or no idea of what may be done to them. Uninformed about their rights (which are almost nonexistent) or even about the kinds of decisions the judge can make, they are passive recipients of whatever kindness or harsh punishment is doled out to them. Many are cowed and fearful of the institutions to which they may be sent, others feign bravado, but few really know what might happen to them. Thus, the courtroom experience can be an overwhelming and frightening one.

THE COURT

The impact of the court experience on kids can only be understood by a careful consideration of the atmosphere in the courtroom. This atmosphere depends partly on the physical appearance of the courtroom, but even more on the actions and demeanor of the officials of the court, particularly the judge.

When a runaway is brought into court there are several elements of the situation which necessarily influence the interactions that take place while he is there. To begin with, the reason he is in court at all is that his parents have sworn out a warrant against him, and he and his parents are consequently in the position of adversaries. Secondly, the judge is the final authority in the outcome of the hearing and is therefore in a position of great power. Clearly the power of the judge and other officials and the relative impotence of the child have a marked effect on how they respond to each other. The interactions that take place between the judge and a runaway depend as much on personal factors as on laws and procedures. The image each presents the other, as well as their preconceived stereotypes about one another, can influence the outcome of the case. One juvenile lawyer we talked with said that, in general, juvenile judges are authoritarian but not punitive. They are often very confused about what to do with the kids who come before them, so in many instances judges appear stern to mask their own uncertainty. Thus some juvenile court hearings are a kind of charade.

In some instances the attitude of the judges and other officials toward runaways seems to be influenced by their impression of "delinquent" kids in general. At least, it is easy for them to regard runaways as criminals, because of the way the system of juvenile justice is presently structured. This attitude in turn may influence the ways in which runaways perceive, and respond to, these officials. In his study of "Juvenile Offenders' Perceptions," Paul D. Lipsitt has suggested that the court experience may be more positive for young people from higher socioeconomic circumstances because their class enables them to identify with the judge.[7] We also feel that judges may respond more sympathetically to middle or upper middle class kids.

Jake, one of the runaways we talked with, had been in juvenile court a few years earlier on a charge of "breaking and entering." He recalled being terrified by the experience. "It was a big old building," he said, "and there were all these people around, and I wasn't sure who any of them were. The judge sat way up in front. I guess he wasn't too bad, but he sure looked scary." Despite their initial unfamiliarity with courtroom procedure, some of the kids we have talked with, or observed in court, seemed to understand intuitively how important the persona they presented could be in determining the outcome of the case. One boy said, "If you act soft in court you can be examined by a shrink and found 'unfit.' Then you can only be sent away for thirty days." A runaway from Maryland who was picked up in Boston on a charge of "Vagrancy" and "Idle and Disorderly Conduct," told the judge, "I'm gonna go back home." He had no real intention of returning home, but the judge let him off.

Two of the Massachusetts juvenile courts we visited, Boston and Cambridge, differed greatly in appearance and in the ways the judges handled the hearings. The Boston Juvenile Court is in the Suffolk County courthouse, a huge old building imposing in its dingy grandeur. Marble pillars and balconies surround the great dimly lit lobby where one enters. Numerous guards sit behind information desks, lawyers exchange anecdotes, and people looking bored or nervous lounge or lurk against the walls. The Juvenile Court itself is crowded into a few small rooms on the mezzanine level. Behind the door marked "Juvenile Court," a narrow hallway is jammed with kids, parents, and officers of the law. The exact hierarchy of titles and positions—"probation officers," "court officers"—is difficult to distinguish, but from the way people dress and talk to each other, some pecking order can be seen. This order is presided over by one full-time and a few part-time juvenile judges. When a judge speaks people jump, saying, "Yes, your Honor" and "No, your Honor" and "If it please the court, your Honor." When the judge walks into the courtroom everyone must rise and whenever anyone speaks to the judge the person must stand up.

In the hallway an officer of the law marched back and forth with a schedule of all the cases that were to come up that day. While the court was in session he was the person responsible for seeing that people were in the right room at the right time for the right case. The hearings are closed, so between cases everyone has to leave the courtroom before the next set of people come in. Those who are there for trial on a particular day *all* have to arrive by 9:30 although the session does not start until after 10. For many of them the wait is long, because some cases are not heard until the afternoon. On the morning we visited, the children and parents who were waiting all looked very confused and unsure of where they should go and what they should do. It seemed that from the court's point of view they were supposed to be waiting around, looking humble and intimidated.

The two courtrooms themselves were very small, with three benches facing the podium of the judge. The small desk in front of the podium was for the lawyers and court officers and the chair off to the right for the "defendant." When a boy was brought in who had been in "care and custody" (i.e., locked up) the guard took hold of his jacket sleeve and twisted it around his arm, to have a firm grip on him. In the "second session" which we observed, the judge's enormous chair was electric blue plastic and an American flag hung next to the worn velvet curtain behind the chair. The harsh fluorescent light and the hard benches gave the room an air suggestive of a modern inquisition. In fact, what went on in the courtroom was hardly an inquisition since no one seemed to care much about asking questions. The police (not an attorney) prosecuted the government's cases and asked only enough questions to establish that the defendant had some involvement in the case being heard, certainly not enough to prove "guilt beyond a reasonable doubt." In every case some court official, who acted as an information coordinator, was responsible for introducing the defendant. This official was also responsible for providing information on the kid's previous record, if he had one, the parents' financial status in the event of their requesting a Public Defender, and any psychiatric information available on the kid.

The presiding judge on the day we observed looked bored but also tough and not to be challenged. When there were no kids in the courtroom his face would relax somewhat but just before they came in he would mold it into an expression of severity which he would maintain throughout the hearing. His manner throughout the session was scornful, cold, awesome, and degrading to the defendant and his relatives. Everyone connected with the defense side of the cases seemed terrified of him. Even the government officials appeared awed by him. His only evident purpose in speaking to the kids was to make them feel "bad" or to frighten them into "good" behavior. He turned to one boy after two minutes of testimony from a truant officer and said in a very menacing voice, "Well, are you going to go to school, or shall I send you to *my* school?" To another he said in a very offhand but patronizing way, "A word to the wise is sufficient; go to school."

There were a variety of ways in which the judge could demonstrate his power over the kids and their parents. One of the most obvious was making dispositions. "I find this boy to be an habitual truant: probation six months." "I find this girl to be a stubborn child: probation one year." There were also more subtle ways, such as whether he would adjust the date of a hearing so that it would be more convenient for a mother to appear; whether he would allow a kid to go home after an arraignment or prevent him from doing so by setting very high bail. In all cases this particular judge tended to take the hardest line possible.

The judge treated the parents in the same manner as the kids. After the charge against the kid was read, the judge said to the parent in a very bored way, "I must inform you that you have a right to a lawyer. If you need time to get a lawyer I will give you time. If you want a lawyer and feel that you cannot afford one, and I so find, I will appoint one. If you want to continue without a lawyer, we will proceed now and you will sign a waiver of counsel." This option is now a legal requirement because of a recent Supreme Court decision—*In re Gault,* 1967—that even juvenile offenders have the right to counsel. Nevertheless, the option was offered to the parents—and in Runaway and Stubborn Child cases this is particularly ironic: those who bring the charge against the child may decide whether he has legal representation. In fact, even in those cases for which Public Defenders were appointed, the lawyers seemed to make little effort to be real advocates for the kids and treated the hearings more as formalities. Unfortunately the case loads of most Public Defenders prevent them from spending more than a few minutes with each client.

The lack of adequate legal aid for the kids was equally apparent in the Juvenile Session of the Cambridge 3rd District Court, although the atmosphere of the court was different. The Cambridge Court is less crowded than Boston's. There were places for people awaiting hearings to sit down, and the general pace seemed less hurried. The probation officers, in contrast to those in Boston, seemed to have a sense of humor and to be genuinely interested in the kids who were assigned to them.

The juvenile judge in Cambridge is elderly, and by his own admission "very old-fashioned." He said that he tries to keep the hearings as informal as possible and when we were there he made some effort to do so. He did not wear a black robe in the courtroom and dispensed with making people rise when they spoke to him. Nevertheless he seemed completely out of touch with young people and their interests. In an attempt to express concern about the welfare of each kid—all urban dwellers—whose case we observed in his court, he asked every one of them whether they had ever thought of going into forestry as a career. He made no distinctions according to their individual interests, but appeared to think they were all perfect potential foresters!

The judge told us that he was reluctant to send kids to correctional institutions if he could avoid it. Under certain circumstances he did so, however. He sent some kids away between an arraignment and a hearing in order to frighten them into compliance—"sometimes just a week at the Board works wonders," he said. He also committed kids whom he thought were "seriously dangerous to others" or "incorrigible," "dope addicts," or "really violent" kids. Although the judge seemed unenthusiastic about the closing down of juvenile reformatories in Massachusetts, he admitted that many kids come out of them "far worse" than they went in: "That's where they really learn to be criminals." In contrast to the Boston judge, the Cambridge juvenile judge claimed to like most of the kids—"unless, of course, they are fresh, and then I can get nasty." And of course, one way of getting nasty is to send a kid away to an institution.

LOCK THEM UP AND THROW AWAY THE KEY

In 1847, Massachusetts established the first state-supported correctional institution for young people, and by the end of the nineteenth century had built two more. The purpose of these early schools—Shirley, Lyman, and Lancaster—was to reform the "idleness" and "waywardness" of children. Any semblance of moral treatment quickly degenerated into mere custodial care. Then, as now, a majority of those children subjected to the degradation of such institutions were from poor families. Children of wealthy families who run into trouble with the law usually escape being locked up, because their cases are dismissed or their families can arrange, and pay for, alternative forms of treatment. At present, ninety percent of those kids who are committed to Massachusetts' Department of Youth Services (which runs the institutions) are from families receiving some kind of welfare.[8]

Although the Department of Youth Services has been closing down the Massachusetts Juvenile Reformatories (see "Changes," this chapter), a few are still open. For this reason, and because other states still institutionalize young "delinquents," we feel that a discussion is warranted of what happens to kids who are incarcerated. The experiences of those runaways (and other "offenders") sent to institutions are determined by the behavior and attitudes of the staff and other inmates, as well as by the physical setting and the activities available—or unavailable.

If a runaway is held in custody after his arraignment, before the hearing takes place he is sent to a detention center. If committed to the Department of Youth Services after his hearing he might be placed temporarily in a detention center and eventually in an institution. (Current changes in this practice will be discussed in "Changes," this chapter.) Two of the institutions we visited were the John Connally Detention Center in Roslindale and the Industrial School for Girls in Lancaster.

Roslindale was the detention center to which Jill Ware was sent before going to Madonna Hall. Since that time the center has been used only for boys, for reasons later explained to us by the staff psychologist. The center, located at the end of a nearly unnegotiable dirt road, looks from the outside like a jail—which, in effect, it is. The building is very dilapidated and depressing, undisguised by halfhearted attempts at painting some walls in bright colors. The ground floor houses offices, the cafeteria, and the infirmary. The dormitories are on the second floor with a small gymnasium and the "recreation" room, a large room containing numerous chairs and a television. If the facilities were more extensive, we were not permitted to see them.

The psychologist explained that the months when girls had been detained at the center had been the worst time he could remember. Violence broke out continually between the girls and the staff and among the girls. Fires were often set in the building and several escapes took place. The psychologist's interpretation of these difficulties was that girls were less able to cope with the lack of privacy. Our impression was that the lack of activity, lack of privacy, and closed-in atmosphere of the place would be sufficient to provoke violence in adolescents of either sex; and two weeks after our visit the boys rioted.

Lancaster was far more pleasant in its physical appearance. Located in a beautiful rural setting it could easily be a private boarding school, except that on the lovely spring day that we visited there was no sign of outdoor activity. The warden, a husky athletic-looking woman, arranged for two girls to give us a tour of the grounds and buildings. A staff member of the Department of Youth Services had informed us that during a recent week two-thirds of the girls admitted to Lancaster were there on "stubborn child," "runaway," and truancy charges. These statistics were confirmed by records the warden showed us for 1971.

The two girls who showed us around were both runaways: Cora was a sixteen-year-old white and Annette, a thirteen-year-old black. In talking with Annette, we sensed that she was anxious to return to a normal life with her family. Before doing so, however, she thought she might go to a "concept" house (see Part II, chapter 4), where, she explained, as though quoting from the handbook, "the intention of the place is to make somebody of yourself." Lancaster did not seem to be doing that for her and all she could muster were self-critical comments about how she was too young to be doing such bad things as drinking and running away.

The first stop on our tour was the child care center for children of the staff and the townspeople. Some "inmates" were allowed to work there as a privilege and were paid a small stipend. We saw there the last signs of vitality. The school at the reformatory was deserted and the two teachers, the only people there we talked to, expressed little enthusiasm: the girls were at Lancaster too briefly to go very far, they said.

The hospital, where Cora lived, housed the "difficult" girls and those who tried to run away. We saw Cora's room, a barren cubicle, bed bolted to the floor. She mentioned being locked in there and pounding on the door in frustration. In the "hospital," girls have to eat meals alone in their "rooms." The other cottages were slightly less confining but equally lifeless, with dark corridors, tiny rooms and a "security room" (which we were assured was rarely used) at the end of each hallway. All the girls were locked into their rooms at night and had to pound on the door to get permission to go to the bathroom. A chart of privileges (weekends home, late bedtimes), which are granted according to levels (0 to 6) of "good behavior," was posted on the bulletin board. Sometimes the girls were tested by being given an errand to see if they would run away.

The daily schedule offered little variety or stimulation. Girls rise at seven, go to school for two hours in the morning, then return to their cottages until lunch. They spend from two to three o'clock in the cottages or at "optional gym." From three until four they are assigned to an activity (sorting laundry, arts and crafts) which they must attend or be locked in their rooms. At 4:30 there is a "cottage meeting" and the rest of the day is spent in the cottages with no activities planned or available. The utter lack of anything interesting to do seemed to channel all constructive energy into restlessness and boredom. This process of dehumanization was reinforced by some of the degrading practices which were used to control the girls. For example, in the dining room they had to sit absolutely straight with their feet flat on the floor and if they swore during a meal, they had to eat the next three meals locked in their rooms.

The warden met us at the end of the tour and led us into her office. She made a subtly vindictive comment, covered with a joking manner, about how surprised she was that Cora had completed the tour without running away. Most of the girls, she said, were committed to Lancaster on runaway or stubborn child charges because so many judges were reluctant to use a charge like "lewd and lascivious person." Her information was that some of the girls were really in "more serious trouble" than their commitment papers indicated. The warden's veiled animosity toward the girls seemed in keeping with the general atmosphere of Lancaster.

There was no blatant violence in evidence as we toured the place, but the lifelessness and inactivity were depressing. Even with the Department of Youth Services' current practice of placing girls at Lancaster for only three months, they still run away—the week before our visit four girls had taken off. The warden nonchalantly ran down the procedure set in motion when a girl was missing: "The security guards look around the grounds for thirty minutes. Then, in all fairness to the community, we have to notify the local police. After one hour we notify the state police and the girl's parents." In justifying the procedure in terms of obligation to the community, the warden seemed to ignore the minimal likelihood of runaway girls being dangerous to the community. When apprehended, a runaway is confined to the hospital for a few weeks.

Other juvenile institutions mete out harsher punishments, particularly to kids who run away from them. The County Training Schools for boys, which are not under the jurisdiction of the Department of Youth Services, have been subjected to strong criticism recently for their cruel treatment of adolescent inmates. Although boys are seldom committed to them for running away, we have talked with several runaways who spent time in the training schools on other charges. One boy from Cambridge mentioned a practice which he considered particularly nasty. When a boy tried to run away he had to write "I will not run away from Middlesex School" on a clipboard one thousand times while standing up. Kids who have been committed to institutions such as these often become cynical about them, and speak of their experiences there in offhand, joking ways—"Oh yeah," one boy said, "that's where I learned how to steal cars."

CHANGES

A number of actual changes in the handling of juvenile offenders and modifications of legislation regarding runaways have been proposed during the last two years. These changes affect the situation of runaways both in court and in institutions. One of the proposals which pertain to court procedure for runaways is a "diversion-from-trial" experiment being tested by the Blue Hills Program in the Boston Juvenile Court; another is an act currently before the Massachusetts State Legislature. The major change in juvenile corrections, however, has been a decision by the Massachusetts Department of Youth Services to close the institutions.

In the early winter of 1972 the Blue Hills Program of the Boston Juvenile Court arranged that all children charged for the first time with Stubborn Child, Runaway, and Truancy offenses would be offered the option of proceeding with their hearings in the usual way or in participating in the diversion program. If they chose the latter they would be offered a wide range of "treatment alternatives" including one-to-one psychotherapy, group therapy, academic and vocational counseling. Individual or group therapy would also be available to parents of these children. The stated goals of the program were: "reduction in the number of cases going to trial; reduction in the number of cases requiring probation, thereby reducing overloading; reduction in the rates of institutionalization and recidivism; and increased and more problem-specific services for youth and family." The program was premised on the idea that Runaway, Stubborn Child, and Truancy offenses were indications of psychosocial problems, and not of crimes. Furthermore, those who designed the program thought that to stand trial, be convicted, and be labeled delinquent put an "unnecessary stress on an already troubled child" and possibly contributed to the development, and acceptance by the child, of a negative or "criminal" self-concept.

Children should certainly not be subjected to the kind of procedure we observed in the Boston Juvenile Court. However, any programs to which they are "diverted" deserve close scrutiny, for we do not assume that *any* alternative is preferable to the present courtroom experience. Our impressions following discussions with staff members at the Blue Hills Program and attendance at one of their "disposition" meetings (in which they decide on the treatment to be prescribed in each case) was that in general the program made excessive use of psychiatric interpretations and procedures. The program subjects diverted youths and their parents to a complicated diagnostic and referral process.

In the disposition meetings lengthy descriptions of each case were presented: a social worker gave the "longitudinal" history of the family; the psychologist reported the results of psychological tests; and a psychiatrist's evaluation was read. Although some of the case workers seemed to have specific insights about the individuals they worked with, the head psychiatrist insisted that they apply psychiatric labels to their clients. He asked repeatedly, "How would you label him?"

Although psychological and psychiatric skills can be helpful in working with adolescents and their families, this particular program's emphasis on "professionalism" and extensive analysis of the past seemed to obscure the relevant issues in the lives of their clients. Parents were consistently discussed in patronizing ways— "Let's get mother in business." Most troubling, however, was the prevalent assumption that many, if not all, of the kids (*and* their parents) were disturbed: there was something wrong with them which the program would put right. Thus, the program tended to focus more on the weaknesses of personality and psyche than on the strengths. With runaways this is particularly problematic because they are not (except in a strictly legal sense) criminals, and people are already prone to think that they are more disturbed than they may actually be. Thus, to offer them, as an alternative to processing as a criminal, a plan which assumes that they need psychiatric treatment may only intensify and irritate feelings they have of being considered strange.

Despite the Blue Hills Program and other similar attempts at keeping runaways out of court, there seems little likelihood at present of any substantial change in the runaway laws. One state representative, who is sympathetic to the legal plight of kids on the run, said that most state legislators are overly influenced by public opinion in their home constituencies: fear of "crime in the streets," and a prevailing attitude that kids should be sent home where they belong, supports efforts to uphold "the crumbling bulwark of the family by merely treating outward symptoms." In fact, apathy is significant as a cause of failure to change the runaway laws: "If you made a list of one hundred issues of concern to legislators," he said, "runaways would go at the bottom."

Despite the Blue Hills experiment in diversion from court, there is a "proposed reform" of the runaway law before the Massachusetts legislature which would nevertheless continue to require runaways to appear in court. The proposed legislation is called "An Act Providing for the Care and Supervision of Certain Children." Basically it abolishes the classifications Stubborn Child, Runaway, and Truant, calling them instead "Children in Need of Supervision," but defining the new classification in the same terms as the old three. The dispositions which a judge can make for "children in need of supervision" are somewhat more clearly defined by the act, the most important stipulation being that such children "shall not be committed to an institution designated or operated for delinquent children." Although this act has the support of the governor, the likelihood of its passing is rather slim. A similar act has been passed in Maryland. Major Bechtel of Montgomery County, in testifying before the Senate Subcommitte on Juvenile Delinquency, said that "children in need of supervision, i.e., runaways and out of controls, cannot be placed with adjudicated or alleged delinquents . . . you ought not to have a runaway juvenile put in with hardened criminals."

This statement is reminiscent of the original motivation for establishing the juvenile justice system—to separate young offenders from adult "criminals." Now it seems that some juveniles are considered "hardened criminals" in their own right. It is our view that, commendable though it is for authorities to recognize that runaways do not belong in reformatories, no adolescents should be committed to the juvenile insitutions as they presently exist.

Fortunately the Massachusetts Department of Youth Services, headed by Commissioner Jerome Miller, has acknowledged this and has proceeded to close down the juvenile reformatories in this state. These institutions were formerly under the jurisdiction of the Youth Service Board, but in 1969 this entity was abolished and control of the institutions was transferred to the newly created Department of Youth Services. As explained in a report issued by the Department, it "has closed its large institutions across the state which have traditionally housed committed and court-detained children. Due to their size and location, these institutions were unable to provide the individualized treatment vital to the child's successful reintegration into his home community." The Department (DYS) has decided to replace the institutions with treatment programs in a variety of community agencies, public and private. By using funds which would previously have been allocated for maintenance of the institutions to purchase treatment on a fee-for-service basis at agencies throughout the state, DYS feels that more effective, "real" service can be provided for the youth who are committed to their jurisdiction.

The intention of DYS is to provide integrated services for adjudicated delinquents (and, if the "care and supervision" act were to pass the legislature, for "Children in Need of Supervision"). A key tenet of their philosophy is that these services should be offered in the community from which the child comes in order to facilitate his return to that community. At present there has been considerable resistance to the closing of the institutions, partly due to the speed with which they have been eliminated, but mainly because of the reluctance of many communities and agencies to take on responsibility for "problem" children. In addition, many people who have worked with delinquent kids in the past feel that their "big stick" has been taken away: no longer can they threaten a "difficult" child with being "sent up."

DYS has organized a wide range of treatment possibilities for adolescents who run into trouble with the law. Like the Blue Hills Program (which is not officially affiliated with DYS) some of these options involve diversion from trial, in order to eliminate the stigma of being judged "delinquent." Other programs vary widely, from individual counseling on a parole basis, to group homes for those who are considered in need of a residential situation. Two of the detention centers—Roslindale and Worcester—will be maintained as "secure intensive care units" for the treatment of "dangerous and highly disturbed youth." Although the question of how to handle violent or "dangerous" young people—whether or not to institutionalize them and in what settings—has certainly not been resolved, we feel that it is essential that places like Roslindale be eliminated if any truly humane modes of treatment are to be found.

Although we have seen signs of potential danger in some of the treatment alternatives under consideration by DYS (see chapter 4), in general the reforms are being carried out by a staff that is apparently caring and sensitive to young people who have run afoul of the law. One staff member said that DYS intends to use the money at its disposal to pressure agencies into delivering the necessary services. "One way that we will know whether, say, a group home is doing a good job is by whether kids stay there. Kids generally have pretty good intuitions about these things. If they aren't getting what they need they'll take off. Should several kids run away from one place we'd take a hard look at what was going on there." By giving kids some credit for knowing what can really help them, such a promise, if kept, could make a significant change in the way delinquents are treated.

THE IDEOLOGY OF TREATMENT

The Department of Youth Services said in a recent report, "Institutional systems have been made by people and can be unmade by people." This is as true for the juvenile justice system as it is for any other, but the question remains whether people are willing to unmake it. Clearly, there have been and are continuing attempts to *change* this system, but it is our impression that the proposed modifications, even if carried out, would leave many of the fundamental principles of the system intact.

The language used to express those principles is, of course, altered. No longer do the authorities talk of "reform," or of instilling a sense of conscience in delinquent youth. Some efforts have been made, particularly by the most "liberal" in the field of juvenile corrections, to call attention to the ways in which so-called delinquents are actually victims of poverty or emotionally deprived backgrounds, and not criminals in their own right. Consequently, the late-nineteenth-century concept of juvenile "reform," and its more archaic form "punishment," are presently being supplanted by an ideology of "treatment." Either the delinquent is considered disturbed and therapeutic measures are prescribed, or his family is deemed troubled—and therefore in need of treatment—or both. In any case, it is society which makes a judgment that something is wrong with the individual, or his family, and then proceeds to use social criteria in determining how to set him, or them, straight. We do not mean to deny that some kids and some families have problems; many do. What we wish to criticize is the ways in which children and families, because their behavior is seen as antisocial, are forced to accept therapy in the interest of social conformity. Such treatment denies people the right to take responsibility for themselves, and is rarely in the interest of the individual.

The way in which runaways are currently being dealt with by the legal system is an excellent illustration of how this process works. Whether or not a runaway is classified as a "criminal," a "delinquent," or a "child in need of supervision," running away continues to be against the law. The fundamental reason for this is society's desire to maintain and support the institution of the family for the sake of social stability. An administrator of the national department of Health, Education, and Welfare, testifying at the Senate subcommittee hearings on the Runaway Youth Act, said, "What we need is a comprehensive program that deals with families and children, that keeps families together."[9] The assumption underlying this statement is that, at almost any cost to the individuals, families should be maintained. There is a prevalent fear that if runaways remain apart from their families, an important means of socialization will be lost, and the alienation of runaways from society will be increased. This attitude is summed up by a chief probation officer's statement, made at the same Senate hearings, that "if the causes [of running away] can be dealt with and adequately resolved, his [the runaway's] pattern of behavior can be redirected and he can be helped to become a good citizen."[10] Our view is that becoming adjusted to, or a useful member of, a society beset with ills is not necessarily the same as becoming a fulfilled or happy individual.

The prevailing attitude toward runaways is no longer "lock them up" but "send them home," and numerous therapeutic alternatives are being proposed to facilitate the reconciliation of runaways with their families. When asked by Senator Bayh what the responsibility of the police was when they saw a runaway on the street, Major Bechtel replied, "Our responsibility is to pick them up . . . the next step is you go to the police station and try to contact the parents and try to make some kind of arrangements so they can go home. We are not professional counselors . . . but we try to solve the situations, to have them go back home."[11] It is ironic that the first place people try to send a person who is running away from home is back to his parents. But this is not surprising if we remember that runaways are not just people. They are underage, "juveniles," with few legal rights, and are considered sick, if not bad.

Slowly stripped of their criminal status, but still in violation of the law, runaways are increasingly being thought of as kids with emotional problems. The same HEW administrator said, "The experts agree that runaways are not involved in a healthy search for a new, mature self-identity . . . instead they are escaping from the problems of the realities at home, at school, and within themselves."[12] Running away is seen as a self-destructive form of "acting out." Several of the parole and probation officers we talked with, as well as the staff at the juvenile institutions, made a distinction between kids who act out "in the community"—stealing cars or setting fires—and those who do so in self-destructive ways like drug use or promiscuity. Runaways are the latter sort. "Acting out" is one of the psychological terms which is currently in vogue for talking about delinquents. Although the term may be a valid description of a psychological process, we have heard it used all too often to label behavior that is confusing to those who work with these kids. Use of this kind of language characterizes the change from thinking of delinquents as bad to thinking of them as sick.

Not all juvenile corrections personnel have made the transition completely, however. One supervisor for the Department of Youth Services maintained that there were some kids who were "bad," unwilling to help themselves. He characterized this type as "oversexed, fourteen-year-old girls with low IQs, who run away and hang around with twenty-five-year-old men."

Although most kids would prefer to avoid being sent to "jail" under any circumstances, most also dislike being labeled as sick, a stigma which is in many ways worse than "bad." At least among some adolescents, being "sent up" carried some status because it is a sign that one is "tough." Being sent to a mental hospital or to see a shrink carried no such "dignity," however. Some kids in treatment do joke about it, though. One boy, who had been in both a training school and a mental hospital and was currently being sent to a psychiatrist once a week, said, "Yeah they always ask 'How are you?' There you are down at the Youth Service Board trying to climb out a window and you're halfway out and you've got to pull your ass through the broken glass, and your buddy's saying 'Hurry up or they'll catch you' and when you go to see the headshrinker he asks 'How are you?'" Humor aside, however, the label of "sick" which many runaways are given by the legal authorities is as difficult to live down as the stigma of a police record. It follows them around to school and into their families where often they are already considered strange.

In some cases, runaways are seen as justified in leaving home, and in such situations, the families become the target for treatment. For example, unsolicited family counseling or individual therapy for the parents may be strongly "recommended" by a court clinic. One judge told us that there was no such thing as an habitual runaway, "kids who run away a lot just have weak superegos because of their chaotic family situations." If family therapy is feasible and effective, it is seen as the most desirable solution. Some families, however, are seen as "incorrigible." In such cases, the state will step in *in loco parentis* and place the kid in a foster home or group home. This is considered as an unfortunate circumstance by many, since great value is still attached to the social norm of children living with their families.

In conclusion we can say that whether runaways are viewed under the law as criminals or emotional problems, and whether or not their families are seen as sick, they and their parents are forced to relate to a vast network of agents and agencies of "punishment" or "help." Many are bounced around from one agency, institution, clinic, or court to another; but although the current trend seems to be toward socialization under the guise of social work, the battery of judges, probation officers, and psychiatrists which runaways come in contact with are inevitably forces of social control.

We recognize that this society has established laws to control the behavior of all its members—old and young alike—yet many of these laws are anachronistic or unjust. We believe that the "Stubborn Child" and "Runaway" laws are particularly so. Although running away is not a crime and should not be illegal, until the statutes are changed, runaways should, at the very least, be guaranteed judicial procedures which safeguard their rights. Most adult offenders have mediators to act in their interests, but despite the *In Re Gault* decision, runaways and other juvenile "offenders" do not, except in the most perfunctory sense and at their parents' choosing. We feel that it is essential for all these young people to have advocates who will act on their behalf to insure that they are treated justly.

4
ROOM
TO
MOVE

When an adolescent walks out the door of his parents' house, intending not to return, at least for a while, the problem of where to stay even for one night can be overwhelming, and a runaway who is determined to remain away longer—for a few weeks or months—or who can never return faces an even more difficult task. Under such circumstances many of a runaway's needs—for independence and support, for friends and things to do, for continuity and experimentation, for a place to live—are similar to those of an adolescent who lives with his family.

We have heard kids talk of sleeping in dark alleys or camping out in the basements of apartment houses. Some choose to do so because they are afraid of going anyplace where people might force them to return home, a fear that is not ungrounded since anyone who helps a runaway can legally be prosecuted for "contributing to the delinquency of a minor." With few exceptions, places where adolescents can stay require either a disposition from the court or parental permission. Some runaways remain away only a day or two, sleeping at a friend's house or living on the street, and then, having had their brief "time out," return home. For those who stay away, however, finding shelter is only the beginning of the adventure—or the nightmare. Whether the experience of an adolescent away from home turns into a bad dream, suddenly all too real, depends upon the alternatives which he can find once he steps outside the door.

PROJECT PLACE RUNAWAY HOUSE

The Runaway House, one place in the Boston area where an adolescent can go for short-term crisis counseling and temporary shelter after he leaves home, is located in an old townhouse in the South End of Boston (described in Part I, chapter 8). The House has room for twenty kids to sleep, dormitory-style, in bunk beds. In the basement there is a kitchen and a "living room," where the kids can talk, play music, and be away from the counselors. The first floor houses the office and switchboard, and the boys' sleeping quarters; counseling rooms are on the second floor, and girls' sleeping areas on the third.

In order to stay at the House for more than one night, runaways must obtain consent from their parents. Many kids are fearful of calling home, thinking that their parents will deny them permission. Some parents do refuse, and counselors have to persuade others to agree, but most are relieved to hear that their child is safe, and accept the idea that he can stay at the House for counseling. One argument, which is often used successfully with reluctant parents, is that the House is a better place for a kid than the street. There is a two-week limit on stays at the House because initially, when kids were allowed to remain longer, they tended to make the House their new home. Their desire to do so was understandable since the place was so supportive in contrast to the environments which they had left behind. Kids still talk about wanting to stay for good.

When he arrives at the House, each kid is assigned a counselor to work with for at least a two-week period. Although the counselors work in teams and support each other, one has primary responsibility for each runaway. The counselors try to help kids clarify what made them run away and what they want to do next. Family conferences to talk things over are often arranged, and the counselors may try to set up either individual or family counseling for after a kid returns home. If the runaway and/or his family are determined not to be reconciled, the counselor has a more complicated task: he may have to arrange an alternative living arrangement (see Part I, chapter 8).

Sometimes the counselors become involved in strong personal relationships with the kids. One, who was particularly sensitive to the needs of delinquent boys, continued to see many of the runaways he had worked with after they had left the House. He visited them weekly wherever they had gone—back home, to special schools, or foster homes—took them bowling, and talked with them about his interests as well as theirs. Particularly when this kind of support from an older person is genuine, it can be valuable to an adolescent.

Many of the runaways found it hard to leave the House after two weeks, often because the work which could be done with them and their families was so severely limited by time. Yet there are so many runaways and there is room for so few at the Runaway House, the only one in the metropolitan Boston area, that the two-week limit is a necessity.

During our final month at the House, it faced a severe funding crisis. Little public money is available at present, although the public need is clear: 500,000 kids, maybe more, run away each year. Thus runaway houses are dependent on private money and when foundations stop funding them, they are in trouble. Throughout the spring, all counselors at the Runaway House worked without pay.

It is tragic that when the need for such services is so great, money is so scarce. In the face of such extreme adversity, only the perseverance of those who know how essential such programs are keeps them going. Still the specter of "folding" haunts the Runaway House—a particularly ironic situation since the staff is trying to figure out what to do with all the kids who call up and come in every day.

"SOMEONE YOU CAN LEAN ON"

Many runaways need some kind of counseling either while they are on the run or after they have returned home. Ironically, once a runaway has been taken into court or has found his way to a social service agency, there is often no dearth of counselors to take on his case, but for several reasons this is not always advantageous for the runaway. First of all, many social workers are all too ready to act *in loco parentis*, to draw up plans of what their "clients" should do and to make choices for them, at a time when most runaways are both confused about what they want and seeking to define or discover it for themselves. Thus a counselor who is too hasty in suggesting and carrying out a course of action may undermine a young person's tentative but nonetheless real struggle for independence. This kind of sabotage is unwittingly reinforced by a tendency to shuffle runaways around from one agency or counselor to another. Sometimes the runaway himself contributes to this by seeking help in several places at once.

The sense of trust and continuing support which is crucial in a good counseling relationship is often lost in an endless chain of referrals. The common claim of "overburdened case loads" is unfortunately, but undeniably, true and does prevent many social workers from devoting adequate time to each case. (This overloading merely increases, however, as runaways are bounced around from one place to another.) Even so, some social workers seem to value the subtle kind of power they have over kids' lives and are reluctant to relinquish a runaway once he is within their jurisdiction.

We watched this process unfold with Johnny, one runaway we heard about, who had had no fewer than ten counselors in as many months. He was committed several times to the Department of Youth Services, had been in and out of a number of institutions, and had spent time in several group homes and halfway houses. Dissatisfied with these arrangements, he kept running away from all of them. Finally at Project Place he found a counselor, Bill, who was concerned enough to spend time trying to help him find a place to stay and to support his strengths rather than his weaknesses. Bill commented, "Everybody thinks they've got a handle on him and nobody does. They only relate to him as a runaway." This single-minded focusing on a salient weak point is a common pattern in working with adolescents. Too often people either dismiss a young person as a "drug problem," a "runaway," or a "truant," or zero in too closely on one particular negative attribute, while failing to credit the young person for his strengths.

Bill realized that Johnny had weaknesses: his inability to handle decisions had catapulted him "out of control," and he was locked into a pattern of running away. But his being assigned a new set of counselors by the Department of Youth Services each time he ran away did not help. Bill tried to break that pattern by helping Johnny develop his ability to trust and to meet challenges head on. Others had assumed that Johnny would simply flee when situations became difficult. A counselor at a halfway house which used a lot of heavy "confrontation" techniques explained Johnny's running away by saying, "The kid couldn't make it because we were getting too close." Johnny's reason for leaving the house was revealing: "I didn't like the yelling—it hurt."

Even though foster homes for adolescents are extremely difficult to find, and Johnny was a "bad risk" since he had run away so often, Bill tried to find him a foster placement, respecting his apparent desire to return to a normal home, despite his confusion about what he wanted. Another of Johnny's many counselors thought Bill naïve in his approach. "The kid's a manipulator," he said, to which Bill answered, "They all are." The ability to lay aside jaded or cynical preconceptions and to respond to each runaway with the renewed, sincere expectation that an honest relationship can be established is essential for successful counseling. Despite the good work which Bill had done with Johnny, several of the other social workers had the case taken out of his hands. It seemed they all wanted to have control over the boy.

Group therapy is another counseling option which exists for runaways. Sometimes when a kid leaves home he has decided to talk about things that have been on his mind for some time. Whatever the reason, some kids do not talk to anyone about pressing emotional concerns—even to their good friends. Some of the talking they do as runaways, with counselors and other kids, may be their first experience of a particular kind of communication in which they discuss their feelings and help others do the same. As we have seen it in action, this is a natural process which can be helped along by those who have had more experience.

Some runaways we know have taken this experience home with them and continued it by taking part in groups run by counselors. We talked to kids from two of these groups (and heard about many more). One such group was run at a suburban drop-in center. Another, which we sat in on for a month, met at a child guidance clinic in Boston. A common problem in both groups was attendance—several kids came regularly while others were more sporadic. There would be weeks in a row when most everyone would show up. Then the numbers would go down. Nevertheless, in the group we observed, it did not seem to matter how many people were there. Important things could happen if only two showed up.

All the kids who took part in the clinic group had some kind of stable living situation in which they were uncomfortable: David, fifteen, was the only one who lived with his real parents; Rebecca, sixteen, had run away from her home in another eastern city and now lived with her grandparents; Phillip, nineteen, lived in a Boston dormitory for young people. While much talk concerned home, kids often spoke of everyday issues—movies, a recent rock concert, school—told jokes, and played games. The valuable thing about the group, one girl told us, was the "different kind of talking" that went on there. Other kids agreed with her—friends back home did not talk like this, though one boy said he was teaching his friends how.

By the time we came, the group had been running for almost six months and was in its final few weeks before summer vacation. One measure of how much these kids wanted to come was the distance they traveled to get there—some lived in faraway suburbs. Most arrived early, talked with each other before the group began, and left together afterwards.

The kind of interplay which takes place between the kids themselves and kids and counselors can only be appreciated by direct observation. There is too much movement, too many expressions and gestures, to capture it all on paper. For our purposes, however, transcripts of several discussions will be sufficient. The first concerned the conflicts Rebecca was having with her grandfather. Although few children live with grandparents, the problems she discussed are typical of ones adolescents have with parents. Other kids in the group sensed this and talked with her. Two counselors (one from the Runaway House, another from the clinic) took part in the group, but for the sake of simplicity we shall refer to them as one.

David: I hear you've been having trouble getting here.

Rebecca: My grandfather won't let me come. He doesn't want me to leave the house and come here.

D: Ever try talking to your grandfather?

R: Yes, I tell him I'm unhappy because of the restrictions. I tell him it feels like a prison at home, and he tells me I need direction.

D: Parents are real con artists. They can talk you into anything.

Bob: I win. I always get the last word.

D (to R): If you want to get them mad, call them a bunch of paranoid hypocrites.

Counselor: Will that help?

D: It gets them madder at you. I've been in arguments like that.... Get yourself a boyfriend who's thirty.

R: I have one who's nineteen, that's as high as I'll go.

D: Use a foster home as a threat. If you don't use threats you'll be doing sneaky things, getting in trouble.

R: I'm already doing that and I don't like it.

· · ·

Counselor: What do people think Rebecca can do?

Phillip: Split. They'll worry after you're gone for a week.

D: Fight harder.

R: If I leave, my grandparents would take out a warrant on me.

D: Act like a freak. I used to pretend I was on drugs; got my parents all worried. Go home with a girl one night and hold her hand.

(Laughter)

Counselor: What will all this get Rebecca?

D: Put in an institution.

Counselor: Where does this get you?

D: Out of the house.

. . .

D: Call him worse names.

R: I have. I called him a conceited hypocrite.

D: How about obnoxious?

R: He doesn't understand big words.

D: Bug him enough. Make him feel what you're feeling by repetition.

R: I can't make him feel what I feel. I sit for a whole hour making the same points.

D: If he treats you like a child, act like one. Do the opposite.

R: That's an idea.

Counselor: You really think he's going to change?

D: When I attack people I attack the opposite way . . . ask for toys and play with them . . . if he sees you're a little kid then he'll treat you like you're older.

Counselor: Or like you're a little kid.

David then went into a long discussion of how parents did not realize that kids were growing up, which the counselor reacted to by saying parents were only too well aware of that. He then asked the kids what kinds of things their parents might be worried about.

> D: Drugs, sex, pimps—all those bad kinds of things out in the world.
>
> Counselor: They know that—that's why they're all the more worried. They're trying to be concerned.
>
> R: But they do it the wrong way.

What appeared to us to be happening in this group was that Rebecca talked about her own frustrations and a number of strategies for dealing with the problem of parental restrictions. She was upset about what had been going on and did not know what to do. The role of the counselor was to get kids to look more critically at what they were doing. In the latter part of the discussion he tried to get kids to see that their parents had their own reasons for being so restrictive and that it might be asking a lot to get them to change.

At other times one kid would talk about a crisis in his family. During the same session he had suggested to Rebecca different ways of dealing with her grandfather, David mentioned that his mother had just filed for divorce.

> D: I'm going to court to stick up for my mother; my sister's going to stick up for my father. I want to go so I can have a say in it. I don't want to live with either really. My mother's already pushing me to get a "big job." All I have is little odd jobs mowing lawns. . . . My mother wants me to stay. . . . I'll be depended on to help raise up the other kids. . . . My sister wants to live with my father. . . . Can I go to court and ask not to live with either?

Counselor: It sounds like you're trying to laugh off your parents' divorce.

D: I was laughing the other day about it. They're supposed to be in love with each other. I read the summons that came from court and it's sick.

Counselor: Sounds sad.

D: It's sad for my mother. She still loves him and doesn't want to see him go. Without a guy she's nowhere. She needs a guy to back her up.

Counselor: So you feel that will be you.

D: No . . . that's my little brother (laughs). . . . If I stay with my mother I probably won't be able to handle it. That's too much responsibility. I don't want to get a job at fourteen. My mother doesn't work.

R: She can go get a job. . . . She'll have to get a job. They don't pay alimony if they don't want to. It takes a long time to collect.

D: My father's the kind that won't pay.

In the next group, David continued to talk about the crisis. In the past week, his father had moved out of the house and David was thinking of running away again.

D: My father came into the house one night, took his stuff, and didn't say anything. I'm glad my mother took the initiative against him. I think maybe now he'll come back and change a little.

Counselor: Will he?

D: . . . for a while, but the change won't last. My father needs the family. He won't be able to make it alone.

Counselor: Sounds like you're lonely too.

D: I was for a while. Sunday when I was tripping for the first time, I got really scared. I put myself in my mother's place, then in my father's place. I know my father is unfit, but my mother needs my father. It started ten years ago, but it's been pretty bad for the last two.

Counselor: What do the rest of you think about this?

(Silence)

R: Not much you can say.

D: It's common in my neighborhood . . . it's full of divorces.

Counselor: Sounds like you're quite affected by your father's leaving.

D: You know something's missing.

Counselor: Not you know, *I* know.

D: All right I know . . . I want to live with my mother, but I'm not sure I can make it living with her.

Counselor: Is that why you want to run away this summer?

D: Maybe.

Counselor: Do you sometimes feel yourself liking your father?

D: I miss him now that he's gone.

During these discussions, David was able to focus on and express some strong though confused feelings. He talked quickly and in a lighthearted manner about the divorce, yet the counselor sensed his underlying sadness as well as his fear of the new composition of his household. There was nothing anyone could do about the facts of his life, but they could help him think about his reactions to all that was going on in his family. That everyone recognized that he was going through a difficult time helped David. Although he tended to be disparaging of his father and side with his mother, after the preceding discussion, David was able to express the ambivalence of his feelings.

D: It's hard because I feel both ways. He's not a good parent, but he's my father. . . . As a little kid I saw little things, and as I've grown older, I've seen more and more things wrong.

This comment led others in the group to talk about how their perceptions of parents had changed with time, after which the counselor said, "One thing we never have any choice about is who our parents are."

Another kind of event we observed was a crisis within the group itself, which all members were affected by. Throughout the month we sat in on the group, Phillip came regularly, but said little. Every now and then he spoke bitterly of the "assholes" who lived in his building and the landlord who kept trying to evict him. At nineteen, he was the only member of the group not living with a family (although his parents still supported him financially). While he attended school and was surrounded by people his own age in the dormitory, he had few friends. One night Phillip finally started talking about his own parents. He felt they had exiled him and now wanted nothing more to do with them.

Counselor: I suspect you're lonely now.

P: I want a roommate. . . . My partner, my partial roommate, is in Europe. He lives with me some of the time.

Counselor: What do the rest of you feel about Phillip?

D: When a kid runs away from home, he really wants his parents. I ran away for attention.

P: I'm beyond that stage. The first time I felt that way. . . . Now I con them for their money. . . . What else do I need them for?

D: For their love. That's what all kids need from their parents.

P: I admit I've been tossed away, but I don't have anything to do with them.

D: You want them back.

P: If they came fifty-fifty.

D: If they didn't give you the money, you'd feel more like a piece of trash.

P: They only maintain me because otherwise people would talk up in a little town in Maine. Just like your parents getting divorced. People will talk.

D: Tough. They'll talk and see my mother's right. I sit here and talk about how much I hate my parents, but deep inside I love them.

P (angry now): My parents used me for a showpiece.

D: Mine did too. . . . They all said, "Oh, he looks like his uncle."

P: I was put away in schools, shut there. They put me out.

D: Did you find out why?

P: I was one less problem.

D: They say that but don't mean it. It's an unsolved joke between kids and parents.

P: My parents didn't send out a warrant when I ran away. They just didn't care.

D: My parents didn't send out a warrant either. They wanted to do it their way, our way, no courts and things.

David then continued to ask Phillip how he felt about his parents, saying he understood what they had done to him, but wanted to know what he felt for them. Suddenly Phillip's anger turned to belligerence and despair.

P: Maybe I never should have fucking existed. I've taken a lot of crap, but now I'm going to get . . . I've taken shit for too long, and I'm going to get my revenge back.

Counselor: There are more positive ways to live.

P: I've tried that way, but it doesn't work. Turn the other cheek.

Counselor: That's still taking shit.

P: I've got to step on somebody to get ahead. I'm the kind of person who's had to fight for every break he's ever had.

Counselor: Let's get back to the question. Are there ways of proving to others that you're okay without being destructive?

P: Some people have to be taught, snapped to ...

When the group ended for the evening, Phillip left the room quickly without speaking to anyone. Usually he stuck around and talked awhile, but that night he seemed angry at everyone in the group; we had the feeling that in his own mind, he had been "taking shit" again from other people and was actively fighting with them. The next week he arrived very late. Toward the end of the group, the counselor turned to Phillip and said that he was concerned that the previous group had upset him.

P: I was pissed.

D: We knew it.

P: You were going too far into my own business. I don't have nothing to do with them. Thing is they never had anything to do with me. . . . Either I get a good break this year or *phhht*—I end it. . . . What's the use of going on with a lot of shit. . . . I've had too much.

Counselor: I'm concerned about last week. You were angry and couldn't share that with us.

P: At least I didn't explode.

Counselor: What were the rest of you trying to do?

D: I was talking from the feeling that all kids need parents and how you can sometimes feel both love and hate for them.

P: I don't want to go back into the past.

Counselor: Do you know what David's saying?

P: No.

Counselor: He accepts that you don't want to go back but wants to know how you feel. . . . They're trying to get to know you better—around this one issue.

D: I want to know how even though he hates them as parents, how he felt about them as people.

Counselor (to everyone): Were you trying to get to know Phillip better?

P: When I get depressed, I keep it inside . . . people don't want to hear problems.

R: That's what this place is for.

Counselor: They're trying to get to know you better. People sensed anger but didn't know what it was you were mad about.

D: We don't know anything about you other than the hate you feel.

P (somewhat angry): What do you want to know? [As if they were prying.]

D: He's never really talked to us.

P (quieter, almost gentle): At this one school I was at, something like this happened to me. They sensed something about me. It's not that I didn't like them, only that I didn't feel like talking to them.

The group ended on his statement, which indicated to us that, in part, they were beginning to resolve the crisis in the group. Phillip had acknowledged their concern by referring to the past ("they sensed something about me") and stated clearly that he didn't feel like talking. He no longer thought the others were "shitting on him" by trying to get close. At the time, however, he did not want to be "known," not by these people at any rate.

We have heard that such groups are becoming more common in schools and other institutions that deal with young people. Despite our positive feelings about the group we observed, we are uncertain that such proliferation is a good thing. The kids we got to know all chose to attend the group. That is not true of other "feelings" groups of which we have heard. In one instance a high school substituted such a group for detention hall as a punishment for misbehavior. At another school, such groups were a part of the curriculum. Our misgivings about such widespread application of the idea come from the conviction that people should not be forced to feel but should be free to choose when they want to deal with feelings in such an intense, structured way. We also feel that those who run these groups must be trained. Many situations which arise—such as the final event described in this section—need to be handled with care if the young people involved are to be helped rather than harmed by this process.

LIVING WHERE YOU HAVE TO

If a runaway is persistent in refusing to go home, or if his parents refuse to take him back, an alternative living arrangement must be found. As we have discussed in earlier chapters, runaways often have no choice about where they will live but are sent places against their will by parents, schools, social workers, or the courts. Sometimes the decision of where to send the young person is made on the basis of how "disturbed" these others think he is. Some runaways are sent to mental hospitals, others to treatment centers or "therapeutic communities," and still others to "group homes."

When we visited one of the mental hospitals, the Children's Unit of Metropolitan State Hospital, an administrator told us she was disturbed by the increasing tendency of courts and families to commit children who had "behavior problems" rather than severe "emotional disorders." She said that runaways are initially only committed to Met State for short periods of diagnosis or evaluation, to remain longer only if they are seriously pathological. Another hospital worker told us, however, that these "observation periods" sometimes extend for several months. Just as many mental hospitals become dumping grounds for lonely or unwanted adults, the Children's Unit is sometimes used as a convenient receptacle for problem children; but the kids themselves often display more energetic efforts to "get out" than adults do in similar situations.

We believe that the tendency of families and courts to make unwarranted commitment of runaways to mental hospitals and of the hospitals to keep them there for longer than necessary is a potentially dangerous one. Administrators at the Department of Youth Services have recognized the possibility that when the reform schools are closed, mental hospitals will be seen as the only remaining form of "institutionalization," and therefore might be "inappropriately used by those wishing to lock kids up." They are trying to guard against this by providing more viable "community-based" programs; however, one of these programs, Mass Transition, seemed a poor alternative to mental hospitals.

Mass Transition occupies a former sea captain's manor house, a huge brick mansion in excellent condition. The atmosphere on the inside contrasted surprisingly with the pleasing decoration of the rooms. Although we only talked with two of the counselors and one of the kids in the program, we got a strong impression of what the place was like.

According to the counselors, Mass Transition began as a "concept" house for heroin addicts, but recently shifted to using similar confrontation tactics on "fucked-up kids, and kids with behavior problems." "Problems, that's what we're about," one of the counselors said. The program is supported primarily by funds from the Department of Youth Services, which pays for kids whom it places there on a fee-for-service basis. Although Mass

Transition staff say they do not limit their intake to kids who are in trouble with the law, most of their referrals come from the Department, and the money which supports them is "delinquency prevention" money. They did not explain to us exactly why they had decided to use the same therapeutic techniques which they had used with twenty- and thirty-year-old heroin addicts on adolescents with a variety of problems.

The structure of the program is extremely rigid; it demands strict adherence to a daily schedule and inflexibly enforces a long list of duties and expectations. The intent is to enable an adolescent to change his bad behavior patterns by forcing him to confront them; the assumption is that his behavior patterns are bad. A recurrent theme in the comments of the counselors was the ways in which kids "fucked up," in the program and out in the community. Every aspect of the kids' lives is subjected to scrutiny once they have joined the program: personal habits like styles of dress and ways of talking, as well as past and present actions, are open to question. Whether or not an ashtray has been emptied or a bed made is considered a reflection of deep-rooted attitudes toward self and others. "Everything about this place is therapeutic," the counselor told us proudly, "every detail."

The program has three cardinal rules: "no violence, no drugs, and no male-female relationships." The reason for the final rule is that "you should first develop the strength to get along without something because you never know when you're going to lose it."

The techniques used to enforce these and other more minor rules rely heavily on peer-group pressure and seemed to us rather harsh. The most common form of punishment (or therapy) for a bad attitude is "pull-ups": all the members of the program publicly confront the deviant with what he has done and try to make him understand how it is reprehensible. One counselor said, "Kids show off a lot to gain acceptance. When they get in here, other kids pick up on that and tell them what's wrong with their behavior." When pull-ups fail, "hook-ups" are tried; the person is forced to wear a sign, such as I AM A BABY, around his neck. Only "in extreme circumstances" does anyone have his head shaved. Although the counselors claimed that participation in the program was voluntary, one added that "if a kid has a shaved head, he'll think twice about walking out the door."

The boy we talked to who was in the program had run away from home and come to Mass Transition in January when the weather was cold and he needed a place to stay. He walked stiffly upright and talked in a thin monotone: "I wasn't very happy with myself before I came here. I feel a lot better about myself now, I can do things for myself . . . the program has helped me a lot . . . I can't go home to my parents for good until my counselor decides it's okay, but sometimes I go home for weekends." The counselors had explained that their intention was to change kids' self-images and make them more independent by forcing them to recognize their bad attitudes and behavior patterns. We felt that their techniques undermined the kids' characters and encouraged dependence on the program rather than self-reliance. What the program actually seemed to accomplish was to enforce its own rigid sense of hierarchy, which was dramatized by a chart, detailing every member's "rank," that hung on the living room wall.

As the boy finished showing us around he pointed to an office and said it belonged to the "expeditor": "It's the expeditor's job to know where everyone is in the house and what each person's attitude is." Although the counselor has assured us that the program "didn't just take kids in and spit them out the side door," and that young people "really learned to love each other while there," we could not avoid the impression that the harshly repressive discipline and excessive emphasis on failure could not help but break down a young person and reshape him in the program's own image.

Groupways, one of the group homes to which male runaways are sometimes sent, was, without advertising the fact, a supportive environment. Groupways is located in an old townhouse in South Boston and like Mass Transition is funded mostly by "delinquency prevention" money. Alex and Jeanne, the "houseparents," who had been working with troubled young people for nearly ten years, reminded us by their warm and friendly manner of how particular *people* may be more important for the success of a program than the *structure* of a group residential situation. Alex and Jeanne seemed to take a personal interest in each of the boys who lived at Groupways, and were able to be relaxed and humorous even while talking honestly with them about a serious problem.

While at Groupways the boys, who may live there for only a few months or as long as a year or two, either work or go to school. Tutoring and individual counseling are available for those who desire them. Even those who have been committed by the court are free to come and go at times when they do not have any specific responsibilities to meet. The trust which Alex and Jeanne had evidently established with them made this kind of open structure a viable one. One boy we talked with there, a runaway who did not wish to return home, had been drunk one night at a party and had gone to a friend's house in his old neighborhood until the next day when he returned to Groupways. The houseparents were able to laugh sympathetically about his hangover while pointing out the ways in which he had transgressed the rules by violating his curfew and staying out overnight. The openness, understanding, and friendly guidance which we observed at Groupways made us realize that some of the places to which runaways and other "problem" adolescents are sent can be environments in which they can grow on their own, away from their families.

GO WHERE YOU WANT TO GO

One of the "alternatives" we visited where young people can choose to live for a few months was Newton's Freeport House, a community set up and run by students at the local high school. The house was supervised by two "houseparents" and a director, all of whom the young people had hired after interviewing a number of adults.

The most striking thing about this community was the responsibility and energy which the students displayed in creating a place where many of them could share experiences and help each other with difficult concerns. When we visited Freeport, nine boys were living there. A few of them felt compelled by difficulties at home to get away, while some simply wanted to experiment with a new style of living. Thus, there was no stigma attached to being part of this community and many other young people from the town were actively involved in what happened there. They participated in house meetings, helped raise money to support the place, shared the work of keeping the house in good condition, and above all came to make close friendships in new ways.

The kids had made extensive efforts to interest adults in the town and keep them informed about what Freeport was doing. From the beginning, however, they had to deal with the oppositon of some adults who objected to the idea of a houseful of young people living in one of the town's most expensive residential areas. According to town law the house could not be coed; it was only after a series of town council meetings, and serious "politicking" for support, that the students convinced a sufficient number of their elders to approve the project at all. Freeport House provided an alternative way of growing up for all young people in the town. The house was a place which they could be responsible for and where they could learn about one another. Several students told us that before they had become involved in the community, they were bored and unsure of what to do about that feeling. Now they had something to which they could devote as much or as little of their time as they pleased.

In this chapter we have tried to point out that when a young person runs away his options are limited. Some of the alternatives which exist impede rather than encourage the development of inner strength necessary for the task of growing up. Adolescence is a time of growing in new and strange ways, and for many kids who have left home the choices can be especially confusing ones.

Often adults—parents as well as those who are trying to "help"—feel they must take on the entire responsibility of making decisions for young people. While runaways and other adolescents may need counseling or adult advice, ultimately they must make decisions for themselves. Whether a runaway returns home or stays out, whether he chooses to work through his concerns in therapy or in other ways, we believe that he must be supported in learning to choose for himself, and that he can only do so if he has room to move.

NOTES

PART II
Chapter 1

1. Kagan, Jerome, "A Conception of Early Adolescence," *Daedalus.* (Vol. 100, no. 4) p. 1010.

2. Stierlin, Helm L., David Levi and Robert Savard, "Parental Perceptions of Separating Children," *Runaway Youth*, p. 186.

3. *Ibid.*, p. 188.

4. *Ibid.*

5. Unpublished study done under the auspices of Dr. Mary Howells and the Street Youth Program of the Massachusetts General Hospital, 1972.

6. Stierlin, Helm, "Characteristics of Suburban Adolescent Runaways," *Runaway Youth*, p. 171.

7. Ackerman, Nathan, *Family Therapy in Transition*, p. 9

8. *Ibid.*

9. Stierlin, Levi and Savard, *op. cit.*, p 191

10. *Ibid.*, p. 192
11. *Ibid.*

Chapter 2

1. Shellow, Robert, et al., "Suburban Runaways of the 1960s," *Runaway Youth*, p. 222.

2. Task Force On Children Out of School, *The Way We Go to School*, p. 65.

3. Friedenberg, Edgar Z., *Coming of Age in America*, p. 232.

Chapter 3

1. Bakan, David, "Adolescence in America," *Daedulus* (Vol. 100, no. 4), p. 986.

2. *Ibid.*, p. 987.

3. *Ibid.*

4. *Ibid.*

5. *Ibid.*, p. 988.

6. Senate Subcommittee Hearings, *Runaway Youth*, p. 49.

7. Lipsitt, Paul D. "The Juvenile Offender's Perceptions," p. 50.

8. According to the Department's own statistics.

9. Senate Subcommittee Hearings, *Runaway Youth*, p. 21.

10. *Ibid.*, p. 125.

11. *Ibid.*, p. 49.

12. *Ibid.*, p. 21.

BIBLIOGRAPHY

Ackerman, Nathan (ed.). *Family Therapy in Transition.* Boston: Little, Brown and Co., 1970.

Blum, Jeffrey D., and Judith E. Smith. *Nothing Left to Lose.* Cambridge, Mass.: The Sanctuary, 1972.

Erikson, Erik H. *Childhood and Society.* New York: W. W. Norton, 1964.

———. *Identity: Youth and Crisis.* New York: W. W. Norton, 1968.

Friedenberg, Edgar. *Coming of Age in America.* New York: Random House, 1963.

———. *The Vanishing Adolescent.* New York: Dell, 1959.

Laing, R. D. *Self and Others.* New York: Pantheon Books, 1969.

———, and A. Esterson. *Sanity, Madness and the Family: Families of Schizophrenics.* Baltimore: Pelican Books, 1970.

Runaway Youth: Hearings Before the Subcommittee to Investigate Juvenile Delinquency of the Committee on the Judiciary, United States Senate. January 13, 14, 1972.

Task Force on Children Out of School. *The Way We Go to School.* Boston: Beacon Press, 1972.

"Twelve to Sixteen: Early Adolescence." *Daedalus* (Vol. 100, No. 4). Cambridge, Mass.: 1971.